75p

The Art of KNITTING

JERRY ROGERS

The Art of
KNITTING

JERRY ROGERS

Photography by Bob Baxter

BLANDFORD

To the Knitterati

A BLANDFORD BOOK
First published in the United Kingdom in 1991
by Blandford
(a Cassell imprint)
Villiers House
41/47 Strand
LONDON
WC2N 5JE

by arrangement with CollinsAngus&Robertson
Publishers Pty Limited, Sydney, Australia

First published in Australia in 1991 by
CollinsAngus&Robertson Publishers Pty Limited
A division of HarperCollinsPublishers (Australia) Pty Limited
4 Eden Park, 31 Waterloo Road, North Ryde, NSW 2113, Australia

British Library Cataloguing in Publication Data
Rogers, Jerry
The art of knitting.
1. Knitting
I. Title
746.432

ISBN 0-7137-2311-4

Typeset in Australia by Midland Typesetters, Maryborough, Vic.
Printed in Australia by Griffin Press.

5 4 3 2 1
95 94 93 92 91

Contents

ABBREVIATIONS

alt alternate

approx approximately

beg begin/beginning

cm centimetre/s

cont continue

crab st work as for double crochet, but work from left to right instead of right to left so that sts are worked backwards

dec decrease/decreases/decreasing

foll following/follows

garter st every row knit

inc increase/increases/increasing

incl inclusive or including

K knit

K1, P1 Rib (odd number of sts)
    1ST ROW: K2, *P1, K1, rep from * to last st, K1.
    2ND ROW: K1, *P1, K1, rep from * to end
    Rep these 2 rows

K1, P1 Rib (even number of sts)
    1ST ROW * K1, P1, rep from * to end
    Rep this row

mm millimetre/s

0 zero—no stitches, times or rows

P purl

purl fabric 1 row purl (right side)
                1 row knit (wrong side)

patt pattern

rem remain/remains/remaining/remainder

rep repeat

st/s stitch/es

stocking st 1 row knit, 1 row purl

tbl through back of loop

tog together

ybk yarn back—take yarn under needle from purling position into knitting position, without making a stitch

yft yarn front—bring yarn under needle from knitting position into purling position, without making a stitch

yon yarn over needle - take yarn over top of needle into knitting position, thus making a stitch

yfwd yarn forward - bring yarn under needle, then over into knitting position again, thus making a stitch

yrn yarn round needle - take yarn right around needle into purling position, thus making a stitch

NOTE: When the pattern reads 'cast off 2 sts, K2' (or whatever number of sts the pattern states), the stitch left on the right hand needle, after casting off, is counted as one stitch. The first row of your work is the right side, unless otherwise stated. Always slip sts knitways when working a S1, K1, psso.

Yarn quantities are approximate and may vary between knitters.

KNITTING HINTS

The tension is stated at the beginning of each pattern. Always obtain the correct tension before you begin your garment to ensure that the finished garment corresponds to the stated measurements. This is particularly important because different designers have used varying techniques to give their finished garment an individual style.

The best way to check your tension is to knit a swatch according to the tension quoted, using approximately 10 more stitches and working 10 more rows than the stated tension. Place the sample on a flat surface and measure with a ruler. If the number of stitches/rows is less than the stated tension, your knitting is too loose and you should try needles a size smaller. If the number of stitches/rows is more, your knitting is too firm and you should try a needles a size larger. Continue to check your garment size as you knit to ensure success.

SIZING

The majority of patterns are in three sizes – Small (S), Medium (M) and Large (L). The fit of each of these varies from pattern to pattern and it is therefore important to refer to the Actual Garment Measurement to ascertain the correct size for you. Throughout the patterns the detail for Medium and Large are given in brackets. When only one set of figures is given, it refers to all sizes.

GRAPHS

All of the patterns are accompanied by one or more Graphs. Each square on a Graph represents one stitch and each line of squares represents one row of knitting.

All Graphs are worked in stocking stitch. Each knit row is read from right to left and each purl row is read from left to right, beginning with row 1, unless otherwise stated.

You may find it helpful to colour in sections of colour on the Graph before beginning and for more detailed Graphs, lightly pencil through each completed line. This can then be erased on completion.

WORKING WITH COLOURS

There are two methods of colour knitting used in this book, called Fair Isle Knitting and Wool Wind or Intersia Knitting. Fair Isle knitting is where two or more colours are used repeatedly across a row. The different colours are stranded or carried loosely across the back of your work when not in use.

If it is necessary to carry a colour across more than 5-7 stitches (depending on ply), it should be woven under and over colour in use at centre stitch (see diagram). It is important that colours are stranded loosely across the back of your work at an even tension, otherwise the knitting will pucker. Always carry MC above C1 and C1 above C2 and so on.

For ease of knitting, you may also use the Fair Isle technique for small areas on some garments. Where, for example, in a section of two to three different colours, another colour is repeatedly used across these sections but not necessarily across the whole garment.

Wool Wind or Intarsia knitting is the technique used to knit sections of different colours, which may appear only once or twice across the garment and where stranding across would be impractical. This avoids the bulk of Fair Isle and produces a single thickness of fabric.

A separate ball of colour is used for each section of colour. You may find it easier to wind your yarn on to yarn bobbins for this purpose, to prevent tangles. Alternatively, for smaller sections of colour, if you cut a length of yarn to complete the section, it will be much easier to manage tangles when they arise. The Wool Wind or Intarsia method involves twisting the different colours around each other whenever they meet to prevent holes in the work. When changing the colours, twist the colour to be used (on wrong side) underneath and to the right of the colour just used (see diagram).

Alternatively with some small areas of colour you may wish to embroider this detail on completion using 'Knitting Stitch' embroidery or Swiss darning, as it is also known (see diagram).

With some of the garments in this book, both Fair Isle and Wool Wind methods have been used throughout the garment, depending on the colour placement in the actual design. Use the criteria above to decide on the most suitable method and once you have chosen a method ensure that you keep your work at an even tension throughout.

You may also find it helpful with some designs to knit your ends in as you go. You can do this by weaving in the ends (as in Fair Isle) on every other stitch for about 7 centimetres.

EMBROIDERY STITCHES

The following embroidery stitches are used for various garments in the book. Some chapters will refer to the stitch specifically, while others will indicate that a choice of embroidery stitch is needed.

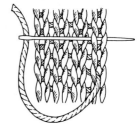

Step 1 Working from right to left, bring the needle out in the centre of the stitch and take it up and around the head of the stitch (as shown), under the stitch above, from right to left.

Step 2 To complete the stitch, take the needle back through the centre of the original stitch and then back up through the next stitch you wish to cover.

Step 3 When working from left to right, follow as for Step 1, but take the needle from left to right instead of right to left.

NOTE: It is important to use a yarn of the same ply or thicker to cover the stitch properly. Do not pierce the fabric of the knitting, because this will reduce the elasticity of the garment.

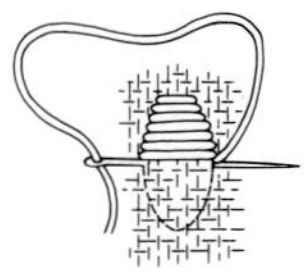

Satin Stitch

Chain Stitch

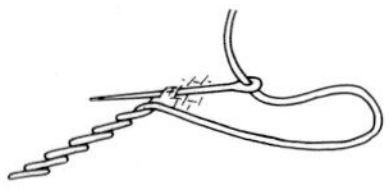

Stem Stitch

Cross Stitch

French Knot

YARNS FOR UNITED KINGDOM KNITTERS

This chart gives United Kingdom yarn equivalents for those Australian yarns specified in the patterns.

Yarns: Where an exact match (colour, fibre make-up, texture or tension) to the original yarn has been impossible we have endeavoured to find the closest match possible. In some cases several yarns are suggested to provide a colour selection equal to the original and an alternatives if one range has been discontinued.

Colour used in these designs can be altered to suit personal preferences and because manufacturers do amend their shade range, we cannot guarantee exact colour matches in every case.
Should some yarns be unavailable due to changes in the manufacturers' range, please contact the manufacturer or your knitting specialty shop for suitable alternatives.

Where there was no satisfactory match available at the time the yarn has been labelled 'Not Available'.

Quantities: Amount of yarn required as specified in patterns relates to Australian yarns only. Please adjust accordingly when purchasing yarns in the United Kingdom.

Tension: It is *imperative* to knit tension squares before starting a pattern. Overall pattern tensions are found at the beginning of each design and you must work up a square using the relevant yarn and the appropriate another sample. Always press your tension square before measuring stitches. If the tension is too tight (too many stitches over the length) use larger needles; if the tension is too loose (too few stitches over the length) use smaller needles and try another sample. Always press your tension square before measuring.

SIZING STANDARDS FOR UK MISSES PATTERNS HEIGHT 5'5"/1.68m

Women	8	10	12	14	16	18	20
To fit (ins)	31½	32½	34	36	38	40	42
in bust (cms)	80	83	87	92	97	102	107
Waist (ins)	24	25	26½	28	30	32	34
(cms)	61	64	67	71	76	81	87
Hips (ins)	33½	34½	36	38	40	42	44
(cm)	85	88	92	97	102	107	112
Back waist	15¾	16	16¼	16½	16¾	17	17¼
(ins)(cm)	40	40.5	41.5	42	42.5	43	44

AUSTRALIAN YARN	**UK YARN**	
Angora Supreme	*Hayfield* Prima Angora—style DK	
Collage 12 ply	NOT AVAILABLE	
Country 8ply	*Pingouin* 4 Pingouins	
	Hayfield Pure New Wool Classics	
Embers 8 ply	*Pingouoin Franace* +	
	Robin New World	
	Wendy Family Choice DK	
Highland 8 ply	*Jaeger* Pot Pourri	Colour range limited
Machine Wash 5 ply		Yarns as for Riverina 5 ply
Machine Wash 8 ply	*Patons* Pure New Wool Crepe DK	Use both ranges for good colour
	Robine New World Crepe DK	selection
Machine Wash 12ply	*Jaeger* Matchmaker Chunky	Not crepe yarn, important that needle size of original be used. Limited colour range
Machine Wash 8ply	*Rowan Fleck* DK	Limited colour range
Merino 8 ply	*Patons* pure wool crepe	
Mohair 12 ply	*Pingouin* Soft Hair	
Mohair Classique	*Sirdair* Mohair	
	Hayfield 80% Luxury Mohair	
Mohair Mystique	*Sirdar* Nocturne Central Park	
Natural 8ply	*Hayfield* Kilmony	Only limited colour range available
Natural 12ply	*Wendy* Orinoco Chunky	
	Texere Yarns Chunky wool	Colour range includes distinctive red required for Preston. Available mail order: College Mill, Barkerend Rd, Bradford W. Yorks, BD3 9AQ
New Caprice 8ply	*Patons* Jasmine DK	
Nostalgia	*Hayfield* Expressions	
	Patons Juniper	
	Emu-Robin Colourdrift	
Riverina 5ply	*Sirdar* Classical Pure Wool	
	DK crepe	
	Sirdar Classical Pure Wool 4ply}	Not crepe yarns. Important that needle size of original be used.
	Wendy Family Choice 4ply	
	Jaeger Matchmaker Merino 4ply	
Sensation 12ply	NOT AVAILABLE	
Woolrich 8ply	*Robin* New World Crepe DK	

English	000	00	0	1	2	3	4	5	6	7	8	9	10	11	12	13	14
Metric	10	8	8	7.5	7	6.5	6	5.5	5	4.5	4	3.75	3.25	3	2.75	2.25	2
American	15	13	12	11	10.5	10	9	8	7	6	5	4	3	2	1	1	00

NOTE: All needle sizes are given in metric and then in English sizes

INTRODUCTION

I fell in love with my first art knit ten years ago at an exhibition at Macquarie Galleries in Sydney. It was Ruby Brilliant's Snugglepot and Cuddlepie jumper, images drawn from May Gibbs classic childrens' series *The Gumnut Babies*. Intricately knitted in a melange of soft colours, it was a garment ahead of its time. I wore it constantly with everything, everywhere. So did my four daughters, whenever they could wrest it from me. Today, teachers of hand knitting in textile courses lecture on this garment as an example of what is possible in creative knitting. Its final destination may well be a museum.

Ruby Brilliant's jumper brought together many strands, which over the years have resonated in my consciousness, for example, the quality of our artists, both as illustrators and painters, and their uniquely Australian sensibility; the quality and history of Australian wool; our remarkable landscape with its wonderfully strange assortment of flora and fauna; and last, but not least, the work of Australian knitwear designers, the largely unsung artists-in-wool.

I wanted to explore how all these factors could be creatively combined in one book. The conceptual idea for *The Art of Knitting* was a knitting together of these strands.

Landscape, flora and fauna were a surreal bounty for the first Europeans settling in Australia. Artists documented and tried to capture these from 1788 onwards. Australia's earliest paintings are of the Hawkesbury landscape, rosellas, black swans and the unique flora.

The Macarthur family introduced the merino sheep into Australia and established the pastoral industry. The Golden Fleece became an icon in Australia's psyche and a mainstay of its economy. It also became a potent symbol on art gallery walls when Tom Roberts painted *Shearing the Rams* and *The Golden Fleece*. These are possibly Australia's most known and loved paintings.

There must have been skilled, imaginative and interpretive knitters during the early days of settlement, but historically there is little evidence of this. Woollen garments are susceptible to the ravages of wear and time, unsympathetic handling and misuse, particularly when accorded little intrinsic worth. It is not surprising therefore that a continuous history of knitting in Australia is undocumented. Although Australia has always grown fine wool, its relatively short history has meant that unlike older cultures, it has not developed any traditional patterning in knitted garments.

The evolution of knitting has spanned thousands of years, and traditions and patterns have evolved along the way. Myth has it that Eve knitted the pattern on the serpent's back and Jacob's coat of many colours is thought to have been knitted. In Homer's *Odyssey*, Penelope knitted a shroud as she awaited the return of Odysseus. She outwitted her many suitors, who agreed to wait until she had finished the garment before wedding anew, by unravelling her knitting each night.

Although there are many such biblical, mythological and literary references to the craft of knitting, it is thought to have actually originated between 2000 and 3000 years ago in the Middle East, before spreading out along the trade routes to Venice and North Africa. The word 'knitting' derived from the Sanskrit 'nakyat', meaning 'net' or 'weave'. The Arabs learnt the technique from the Christian Copts and introduced it to Spain with the conquest of the Moors in the eighth century. In the following centuries, Spain became the cradle of knitting and crafted geometric patterning, an important development that became the basis of almost all folk knitting in Europe and the near East.

By the ninth century, the craft had swept along the sea trade routes as far as Iona, an island off the western coast of Scotland. In the 820AD Book of Kells, one of the most famous illuminated manuscripts in the world, it is recorded that Daniel fed the Dragon wearing an Aran knit pullover and stockings. The intricate pagan patterning on these pullovers reflects designs that were carved out of stone and moulded out of metal by the Celts; these patterns still grace the Aran knits of today.

Christian iconography also records the craft of knitting. In the fifteenth-century altar piece, 'The Visit of the Angels', the Virgin Mary is depicted knitting, using four needles to pick up stitches around the neck of a vest.

From examples found in the tombs of kings and bishops buried between the thirteenth and sixteenth centuries, skilled knitting techniques seem to have gradually spread throughout Germany, Holland, France, Denmark, Italy and England.

In the fifteenth and sixteenth centuries, Knitting and Hosiery Guilds were established in Europe. Male knitters served apprenticeships of six years with a rigorous 13-week qualification period at the end of their time. Examples of their skill were tested by knitting a felt cap, a woollen shirt, a pair of hose (similar in shape and style to men's knitted golf hose of today) with Spanish clocks at the ankle, and a woollen carpet about 2 metres square. Commercial knitting was a fully fledged and lucrative industry in Europe at this time.

Italy became associated with knitted jackets, Spain with gloves and hose, France with fine, fancy stockings, while German and Austrian knitters became known for their magnificent knitted carpets and wall hangings. In England, under Elizabeth I, knitting schools were set up to train the poor and give them a livelihood.

The pattern for Fair Isle is rumoured to have evolved during Elizabeth I's reign. In 1558 a ship from the Spanish Armada was wrecked off the Scottish island of Fair Isle. The crew were wearing brightly coloured, linear-patterned jumpers, with Catholic symbols knitted into them. The islanders adopted the designs and thenceforth the Star of Bethlehem, the Armada Cross and the Sacred Heart (symbols used to ward off disaster) found their way into Nordic knitting and folklore.

Other traditional Fair Isle patterns were those knitted into the now fabled 'Robes of Glory'. The usual practice on Fair Isle was for the grandmother to knit the first Fair Isle sweater for her grandson to wear when he reached adolescence—the garment symbolising initiation into manhood. The pattern on the jumper began with the 'Water of Life' and the 'Seed of Life', which grew into the 'Flower of Life'. This was followed by the 'Anchor of Hope' and then the 'Star' to guide the fisherman on his way. The 'Crown of Glory', symbolising the reward for a good life, was knitted on the shoulder. These garments are now treasured objects in the museum in Lerwick, the main town on Fair Isle.

Traditionally, the diamond pattern in fishermen's sweaters designates wealth, the zig-zag patterns refer to twisting cliff paths, the cables portray fishermen's ropes, the tree of life tells of strong sons and long life, and the trellis pattern relates to stone fences and enclosed fields.

Fishermen of Aran who were drowned inshore could be readily identified by the patterns on their garments, as these varied from family to family and village to village. As Sheila McGregor notes: 'A man could no more wear the gansie of the next village than he could change his name; he might suffer the ultimate fate of being buried among strangers.'

In former times, jerseys and guernseys in the Channel Islands and in Scottish fishing villages often had the wearer's initials knitted into the jersey above the welt before the pattern started.

Sometimes the fisherman's name was knitted in full. In the Hebrides, fishermen wore jerseys with a distinctive yoke, which represented the house or home. In the middle of the yoke was an open diamond representing a window. If there was a heart inside the diamond, it meant that 'the heart was in the home'. Closed diamonds, or 'nets' edged the central design in a double plait that symbolised 'hoof prints in the sand'. 'Steps' to the house on the yoke led up from the middle of the lower part of the jersey. Double zig-zags referred to the 'ups and downs' of marriage and parallel zig-zags to the waves of the sea.

In the seventeenth and eighteenth century, hand knitting became a cottage industry of great economic importance in many areas of Britain and Europe. Because its practice was so endemic, ordinances were even introduced to curtail knitting when other important and necessary tasks needed implementation. On the island of Jersey in 1601, the Royal Court forbade the knitting of stockings, on pain of imprisonment and a diet of bread and water, during the six weeks of harvest and seaweed gathering. Both of these tasks were essential to the economy of the small island. To save heat and light, groups of knitters would work together in the dark, their yarn wound around a hollow rattle containing a few dried peas. If they dropped their ball of wool, they could then 'hear' it in the dark.

With the introduction of knitting machines by the late eighteenth century, hand knitting in a commercial sense almost died out. Small communities in coastal and rural parts of England, Scotland and Ireland, however, continued to produce from necessity, keeping knitting traditions and patterns alive. In the wider community, knitting became a largely unpaid, leisure pastime, which was practised by both men and women. Pattern books were introduced and general knitting skills increased.

During the two hundred years of European settlement in Australia, no traditions or specific patterns evolved. As with needlework, the traditions were handed down usually from the mother

Shearing the Rams TOM ROBERTS

country, Britain, where knitting patterns were propagated through women's magazines. In the twentieth century, it has been mainly women in Australia who have continued to knit in the domestic sphere, for family and friends. It has also been women who have recorded other women knitting. In the 1920s and 1930s, Grace Cossington Smith's *The Sock Knitter*, Vida Lahey's *Busy Fingers* and depictions of knitters by Dorrit Black found their way on to prestigious art gallery walls.

Knitting in Australia responded to overseas fashion trends and the dictates of two World Wars. When the Duke of Windsor sported a Fair Isle vest on St Andrews Golf Course, Scotland in 1922, he gave a much needed promotional charge to the flagging knitting industry in the Fair Isles. As in Britain, Fair Isle patterning subsequently became very popular in Australia. Coco Chanel set fashion trends in both the 1920s and the 1950s, which made fishermen's guernseys and chunky man-size jumpers a chic item of apparel. Fashion knitting retreated during the two World Wars when dedicated knitters focused their attention on balaclavas, mittens, mufflers and scarves for the troops abroad.

With the advent of the mini skirt and Mary Quant's 'Ginger Group Collection' of new, easy-fitting, casual, jersey-style clothes in 1964, knitting underwent a revival. Cling sweaters, sock ribbing and patterned stockings became high fashion items, and the newly found economic power of youth in affluent western cultures allowed them to both buy and dictate their fashion preferences. In the 1970s, young designers turned to hand knitting as a field for creative expression and explored traditional and folk designs from other countries as a source of inspiration.

The craft received attention from male painters and a different aspect of knitting found its way in to the galleries. David Hockney designed a picture sweater that was framed to hang on the wall, and Australian Robert Rooney painted a series on knitting stitches; one of these, *Superknit 6*, is included in this book.

The knitting revolution in England in the late 1960s and early 1970s saw the emergence of innovative and interpretive knitting and this in turn was adopted and adapted in Australia. With the opening of her Flamingo Park shop in 1973, Jenny Kee introduced the concept of uniquely Australian images on her hand knits, including kookaburras, kangaroos and 'Blinky Bill'. Galleries began including hand knits in their exhibitions. A gift from Australia of a kangaroo and a koala jumper to Prince Charles and Princess Diana for their marriage helped promote the international image of originality in Australian hand knits.

Hand knits became art knits and invaded art galleries in their own right when Jane de Teliga curated the *Art Clothes* exhibition at the Art Gallery of New South Wales in 1980–1981, and subsequently exported it to the Edinburgh Festival. Jane defines art knits as 'a style of work that has transcended the traditional boundaries of the craft of knitting to explore the broader aesthetic and expressive concerns of visual art.'

Jane added further impetus to the acceptance of hand knits as an art form when the *Art Knits* exhibition in 1988 at the Art Gallery of New South Wales entranced spectators. Australian art knits were part of the *Contemporary Art of Dress* exhibition at the Victoria and Albert Museum in London in 1989 and this collection was also shown in Australia.

A *Men Knitting* exhibition was promoted by the Wool Corporation in 1988 and shown at the Argyle Centre at The Rocks in Sydney. Not only was the knitting of interest, but the different backgrounds of the knitters oscillated between market gardeners and dam builders to well-paid executives and art teachers. There is a hidden core of male knitters in Australia, which needs to be encouraged.

Interest in the art of knitting fostered an exhibition, *The History of Knitting*, at the National Gallery of Victoria, curated by Rowena Clarke. This exhibition provided a framework within which Australian art knitters could find their place.

Knitting as an art form has had a long evolution. Although images on gallery walls have previously depicted the raw material in the wool, the knitter, the garment, even the stitches, *The Art of Knitting* reverses the roles. Well-known Australian knitters interpret the work of some of Australia's premier artists, taking the paintings off the gallery walls and out on to the streets in highly innovative and imaginative knitwear.

The choice of paintings in *The Art of Knitting* was determined by the intrinsic aesthetic quality of the work itself and the imagery evoked of Australia and its way of life. I would like to thank all artists or their estates for permission to reproduce the paintings used for interpretation in *The Art of Knitting* and their generosity of spirit in contributing to the concept.

In *The Art of Knitting* I have included a profile of each knitter adapted from interviews I have had with them. The knitters have not only generously contributed their ideas, sketches, accessories and art knits to the book, they have also explained in a short essay why they chose a particular painter or painters and how they have interpreted his or her work. They have also submitted a pattern for each garment, which is included in the book. *The Art of Knitting* is a testimonial to their skill.

Summer

JOHN COBURN

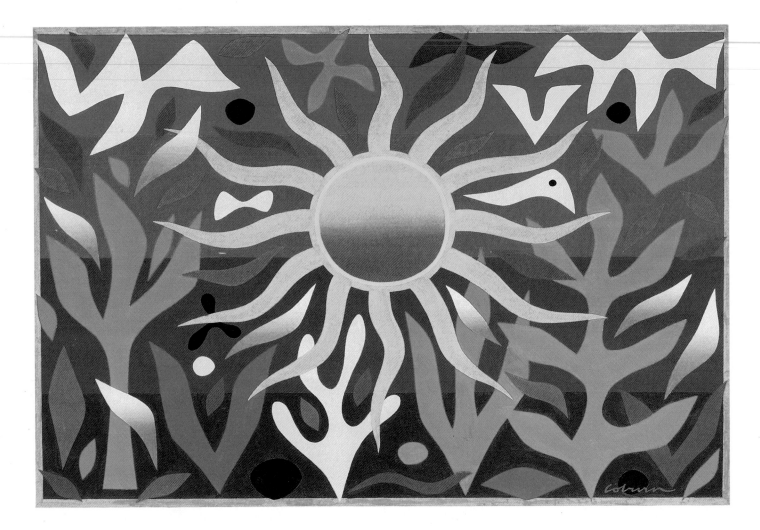

Interpreted by Dariel Brunton

In my cardigan interpretation of Coburn's painting, I have tried to capture the feeling of interacting shapes and colours and at the same time incorporate some of my own particular fetishes.

It would be difficult to find an Australian painter who offers more in his paintings for interpretation into knitting than John Coburn.

He provides a large vocabulary of shape and colour as well as suggestive ideas for the form of the garment itself. The rays of the sun in his painting *Summer, 1987*, for example, lend themselves to draping around a neckline like an enormous necklace. Other seasonal paintings in this group have the same propensity.

Coburn's designs in this series are flat, cut-out shapes plus colour. With his masterful arrangement of these simple, bold shapes and the colour relationships he uses, he achieves a wonderful sense of glowing order and vitality. There is a feeling of being totally immersed in colour, and a sense of everything being linked and unified. I particularly like the way he uses all available space, and how the entire picture surface seems to move.

Coburn's shapes echo the collages and paper cuts of Matisse, but also evoke the same religious feelings found in much mediaeval tapestry and stained glass. He has absorbed and consolidated these influences, and his work conveys his concern with, and belief in, religion and nature.

Tapestry has always appealed to Coburn, though he is primarily a painter. Of this work he says, 'My aim in my work is to create visual images which reflect emotions and feelings about nature and the landscape. I should like to reveal the transcendental mystery of nature, to create harmonies of form and colour that are like mystical experiences—the feeling of awe and wonder one sometimes has in the presence of nature.'

Tapestry has always been a good medium for works of a religious nature, and it is a natural vehicle for Coburn. There is a beautiful quality about the rich depth and glow of coloured wool, which is admirably suited to the visual language of Coburn.

The influences behind Coburn's art are numerous. Gardens, particularly tropical gardens from his childhood, are always recurrent. His shapes are biomorphic and his symbols are often religious in origin—the sun, the garden, the earth, the heavens—and associated with the Australian landscape. The influences of early 1960s abstraction and late 1960s hard-edged Colourfield painting are also evident in his style.

In my cardigan interpretation of Coburn's painting, I have

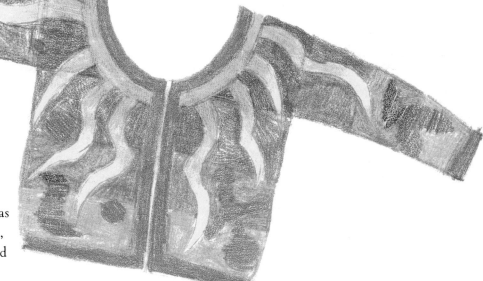

tried to capture the feeling of interacting shapes and colours and at the same time incorporate some of my own particular fetishes.

In my view, the more colours, shapes and textures a knitted garment has, the more likelihood it has of a 'special' status. For me, an empty or plain patch on a knitted garment is a shameful waste of opportunity to squeeze in more colours. I have therefore chosen some basic Coburn shapes, including the centrepiece sunshape, laid them over a little cropped cardigan, and concentrated on colour.

For the knitter, a practical word of advice is to pre-roll balls of multi-colour wools. For this cardigan, for example, I would roll all the blues together, all the pinks/reds together and so on. In the practical sense, we end up knitting with only five colours even though each colour is made up of a variety of tones, shades, textures and intensities of the one colour. It greatly simplifies an otherwise difficult job and has the added bonus of producing some random effects. This technique greatly increases the pleasure of the actual knitting process.

Place all balls of blue tonings in order from the lightest to the darkest shade of blue in front of you, cut an arm's length from each, and tie them together in order of colour gradation. Then reverse the process from the darker to the lighter shade, and you will be able to roll a ball of wool that will knit into a wonderful melange of blues. Just sew in the ends as you come to them. If the other colour groups are treated in the same manner, you can knit a cardigan with 20 colours, while only handling five balls of wool.

This colour technique will combine well with the strong biomorphic shapes derived from John Coburn's painting. I have chosen colours that relate to the work and are deep, intense and glowing. I feel the result is a bright and energetic piece of knitting, which is simple to make and also fun to wear.

The Value of Versatility

'One of my favourite things to do is to rearrange my wools. I like to lay them all out on the floor in different colour groups and move them around. This way I come up with colour combinations I would never have been able to pre-conceive.'

Dariel Brunton is discussing her love affair with knitting, wools and colour. 'I like to use a lot of colour. I've found that by using many shades of perhaps two compatible colours such as pink and green, in a great variety of textures, I produce a rich and complex effect. This complexity is often an illusion, as the patterns I use are rarely complicated.'

Chagall contends that the only movements in art that last are those very rare ones which possess innate colour. He claims that colour and painting are both inspired by the same thing—love. Colour with its lines contains your character and your message. Dariel's message is clear—it is one of joy and celebration in life.

Dariel was born in Melbourne and was exposed to strong and positive artistic influences in her formative years. Her mother is a skilled haute couture dressmaker as well as a weaver and an embroiderer. Her father is an architect and designer. Memories of her very early childhood revolve around her grandparents' beachside residence near Brighton where she spent happy days swimming and playing under the long jetties.

When she was seven, Dariel's parents separated and she and her brother spent the weekdays with her father in Melbourne and the weekends with her mother in

Trentham, a beautiful Victorian country town. Here she lived a communal lifestyle in a large, former gold-mining hotel, as Dariel reminisces, full of memories of the past:

> *The front bar had shelves of former gold rush bottles, the attic was full of old furniture, cards, books and newspapers. The numerous sheds were full of rusting saddlery, blacksmithing gear and machinery. There was an over-population of sheep, goats, horses, cats, possums and chooks. To me it was paradise. In the big ballroom my mother set up a loom and I learnt to weave there. She taught me to knit and crochet also.*

Dariel's life with her father in Melbourne was equally rich and absorbing. Her stepmother marketed herbs partly in liaison with Sunday Reed, the wife of John Reed, both of whom were renowned patrons of the arts at that time. 'Heide Herbs' was named after the Reed's house *Heide*, which Dariel remembers as 'the most magical place of art and nature'. The walls of the house and the gardens were a repository of some of the best Australian art of that period. As Dariel remembers:

> *The Nolan Ned Kelly paintings were on those walls. So too were Percival, Boyd, Hester, Tucker, Vasilieff and Counihan, amongst countless others. As a child I was more interested in the acres of fabulous gardens around the house, but unconsciously I absorbed a lot from the art with which I was in contact. In retrospect I realise how privileged I was to be exposed to such a rich and important period in Australian art.*

Through her father and stepmother, Dariel also mixed with photographers, commercial artists, designers and architects: 'My father loved "modern" things— aerodynamic cars and planes, state-of-the-art ergometrically designed drawing instruments. His favourite colour is white. He taught me a lot about drawing and he's been a fine example to me of dedication and commitment.'

At Unley High School, when Dariel was fifteen, she became interested in ceramic sculpture, and decided, after graduating in 1979, to enrol at North Adelaide School of Art, majoring in painting and drawing. At High School she knitted experimental concepts in jumpers. 'One I made was based on the colours and shades of liquorice allsorts and had to be tied on with straps. It was ridiculous—but it was certainly eye-catching.'

Dariel attended the Royal Melbourne Institute of Technology (RMIT) in 1983 for a further year's training before travelling around Australia for the next two to three years. Settling back into Adelaide, she exhibited drawings and paintings in group exhibitions and painted fabric that her mother made into garments for sale. She sold these at the Designers' Market.

Dariel traces her artistic influences to Matisse, Bonnard and Hundertwasser, whose paintings are like 'precious jewels' to her. She loves the highly decorative nature of his work and his use of pattern and colour.

She finds her inspiration for design in a range of sources, from nature to the kitchen sink. She elucidates:

> *Frogs are an endless source of design material for me—even the dullest, brownest-looking frog will have the most glorious underbelly or inner leg. Conversely, when I'm washing the dishes in the sink, I find that beautiful, oily sheen on the bubbles full of potential colour schemes. My messy cutlery drawer can provide an interesting design of round and long shapes. Wherever I look there are exciting ideas.*

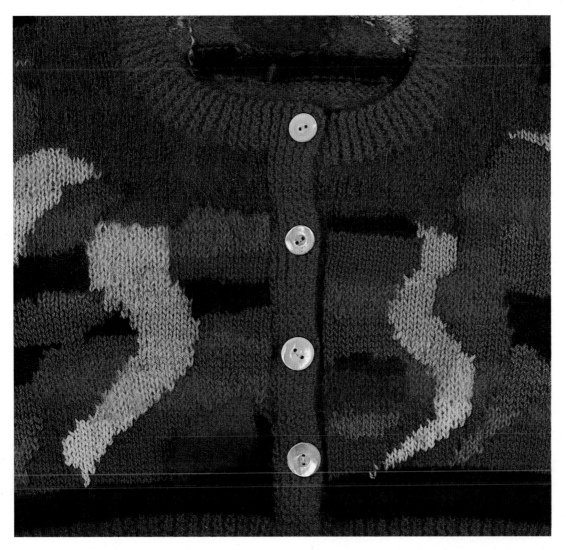

Her mentor in knitwear is Kaffe Fassett. His painterly approach to knitting, his fearless overuse of pattern and the brazen way he breaks all the rules have enormous appeal. His catchcry, 'If it's worth doing, it's worth overdoing' is an attitude with which Dariel empathises.

Dariel is impressed by the cross-pollination of ideas in Kaffe Fassett's work. Because he is adept in many different artistic areas and has many interests, his work is dense and multi-layered. Dariel is cognisant of the value of this versatility, and paints, draws, employs decoupage, knits, gardens and is very attentive to the everyday life around her as a source of inspiration. She also intends to take a course in weaving.

As Dariel now has an eighteen-month-old daughter Lily, she finds her time more fragmented. Knitting is a perfect creative outlet in these circumstances, requiring neither the block of concentrated time that painting does, nor the physical space. As Dariel says, 'Painting is a luxury. Knitting is a more sociable art form. Instead of having to say to Lily, "don't touch", as I would if I were attempting to paint, I give her coloured scraps of wool and she plays with them happily.'

Time has become more precious to Dariel and she is evolving a more disciplined approach to her knitting. To help her fulfil her orders, she now employs regular contract knitters, which leaves her freer to concentrate on design.

In the world of art knits, Dariel is a rising star to watch.

Measurements

	Small	Medium	Large
Actual Garment Measures (approx) (below armholes):	102	111	122 cm
Length (approx):	41	42	43 cm
Sleeve Fits:	43	43	43 cm

Materials

8 Ply Yarn in a Mixture of Yarns and Colours
Approx 350 (400–450) g in a mixture of blues for Background Colour
Approx 100 (150–150) g in a mixture of golds and tan for 1st Contrast
Approx 50 (100–150) g in a mixture of pinks and reds for 2nd Contrast
Approx 50 (50–50) g in a mixture of purples and mauves for 3rd Contrast
Approx 50 (50–50) g in a mixture of greens for 4th Contrast

Note - *Background and contrast colours are worked in random stripes in various yarns and colours as indicated above. Before commencing garment, wind off lengths of various yarns and colours into balls, joining together with knots and leaving ends 15 cm long. This will enable yarns and colours to be knitted in at random.*

One each 4.00mm (No 8) and 3.25mm (No 10) circular knitting needle . . . 80 cm long; one pair 3.25mm (No 10) knitting needles; 3 stitch holders; knitters needle for sewing seams; 5 buttons.

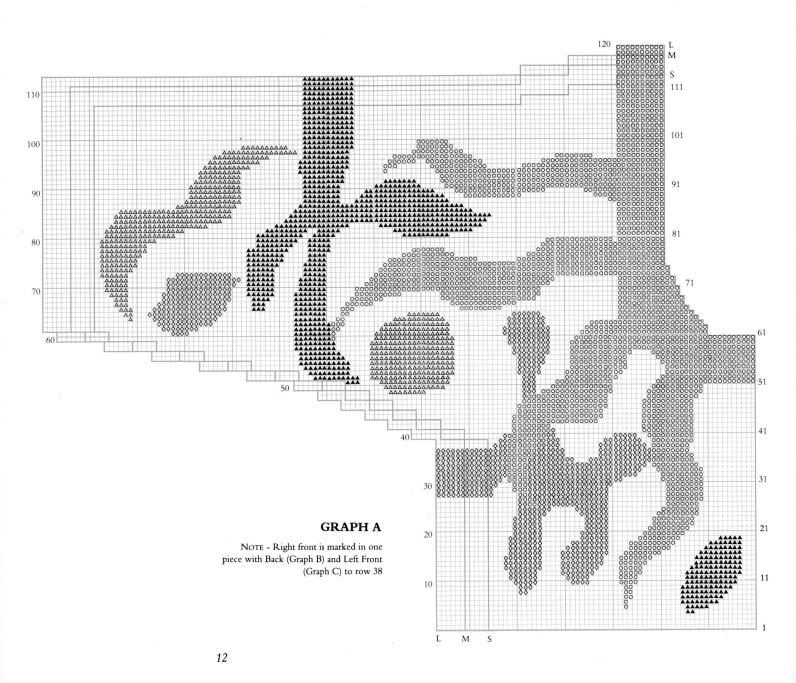

GRAPH A

Note - Right front is marked in one piece with Back (Graph B) and Left Front (Graph C) to row 38

Tension

22 sts and 30 rows to 10 cm over patt,
using 4.00mm needles.

Cardigan (*worked in one piece to armholes*)

Using 3.25mm circular needle and C, cast
on 247 (267–291) sts.
Work 4 rows K1, P1 rib.
5th Row: Rib 5, cast off 2 sts, rib to end.
6th Row: Rib to last 5 sts, cast on 2 sts, rib
5 . . . (one buttonhole).
Work a further 8 rows rib. (14 rows rib in
all)
Next Row: Rib 11 sts and slip these onto a
stitch holder for right front band, using
4.00mm circular needle patt across first

row of Graph A, first row of Graph B
then first row of Graph C , slip last 11 sts
onto a stitch holder for left front band
. . . 225 (245–269) sts.
Cont in patt as shown on Graphs A, B and
C until row 38 has been completed on all
Graphs.

DIVIDE FOR BACK AND FRONTS:
Next Row: Patt across 39th row of Graph
A, turn.
Cont on these 56 (61–67) sts for Right
Front.

SHAPE FOR SLEEVE:
Keeping patt correct from Graph A, cast
on 5 sts at beg of next and alt rows 6
times in all, then 10 sts at beg of foll alt
rows 5 times . . . 136 (141–147) sts.

K E Y

C	=	☐
C1	=	O
C2	=	▲
C3	=	△
C4	=	◇

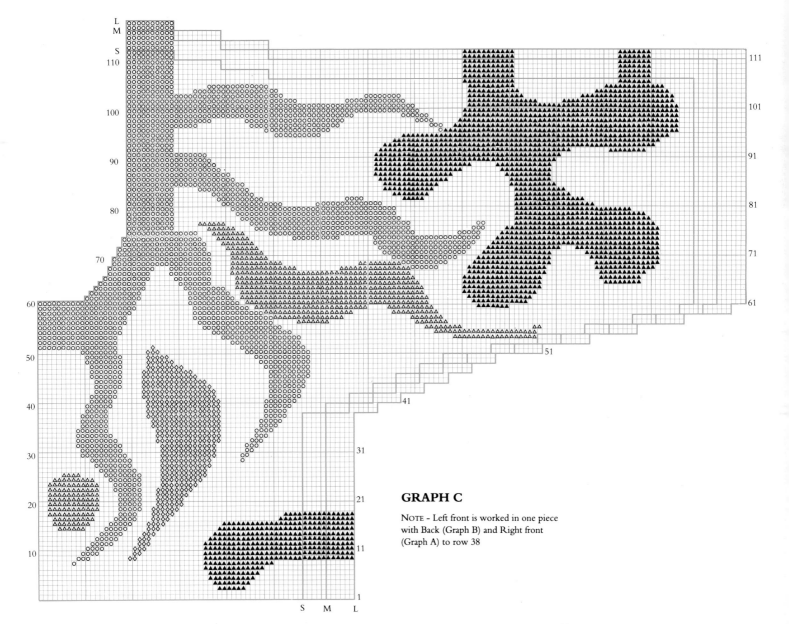

GRAPH C

NOTE - Left front is worked in one piece
with Back (Graph B) and Right front
(Graph A) to row 38

SHAPE NECK:

Next Row: Cast off 10 sts, patt to end.
Next Row: Cast on 3 sts, patt to end . .
129 (134–140) sts. Keeping patt correct
from Graph A, dec one st at neck edge in
every row 5 times, then in alt rows 4
times . . . 120 (125–131) sts.

SHAPE TOP SLEEVE AND SHOULDER:

Cast off 90 (95–101) sts at beg of next
row, then 10 sts at beg of foll alt rows 3
times.
With right side facing, join yarn to rem
sts, cast on 5 sts, patt 118 (128–140) sts
from Graph B (39th row), turn.
Cont on these 118 (128–140) sts for Back.

SHAPE FOR SLEEVES:

Keeping patt correct from Graph B, cast
on 5 sts at beg of next 11 rows, 10 sts at

beg of next 10 rows, then 3 sts at beg of
foll 2 rows . . . 279 (289–301) sts.
Cont without shaping until row 106
(110–112) has been completed.

SHAPE TOP SLEEVE AND SHOULDERS:

Cast off 90 (95–101) sts at beg of next 2
rows, then 10 sts at beg of foll 6 rows.
Leave rem 39 sts on stitch holder.
With right side facing, join yarn to rem 56
(61–67) sts, cast on 5 sts, patt across 39th
row of Graph C.
Cont on these 61 (66–72) sts for *Left Front*.
Cont to correspond with Right Front,
reversing shaping and working in patt as
shown on Graph C.

Right Front Band

With wrong side facing, using 3.25mm
needles and C, rib across 11 sts left on

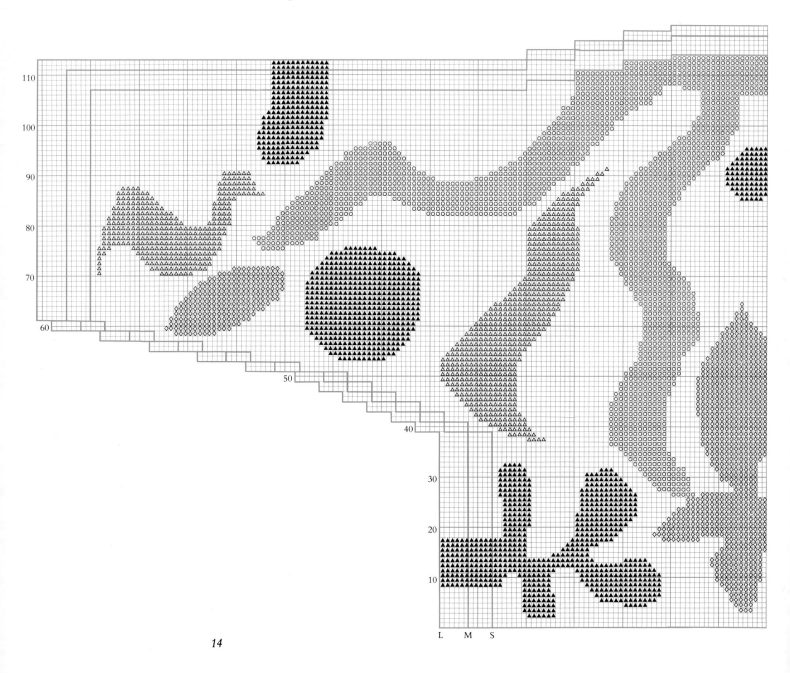

L   M   S

stitch holder on Right Front. Cont in rib, working a buttonhole (as before) in foll 17th and 18th rows from previous buttonhole 3 times in all . . . 4 buttonholes in total.

Work a further 13 rows rib. Leave sts on needle. Do not break off yarn.

Left Front Band

Work to correspond with Right Front Band, omitting buttonholes and working 1 row less. Break off yarn. Leave sts on stitch holder.

Neckband

Join top sleeve and shoulder seams. Sew front bands in position, stretching slightly to fit. With right side facing, using 3.25mm needle holding right front band

sts and C, knit up 143 (151–155) sts evenly around neck, incl sts from back neck stitch holder, then rib across sts on left front band stitch holder . . . 165 (173–177) sts. Work 9 rows K1, P1 rib, beg with a 2nd Row and working a buttonhole (as before) in 4th and 5th rows . . . 5 buttonholes in all.

Cuffs

With right side facing, using 3.25mm needles and C, knit up 47 (49–49) sts evenly along sleeve edge.
Work 23 rows K1, P1 rib, beg with a 2nd Row.
Cast off loosely in rib.

Making Up

Join side and sleeve seams. Sew on buttons.

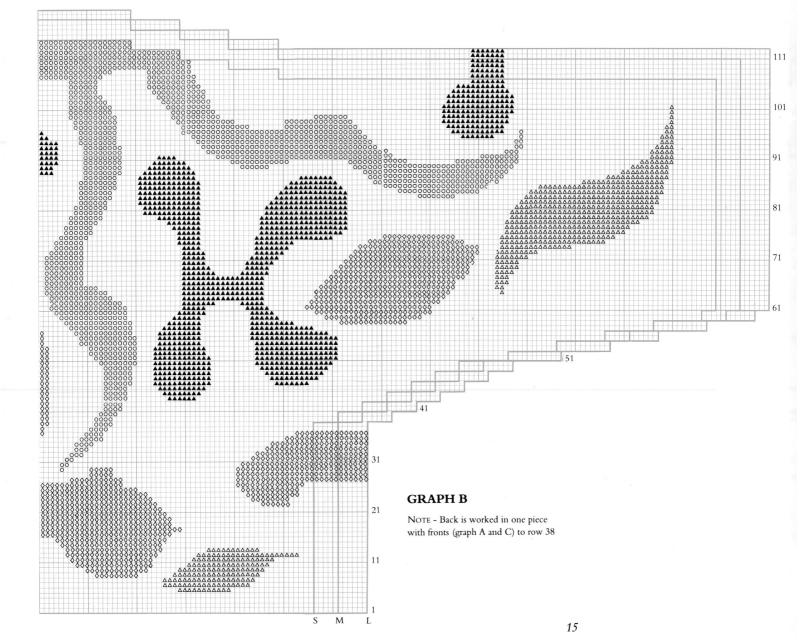

GRAPH B

NOTE - Back is worked in one piece with fronts (graph A and C) to row 38

Spring

JOHN COBURN

Interpreted by Kerry Nicholls

*Even though his work is full of abstract shapes, it is not just a geometric figure—
each shape is a representation of something vital and alive, an organic form of life.*

Tree of Life

Paradise Garden

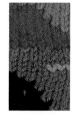 John Coburn was an easy choice to make. I was immediately attracted to his work and could easily imagine how well it would adapt to a knitted garment.

As a knitwear designer, I always look at patterns that tend to be repetitive, seeking a certain form and a definite order to interpret on to a jumper. My mind is very mathematical and when I think of designing a jumper the little squares on the graph paper play a major role in its design. This is no doubt the result of a background in Maths and Sciences with a total absence of artistic endeavours and interpretations.

Graphics and abstract forms, however, are something else. I love John Coburn's work; it gives me a feeling of movement and a joy of living things. I felt I didn't have to pick a particular painting to interpret, I could just look at a group of his paintings and tapestries and easily interpret his style on my jumper.

The first thing I noticed was that even though his work is full of abstract shapes, it is not just a geometric figure—each shape is a representation of something vital and alive, an organic form of life.

There were many common denominators in each of the paintings and tapestries I used. Perhaps the most striking was the green tree-like abstract, which to me definitely signified growth. I had to have this as a main feature in my pattern just as it seemed an important issue in Coburn's paintings.

Most of the forms pointed upwards, once again giving the feeling of dynamic growth just as naturally as nature itself.

The sun seemed the ultimate goal, however, I found this difficult to include without becoming overrun by a huge blob at the top of the jumper. I noticed that Coburn doesn't necessarily have a sun in his paintings; it is symbolised by circles and rainbows, which tend to appear at the midline and top border of his painting.

I also felt that the neck shaping of the jumper would signify the sun. I have used the rainbow on the back where the neck shaping is not necessary, but on the front the collar is an integral part of this rainbow effect.

John Coburn's paintings are very full and animated and involved with form and movement. I was glad not to have to deal with a muted landscape or sunset that wafted off into the background with no intense feeling to it. His paintings have depth and seem to evoke basic feelings of joy, a freedom of spirit and a passion for life; a perfect pattern for a jumper that is a wearable form of art.

Perhaps the changing background colours in the cardigan give it a more earthy feel than just one background colour. It certainly transforms the garment into a landscape or scene and gives a depth of organic life that maybe it would lack without these 'levels' of colour.

It is difficult to stop at one jumper when designing a 'Coburn'. Every time I look at his work, I think next time I could bring out this particular idea or include different shapes that are all undeniably Coburnesque.

Coburn's abstract shapes would not have the same appeal, however, without such intense use of colour. The colours are so vivid and strong that they seem to give a basic understanding to the whole painting. To me the colours are also uniquely Australian, typifying the richness of the earth, abundance of the natural resources and the beauty of the landscape.

Mathematical Designs

Kerry Nicholls is unusual for a creative art knitter. She can neither draw nor paint, nor has she ever taken a lesson in either. Kerry thinks mathematically. All her designs are conceived on graph paper, which is her only mode of deciphering her visual concepts. She is bemused herself: 'It's funny where maths can lead you. I intended becoming a doctor. Now I've ended up an art knitter.'

Kerry is a very energetic 30-year-old, who lives in Merimbula, a south coast fishing town in New South Wales. She produces a range of garments and individual items for boutiques in Sydney, and retails to the public direct from her own premises in the town.

One of five children, Kerry was born in New Zealand, but moved to Sydney with her family when she was ten years old. Her mother taught her to knit and Kerry remembers her first efforts as hot water bottle covers. She knitted intermittently at high school where she concentrated her studies on mathematics, chemistry and physics. Kerry left high school when she was 17 to travel and gain some knowledge of the wider world, before settling into serious study. For the next three years she travelled on her own, working in bars or restaurants throughout Canada, the United States and Europe.

In London Kerry discovered and was entranced by the designs of Patricia Roberts. She knitted her first jumper for herself based on one of Roberts' patterns— a relatively ambitious project for a sometime knitter. Kerry says: 'It was a disaster. It ended up full of holes and about size sixty-four.'

Kerry returned to Australia in 1980, abandoned her idea of becoming a doctor

and for the next four years studied acupuncture. During this time she married, had a baby son and practised knitting in her spare time. She says: 'I needed it. I didn't know why at the time. I was studying intensively—anatomy, physiology and science—and of an evening I'd just turn to

my knitting. In retrospect it was both therapy and a way of balancing the type of study I was undertaking.' As her knitting became more professional she sold her garments to her friends as a source of income.

To complete her studies in acupuncture, Kerry spent six months working at a hospital in China. She took her baby son with her and her sister went along as nanny for the child. The Chinese and their seemingly casual approach to knitting greatly impressed Kerry: 'In the city everyone I visited seemed to knit. They went about their daily business knitting in the street as they did their shopping or walked to the bus stop. They throw their

knitting over their right shoulder and have no problems joining in a sleeve or a leg as they talk to others or just stroll around'.

Kerry's reminiscences evoke similar images and casual attitudes to knitting in other eras and cultures. In the French district of Landes the local people knitted in the most unlikely situations. With a pouch around their necks hanging like a satchel down their backs, they tended their sheep on stilts and knitted at the same time. The peasants were expert on stilts and could even dance on them. The pouches on their backs were used to store the raw wool gathered each day, the spun yarn, needles and the finished knitting.

In nineteenth-century Yorkshire the story is told of a woman who used to walk three miles each week to the local market to sell the family's knitting output, which she carried on her head. She knitted all the way there, bought enough worsted yarn for the following week's knitting, placed it on her head and walked all the way home. Usually she had finished a pair of stockings by the end of the day.

In China, Kerry was not yet as dedicated or as accomplished as these examples, but her apprenticeship was well under way. With her studies completed there, she travelled to London with her son, and began practising acupuncture at a dance studio. Again inspired by Patricia Roberts and the range of wools and colours available, Kerry invested in a knitting machine. She haunted knitting shops and woollen mills, deciding to forgo acupuncture for knitting. She felt the need to spend more time with her small son and this would only be possible if she worked from home. She designed and made a range of children's clothes, which she sold at different markets. She was encouraged and guided by an American designer living in London who suggested shaping and styling suitable for successful marketing.

Kerry returned to Australia in 1985, moved to Merimbula on the south coast of New South Wales and set up acupuncture studios. Knitting again dominated her leisure time. She designed and knitted a huge coat as a gift for her sister's 21st birthday. Her sister, an architect who lived in Italy, wanted 'something fantastic': 'She asked for a Jenny Kee type garment but I was determined it was going to be a Kerry Nicholls original. At that stage when I finished knitting it, I didn't even know how to sew up the seams. I learnt as I went along'. The coat was a huge success and when Kerry borrowed and wore it in London the following year, people followed her in the streets asking her where she had bought it.

Realising the potential in original hand knits, when Kerry returned to Australia she designed, knitted and approached the Dorian Scott boutique in Sydney with four jumpers. She has been making garments for Dorian Scott ever since.

Of her patterns Kerry comments: 'I employed a knitter and I had to do designs that I knew would sell. Australiana was a natural choice and there is still a strong market for it with overseas tourists. Australians themselves are ready for something more sophisticated.'

Kerry feels that Australian knitwear has a very distinct quality about it, based both on colour sense and an uninhibited approach to design and materials. In European and American markets it attracts a lot of attention. Returning to New Zealand last year, Kerry was overwhelmed by the disparity in the aesthetic sense in knitting between the neighbouring countries: 'I was not impressed by either their sense of design or colour. It is particularly distressing when you realise the wonderful Maori designs and colour sense that artisans have to draw on within their own culture.'

Kerry finds her inspiration for design in everyday life, whether it be paisley wallpaper, patterned carpets, a plate or a flower. She fully realises, however, the limitations of design by graph and intends studying drawing and painting in her spare time.

Like other art knitters, Kerry employs a number of piece-makers for whose work she has great respect: 'These women are great knitters and this is often the only way they can earn money. They prefer to work from home often because they have small children. Others live in remote areas or on country properties and knit in their spare time'.

Kerry divorced her first husband, remarried in 1986, and is expecting a child later this year. Her husband, a former mechanical engineer, now assists Kerry in her retail outlet. Kerry feels that what she may lack in drawing skills, she makes up for in marketing. She contends that it is no good being a fantastic art knitter if you can't sell the garments. Next year Kerry and her husband will open their second retail outlet in Canberra, a well-researched decision that will further promote her name as an art knitter.

Measurements

	Small	Medium	Large
Actual Garment Measures (approx):	134	142	150 cm
Length (approx):	58	59	60 cm
Sleeve Seam (approx):	39	39	39 cm

Materials

CLECKHEATON 12 PLY MACHINE WASH (50g balls)

Main Colour (MC) Black	4	5	6 balls
Contrast 1 (C1) Cobalt Blue	4	5	6 balls

Contrast 2 (C2) Green	3	4	5 balls
Contrast 3 (C3) Brown	3	3	4 balls
Contrast 4 (C4) D Blue	2	3	3 balls
Contrast 5 (C5) Apricot	1	1	1 ball
Contrast 6 (C6) White	1	1	1 ball
Contrast 7 (C7) Light Red	1	1	1 ball
Contrast 8 (C8) Dark Red	1	1	1 ball

KEY

MC	=	●
C1	=	△
C2	=	╱
C3	=	▲
C4	=	✕
C5	=	◇
C6	=	─
C7	=	○
C8	=	V

One pair each 4.00mm (No 8) and 5.50mm (No 5) knitting needles; 2 stitch holders; knitters needle for sewing seams.

Tension

18 sts and 24 rows to 10cm over patt using 5.50mm needles.

Back

Using 4.00mm needles and MC, cast on 83 (89–95) sts.
Work 13 rows K1, P1 rib.
14th Row: Rib 4 (4–6), *inc in next st, rib 1, rep from * to last 1 (3–3) st/s, rib 1 (3–3) . . . 122 (130–138) sts.
Change to 5.50mm needles.
Work in patt as shown on Graph A until row 126 (128–130) has been completed.

SHAPE SHOULDERS:

Keeping patt correct from Graph, cast off 11 (12–13) sts at beg of next 6 rows, then 9 (10–11) sts at beg of foll 2 rows.
Leave rem 38 sts on a stitch holder.

Front

Work as for Back until row 110 of Graph has been completed.

SHAPE NECK:

Next Row: Patt 56 (60–64) sts, turn.
Cont on these 56 (60–64) sts.
Keeping patt correct from Graph, cast off 3 sts at beg of next row, then K3tog at neck edge in next 3 rows . . . 47 (51–55) sts.
Dec one st at neck edge in alt rows until 42 (46–50) sts rem.
Work 1 (3–5) row/s from Graph, thus completing row 126 (128–130).

SHAPE SHOULDER:

Cast off 11 (12–13) sts at beg of next and alt rows 3 times in all.
Work 1 row. Cast off rem 9 (10–11) sts.
Slip next 10 sts onto stitch holder and leave. With right side facing, join yarn to rem 56 (60–64) sts and work to correspond with side just completed, reversing shaping.

Sleeves

Using 4.00mm needles and MC, cast on 35 (37–39) sts.
Work 13 rows K1, P1 rib.
14th Row: Rib 4 (2–0), *inc in next st, rib 1, rep from * to last st, rib 1 . . . 50 (54–58) sts.
Change to 5.50mm needles.
Work in patt as shown on Graph B, inc one st at each end of 5th and foll 4th rows until there are 76 (80–84) sts, then in foll 6th rows until there are 84 (88–92) sts.
Work 7 rows without shaping, thus completing Graph.
Cast off loosely.

Neckband

Join right shoulder seam. With right side facing, using 4.00mm needles and C1, knit

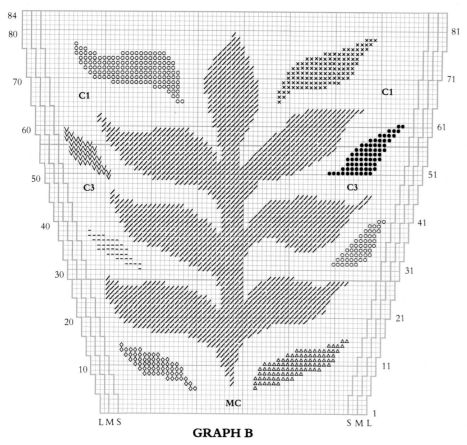

GRAPH B

up 84 (88–92) sts evenly around neck, incl sts from stitch holders.

Next Row: *K1, P1, rep from * to end.
Rep last row 28 times.
Cast off loosely in rib.

Making Up

Join left shoulder seam. Tie a coloured marker 24 (25–26) cm down from beg of shoulder shaping on side edges of Back and Front to mark armholes. Sew in sleeves between markers, placing centre of sleeve to shoulder seam. Join side and sleeve seams. Fold neck band in half onto wrong side and slip stitch loosely in position.

GRAPH A

Waratahs

GRACE COSSINGTON SMITH

Interpreted by Kerry Nicholls

Grace Cossington Smith's painting is bold and dramatic. She has given it a third dimension, painting the waratah against other waratahs that form discernible patterns and shadows where the leaves are all inextricably layered upon one another.

 I felt Grace Cossington Smith's *Waratahs* was a natural choice yet also a challenge.

The instinctive appeal of flowers has long been part of my designing career, having used the waratah as one of my very earliest patterns. My design was bold and graphic (as most of my work is), and two dimensional with little or no subtlety at all. The waratah appealed to me because of its distinct colour and clearly defined shape.

Grace Cossington Smith's painting is much more complex. Her painting is bold and dramatic, yet has a soft and feminine appeal. She has given it a third dimension, painting the waratah against other waratahs that form discernible patterns and shadows where the leaves are all inextricably layered upon one another.

Her distinct use of colour seems to enhance the different dimensions of the painting and gives the background a definitive pattern. This was a challenge in itself, because the colours, shapes, textures, depth and the overall feeling of *Waratahs* had to be interpreted and I did not want to design just a copy of the painting.

The decisions were many, for example, would it be better to create a cardigan or a jumper? The softness and femininity of the painting made me decide instinctively on a cardigan. In my experience cardigans have a far greater appeal to women than jumpers, which always seem more masculine.

I also needed to decide how many waratahs to have on the garment. Even though the painting predominantly features one waratah, it is not the impression the painting conveys. You get the feeling of many waratahs, one on top of the other, giving the painting lots of depth.

I wanted to bring out this third dimension and the feeling of many flowers without making the pattern too cluttered or confusing. Two flowers seemed the logical conclusion, defining each of them against the contrasting background, rather than a mass of red on red.

The background leaves and shadowing was my next hurdle. Being an intrinsic part of the painting I knew they had to be included, yet I felt they needed to be 'tidied up' in a graphic sense. The diagonal crossing of the leaves to form a lattice arrangement seemed the perfect solution to express the shapes within the painting. The two colours suggest the shadowing within this form.

Initially, I had decided to keep the background colour similar to that of the painting, and perhaps include different textures as a means of separating the similarly coloured leaves.

My pattern, however, had little use of black and the background colour was so similar to that of the leaves, it seemed to lose its depth and dramatic appeal even though the wools were of different textures. Black came to the rescue as it often does to 'bring out' a pattern and even though the painting itself has a lighter background colour, I feel the cardigan only does justice to the painting with the black background. It transforms the garment into something special, warm yet dramatic, with a flamboyancy which is suggested by the painting. I was pleased with this outcome.

Choosing wool from a limited selection is always a concern, but fortunately Cleckheaton had a range of colours that included the exact colours I wanted, so the choice proved reasonably easy.

I was also more concerned with what textures I would use to create the right impression. Mohair seemed the logical choice for the waratah and background leaves. Instead of also using mohair for the background, I chose the machinewash 12 ply to give the mohair a definite edge. This also seems to create a multi-dimensional look without having to include bobbles or other forms of texture.

I found the designing of this garment both enjoyable and fulfilling. Everyone who undertakes the challenge to knit it will also find the finished work a credit to themselves and to Grace Cossington Smith.

Measurements

	Small	Medium	Large
Actual Garment Measures (*approx*):	120	130	140 cm
Length (*approx*):	59	60	61 cm
Sleeve Seam (*approx*):	40	40	40 cm

Materials

CLECKHEATON 12 PLY MACHINEWASH (*50 g balls*)

Main Colour (MC) Black	12	13	14 balls

AND CLECKHEATON CLASSIQUE 12 PLY MOHAIR (*50 g balls*)

Contrast 1 (C1) Light Brown	4	5	6 balls
Contrast 2 (C2) Red	3	3	3 balls
Contrast 3 (C3) Turquoise	2	2	2 balls

AND CLECKHEATON NEW CAPRICE 8 PLY (*50 g balls*)

Contrast 4 (C4) Purple	3	3	3 balls
Contrast 5 (C5) Pink	1	1	1 ball

One pair each 4.00mm (No 8) and 5.50mm (No 5) knitting needles; 2 stitch holders; 9 buttons; knitters needle for sewing seams.

Tension

18 sts and 22 rows over patt using 5.50mm needles.

NOTE: *Two strands of Mohair are worked together at all times.*

Back

Using 4.00mm needles and MC, cast on 75 (81–89) sts.
Work 13 rows K1, P1 rib.
Next Row: Rib 3 (2–4), * inc in next st, rib 1, rep from * to last 2 (1–3) st/s, rib 2 (1–3) . . . 110 (120–130) sts.
Change to 5.50mm needles.
Work in patt as shown on Graph A until row 118 (120–122) has been completed.

SHAPE SHOULDERS:
Keeping patt correct from Graph, cast off 8 (9–10) sts at beg of next 10 rows.
Cast off rem 30 sts.

Left Front

Using 4.00mm needles and MC, cast on 41 (43–47) sts.
Work 13 rows K1, P1 rib.
Next Row: Rib 8 sts and slip these onto a stitch holder for front band, rib 2 (1–2), inc in next 1 (0–1) st/s, * inc in next st, rib 1, inc in next st, rep from * to last 3 (1–3) st/s, rib 3 (1–3) . . . 52 (57–62) sts.
Change to 5.50mm needles.
Work in patt from Graph A until row 109 has been completed.

SHAPE NECK:
Keeping patt correct from Graph, cast off 5 sts at beg of next row, then dec one st at neck edge in every row 7 times . . . 40 (45–50) sts.
Cont without shaping until row 118 (120–122) has been completed.

SHAPE SHOULDER:
Cast off 8 (9–10) sts at beg of next and alt rows 5 times in all.

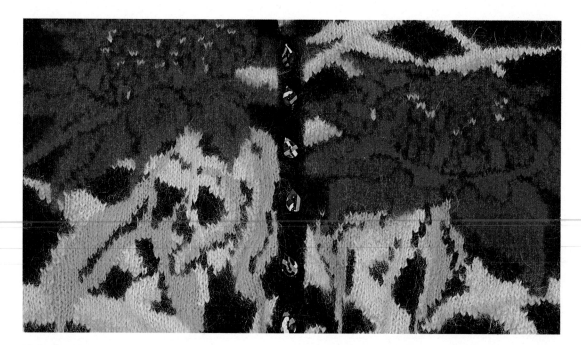

KEY

MC = ☐

C1 = ╱

C2 = ○

C3 = ✖

C4 = ▲

C5 = ⋁

Right Front

Using 4.00mm needles and MC, cast on 41 (43–47) sts.
Work 2 rows K1, P1 rib.
Next Row: Rib 4, yon twice, rib 2 tog, rib to end.
Next Row: Rib to last 6 sts, drop 1 loop, P1 loop, rib 4 . . . one buttonhole.
Work 9 rows rib.
Next Row: Rib 3 (1–3) st/s, * inc in next st, rib 1, inc in next st, rep from * to last 11 (9–11) sts, inc in next 1 (0–1) st/s, rib 2 (1–2), slip last 8 sts onto stitch holder for front band . . . 52 (57–62) sts.
Cont as for Left Front, reversing shaping.

Sleeves

Using 4.00mm needles and MC, cast on 33 (35–37) sts.
Work 13 rows K1, P1 rib.
Next Row: Rib 4 (4–2), * inc in next st, rib 1, rep from * to last 3 (1–1) st/s, rib 3 (1–2) . . . 46 (50–54) sts.
Change to 5.50mm needles.
Work in patt as shown on Graph B, inc one st at each end of 5th and foll 4th rows 18 times in all . . . 82 (86–90) sts.
Work 7 rows without shaping, thus completing Graph.
Cast off loosely.

Right Front Band

With wrong side facing and using 4.00mm needles and MC, rib across 8 sts left on stitch holder on Right Front. Cont in rib, working a buttonhole (as before) in 3rd and 4th rows and foll 13th and 14th rows from previous buttonhole until there are 9 buttonholes in all. Work 4 rows rib. Cast off. Band should fit along Right Front when slightly stretched. Sew band in position.

Left Front Band

Work to correspond with Right Front Band, omitting buttonholes.

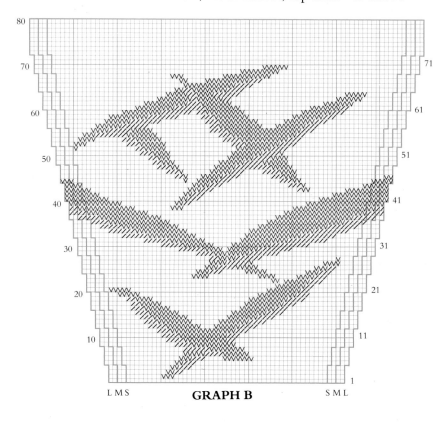

GRAPH B

GRAPH A

Neckband

Join shoulder seams. With right side
facing and using 4.00mm needles and MC,
knit up 83 (87–91) sts evenly around neck,
beg at the 5th st of right band and ending
on the 4th st of left band.
Work 29 rows of K1, P1 rib, beg with a
2nd row.
Cast off loosely in rib.

Making Up

Tie a coloured marker 22 (23–24) cm
down from beg of shoulder shaping on
side edges of Back and Fronts to mark
armholes. Sew in sleeves between
markers, placing centre of sleeve to
shoulder seam. Join side and sleeve seams.
Fold neckband in half onto wrong side and
a slipstitch loosely into place. Sew buttons
in place.

Shearers Playing
for a Bride

A R T H U R   B O Y D

Interpreted by Roz Avent

I first saw Shearers Playing for a Bride *when taking my then four-year-old son to the National Gallery of Victoria to see some of my favourite paintings. When he saw the large dark painting with its menacing overtones, he announced in a loud voice that it was 'just like a nightmare'.*

Arthur Boyd is one of the most important artists Australia has produced since the Second World War. He has been able to synthesise the European experience with the raw, primitive nature of this land to create a new vision, a kind of twentieth-century White Dreaming. Born in 1920, his early years were spent in the Melbourne suburb of Murrumbeena in a house built by his father, the potter and sculptor Merric Boyd. The atmosphere was highly stimulating for a young child with its bohemian spirit, prolific artistic activity and constant discussions on art, literature, philosophy and religion. Very early in his life, Arthur demonstrated a talent for both painting and pottery. In fact, all five children of Merric and Doris Boyd became artists. Arthur's children are also painters, making four generations of artists in the Boyd family.

Merric Boyd was a formidable figure. He combined a Victorian morality with a sensitive artistic nature, and also suffered from epilepsy. He was to be a great influence in his son's art.

Arthur was also influenced by the Old Testament stories read to him by his highly religious grandmother Emma, the novels of Dostoevsky, and the paintings of Van Gogh. Prior to the late 1930s, he painted mainly pastoral landscapes, portraits and interiors. With the influx of European refugees to Melbourne, some of whom became friends of the family, he became aware of expressionist painting and his own style began to change.

The Second World War brought to the surface his feelings of uncertainty and fear, which he painted as macabre fantasies of coffins, cripples and creatures of prey. They represented his psychological rejection of the devastation and futility of the world conflict. These paintings were often set within the structure of a biblical story.

In 1951, Arthur Boyd travelled by train to Central Australia to broaden his vision. Like many city dwellers, it was the first time he had come into contact with Aborigines. He was deeply shocked at the barbarous treatment they received and the poverty and helplessness in which they lived. It was not until six years had passed that he was able to synthesise all that he had seen and felt, and find a way to express it. He then embarked on a series of paintings where he used the symbol of the half-caste bride to represent the people who are rejected by both black and white societies. Each painting can be seen as an image of racial tension or as the unfulfilled dreams of an oppressed people. Seen together, they tell a story of powerlessness.

In 1959, Boyd and his family moved to London. It was to be 21 years before he would return to Australia to live and paint. He now lives on the banks of the Shoalhaven River in New South Wales where he continues to paint mythological and biblical subjects and landscapes, all of which continue to shape the way we see our world.

I first saw *Shearers Playing for a Bride* when taking my then four-year-old son to the National Gallery of Victoria to see some of my favourite paintings. When he saw the large dark painting with its menacing overtones, he announced in a loud voice that it was 'just like a nightmare'.

Does a work of art 'grow' on you or do your perceptions change with the years? When I recently saw this painting again, it immediately caught my eye. I now feel that it is a very exciting painting with its sombre colouring lit by the drama of the white streak of the bride. Throughout the painting, circles are repeated—in the moths' wings, the shearers' toes and eyes, the horns of the sheep, flowers, the black spades on the playing cards and the red dot of the sheep's eyes.

I love the upward sweep of the bride in the painting, but didn't want to have a large area of white in the knitted garment. I decided to knit a large group of flowers across the front of the garment, based on the bouquet in the bride's hand and with the same impression of movement. I chose mohair as the yarn because I wanted the feel of a warm dark night. The white lace collar is my symbol for the bride.

Artistic Traditions

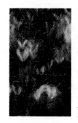

Roz Avent lives in Brunswick, an inner Melbourne suburb, with her husband Pip, and their two young children Indiana and Jasper. The family have recently moved to the city from Castlemaine, a small, former gold-mining town north of Melbourne. They enjoyed life in a country town, particularly in Castlemaine, which is known for its artists' colony, its lovely old houses and beautiful gardens.

The move to Melbourne, however, was precipitated because Pip, a well-known tuba player in a jazz band, found the travelling between Castlemaine and Melbourne for gigs too time consuming and exhausting. Roz says: 'We never seemed to

have any time together . . . It was a matter of priorities.'

During their two year sojourn in Castlemaine, Pip taught music in the neighbouring country towns as well as performing each week in a band. Roz painted, knitted and began dyeing wool:

I was dismayed by the range of colours available that it seemed the only thing to do. When I started experimenting with dyeing I became bewitched by the alchemy of the process. I decided against using natural dyes, such as gum leaves, because you have toxic chemicals such as alum sitting around in your kitchen. I tried a range of dyeing products, but was most satisfied with the results of Landscape dyes. It was like magic. I'd put the wool in, leave it to absorb

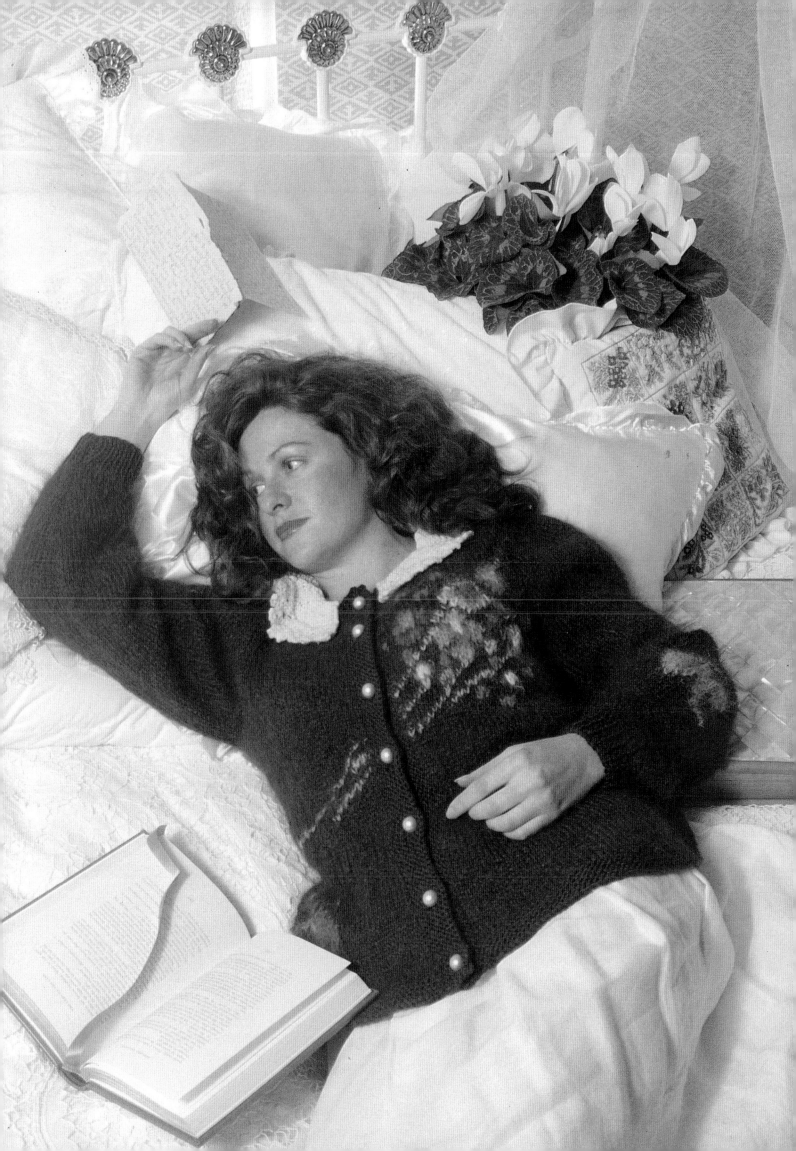

the colour and lift it out. My kitchen was a blaze of colour. Then I had to go through a much more down to earth process to establish that I could repeat the same colour every time. That was more difficult. But I'm good at dyeing wool because being a painter I can match colours. It takes time and care to get a spread of even colour through the wool, but it's worth it.

In her Brunswick studio there is a range of more than 100 colours ready to be knitted into one-off garments. Partly because of cost, Roz is currently dyeing her wools with acid milling dyes. She has a mail order company, 'Wild Dreams', which supplies other knitters. Ken Killeen, a kindred spirit and co-knitter who lives in Castlemaine, has high praise for both her

range of colours and the quality of her wool.

Roz began knitting as a child and thinks her stepmother may have taught her. It took Roz about two years to knit her first pair of bedsocks; the first bedsock was the original pink, but by the time she had finished the second, it was a nice shade of grey and about three times larger. She did not knit again until she was into her thirties. In the intervening years she became an artist.

Roz married when she was 20 and travelled to England with Pip, who was studying music in London. She enrolled at an Aldgate art school, which didn't require a folio. Inspired by the teaching, she worked six days a week to improve her skills. The standard she reached was such that she was accepted at the City and Guilds Art School where she studied full time, gaining a diploma in fine art. Roz then did a post-graduate course at the Wimbledon School of Art and Printmaking.

Pip finished his course at the music school at the same time Roz was accepted into the art school. In 1974–79, London was a very exciting place to be; it was also very expensive. As an overseas student not on a scholarship, nor entitled to discounted fees, Roz's training was contingent on financial support. Pip joined the Coldstream Guards Band, changing the guard at Buckingham Palace until Roz finished her course in 1979.

The Avents returned to Australia in 1980; Jasper was born in 1981 and Indiana in 1982. Motherhood was a shock to Roz. It still is: 'What I've found is that with kids your time is so fragmented. I thought that when the kids went to school this would change. But it hasn't. The phone, the doorbell, the shopping and all the other chores associated with home and family never seem to leave you with a block of time that is your very own'. This fragmentation of time was the reason Roz began to knit again.

Painting requires concentration and a certain amount of space. Since her children were born Roz has rarely had the time or the space in which to paint. Frustrated creatively, a friend suggested that she start knitting again. It was something she could pick up and put down at all odd intervals day and night. Once she began she would knit until 3 am if she could see an end in sight for a garment. Previously she had knitted only for friends and family, but when she decided to knit commercially, she found she was not quick enough. Roz therefore employed knitters to help make up her designs.

Roz sees her art knits as one way of expressing her creativity by exploring colour and design, and making some

income. In the future she would like to make one-off garments, paint again, make masks and sculpt. There is a strong tradition of artistic creativity in her family. Her mother painted, in her younger days her grandmother was a concert pianist and her grandfather, though by profession a sea-captain, was a very good amateur sculptor. One of his busts reposes on top of the piano. Roz says:

> It wasn't until I started taking some classes in sculpture that I understood just how good he was. He took casual lessons at the College of Advanced Education. But he had an innate understanding of form, which I find amazing considering how little time and academic training he brought to his work. He and my grandmother also potted together. My great regret is that today I don't possess any of their ceramics. My grandparents have been quite an inspiration to me.

As we talk Roz's daughter Indiana shows her mother an intricate collage she has just made. Underscoring our conversation, through the walls Pip is practising his musical score. Roz shows me her current imaginative piece of hand knitting. The grandparents are here with us and they are smiling.

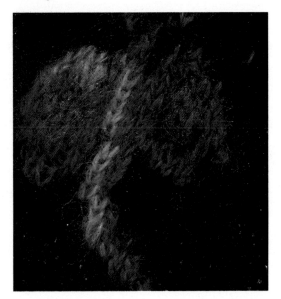

Measurements

	Small	Medium	Large
Actual Garment Measures (*approx*):	90	95	100 cm
Length (*approx*):	61	64	68 cm
Sleeve Seam:	42	43	44 cm

Materials

CLECKHEATON 12 PLY MOHAIR (*50g balls*)

	Small	Medium	Large
Main Colour (MC) Dark blue	7	8	8 balls
Contrast 1 (C1) Red	1	1	1 ball
Contrast 2 (C2) Mid blue	1	1	1 ball
Contrast 3 (C3) Dark green	1	1	1 ball
Contrast 4 (C4) Tan	1	1	1 ball
Contrast 5 (C5) White	1	1	1 ball
Contrast 6 (C6) Light green	1	1	1 ball
Contrast 7 (C7) Pale blue	1	1	1 ball
Contrast 8 (C8) Yellow	1	1	1 ball

AND CLECKHEATON 12 PLY MACHINE WASH (*50g balls*)

	Small	Medium	Large
Contrast 9 (C9) Dark blue	3	4	4 balls

AND CLECKHEATON 5 PLY MACHINE WASH (*50g balls*)

	Small	Medium	Large
Contrast 10 (C10) White	1	1	1 ball

One 5.50mm (No 5) circular knitting needle . . . (80 cm long); one pair each 5.50mm (No 5), 4.50mm (No 7) and 4.00mm (No 8) knitting needles; 4.00mm crochet hook; black shirring elastic; knitters needle for sewing seams and embroidery (if desired); 7 buttons.

Tension

17 sts and 23 rows to 10cm over stocking st using 5.50mm needles and 12 Ply Mohair.

NOTE: *Small areas of colour on Graphs may be embroidered on afterwards using knitting stitch embroidery.*

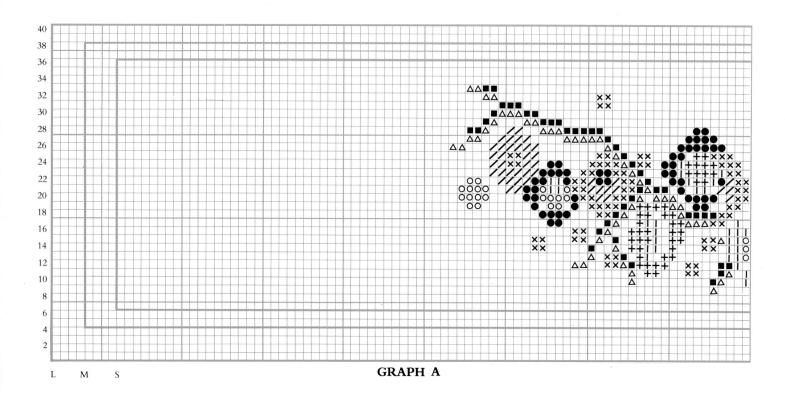

GRAPH A

Cardigan (worked in one piece to waist).

Using 5.50mm circular needle and C9, cast on 200 (208–216) sts.

Knit 7 rows garter stitch.

8th Row: K2 (6–9), * K2 tog, K3, rep from * to last 3 (7–12) sts, K2 tog, K1 (5–10) . . . 160 (168–176) sts.

Using Mohair, work rows 7 (5–1) to 36 (38–40) incl from Graph A.

Using MC, *Next Row*: K7 (11–3), * K2 tog, K4 (4–5), rep from * to last 9 (13–5) sts, K2 tog, K7 (11–3) . . . 135 (143–151) sts.

Work 9 rows K1, P1 rib.

Next Row: K7, * inc in next st, K7, rep from * to end . . . 151 (160–169) sts.

DIVIDE FOR BACK AND FRONTS:

Next Row: P38 (40–42), turn.

Cont on these 38 (40–42) sts for *Left Front*. Work in patt as shown on Graph B until row 40 of Graph has been completed.

SHAPE ARMHOLE:

Keeping patt correct from Graph, cast off 4 sts at beg of next row, then dec one st at beg of alt rows 4 times . . . 30 (32–34) sts. Work 5 rows, thus completing graph.

Cont in MC and stocking st for rem, work 9 rows.

SHAPE NECK:

Cast off 5 (6–7) sts at beg of next row, then dec one st at neck edge in every row 5 times . . . 20 (21–22) sts.

Work 13 (15–17) rows stocking st.

SHAPE SHOULDER:

Cast off 7 sts at beg of next row and foll alt row.

Work 1 row. Cast off rem 6 (7–8) sts.

With wrong side facing, join yarn to rem sts, P75 (80–85), turn.

Cont on these 75 (80–85) sts for Back.

Work 40 rows stocking st.

SHAPE ARMHOLES:

Cast off 4 sts at beg of next 2 rows, then dec one st at each end of next and alt rows 4 times in all . . . 59 (64–69) sts.

Work 33 (35–37) rows stocking st.

SHAPE SHOULDERS:

Cast off 7 sts at beg of next 4 rows, then 6 (7–8) sts at beg of foll 2 rows.

Cast off rem 19 (22–25) sts loosely.

With wrong side facing, join yarn to rem sts, purl to end.

KEY

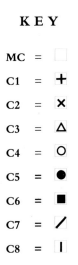

MC	=	☐
C1	=	+
C2	=	×
C3	=	△
C4	=	○
C5	=	●
C6	=	■
C7	=	╱
C8	=	│

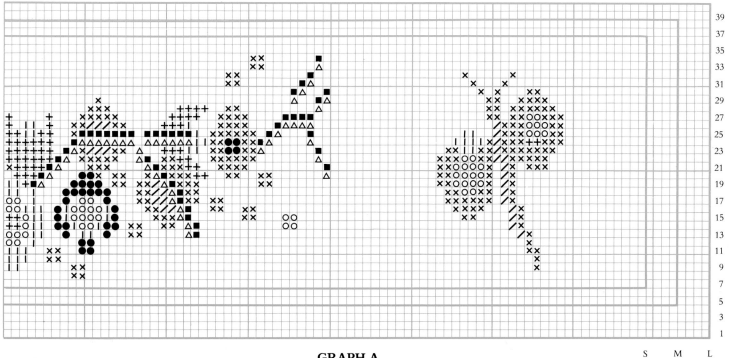

GRAPH A

S   M   L

Cont on these 38 (40–42) sts for Right Front.

Work rows 1 to 22 incl from Graph C, then cont in MC only and complete to correspond with Left Front, reversing shaping.

Left Sleeve

Using 4.50mm needles and C9, cast on 37 (41–45) sts.

Work 13 rows K1, P1 rib.

14th Row: Rib 6 (2–4), * inc in next st, rib 1 (2–2), rep from * to last 5 (0–2) sts, rib 5 (0–2) . . . 50 (54–58) sts.

Change to 5.50mm needles and MC.

Work in stocking st, inc one st at each end of 5th and foll 4th rows 4 times in all . . . 58 (62–66) sts.

Work 1 row.

Place motif—Next Row: K23 (25–27) MC, patt across row 1 of Graph D, using MC knit to end.

Next Row: P31 (33–35) MC, patt across row 2 of Graph D, using MC purl to end. Keeping motif correct from Graph D *as placed* in last 2 rows, cont in stocking st and inc one st at each end of next and foll 4th rows 3 times in all . . . 64 (68–72) sts. Work 6 rows without shaping, thus completing Graph.

Cont in stocking st (beg with a purl row) until sleeve measures 42 (43–44) cm (or length desired) from beg, ending with a purl row.

Shape Top

Cast off 3 sts at beg of next 2 rows . . . 58 (62–66) sts. **

Dec one st at each end of foll 5th then 4th rows 6 times in all . . . 46 (50–54) sts.

Work 1 row.

Next Row: * K2 tog, rep from * to end . . . 23 (25–27) sts.

Work 1 row.

Next Row: K2 (1–4), * K2 tog, K1 (1–0), rep from * to last 0 (0–3) sts, K0 (0–3) . . . 16 (17–17) sts.

Work 1 row.

Cast off.

Right Sleeve

Work as for Left Sleeve to **, omitting motif.

Work 1 row.

Place motif—Next Row: P31 (33–35) MC, patt across row 1 of Graph E, using MC purl to end.

Next Row: K26 (28–30) MC, patt across row 2 of Graph E, using MC knit to end. Complete as for Left Sleeve, keeping motif correct from Graph as *placed* in last 2 rows, until row 16 has been completed.

Right Front Band

With right side facing, using 4.50mm needles and C9, knit up 87 (93–99) sts evenly along right front edge.

Knit 4 rows garter st.

5th Row: K3, * cast off 2 sts, K11 (12–13), rep from * 5 times, cast off 2 sts, K4.

6th Row: K4, * cast on 2 sts, K11 (12–13), rep from * 5 times, cast on 2 sts, K3 . . . 7 buttonholes.

Knit a further 3 rows garter st.

Cast off loosely.

Left Front Band

Work to correspond with Right Front Band, omitting buttonholes.

Collar

Using 4.00mm needles and C10, cast on 16 sts.

Note: *When turning, yft, slip next st from left-hand needle on to right-hand needle, ybk, slip st back on to left-hand needle, then turn and proceed as instructed. This avoids holes in work.*

1st Row: K10, yrn, P2 tog, (K1, yfwd) twice, K2.

2nd Row: K6, yrn, P2 tog, K10.

3rd Row: K10, yrn, P2 tog, K2, yfwd, K2 tog, yfwd, K2.

4th Row: K7, yrn, P2 tog, K8, turn.

5th Row: K8, yrn, P2 tog, K3, yfwd, K2 tog, yfwd, K2.

6th Row: Cast off 4 sts, K4, yrn, P2 tog, K6, turn.

7th Row: K6, yrn, P2 tog, (K1, yfwd) twice, K2.

8th Row: K6, yrn, P2 tog, K4, turn.

9th Row: K4, yrn, P2 tog, K2, yfwd, K2 tog, yfwd, K2.

10th Row: K7, yrn, P2 tog, K2, turn.

11th Row: K2, yrn, P2 tog, K3, yfwd, K2 tog, yfwd, K2.

12th Row: Cast off 4 sts, K4, yrn, P2 tog, K10.

Rep rows 1 to 12 incl 26 times, then rows 1 to 6 incl once, noting to finish with K10 instead of 'K6, turn' at end of last (6th) row.

Cast off.

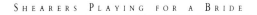

To finish collar ends: Using hook and C10, work 1 row double crochet then 1 row crab st along cast off edge. Work same edging along cast-on edge.

Making Up

Join shoulder, side and sleeve seams. Sew in sleeves. With right side of collar and wrong side of garment facing, sew collar in position, easing to fit. Run rows of shirring elastic through rib waistband on inside of garment, securing firmly into edge of front bands. Sew on buttons.

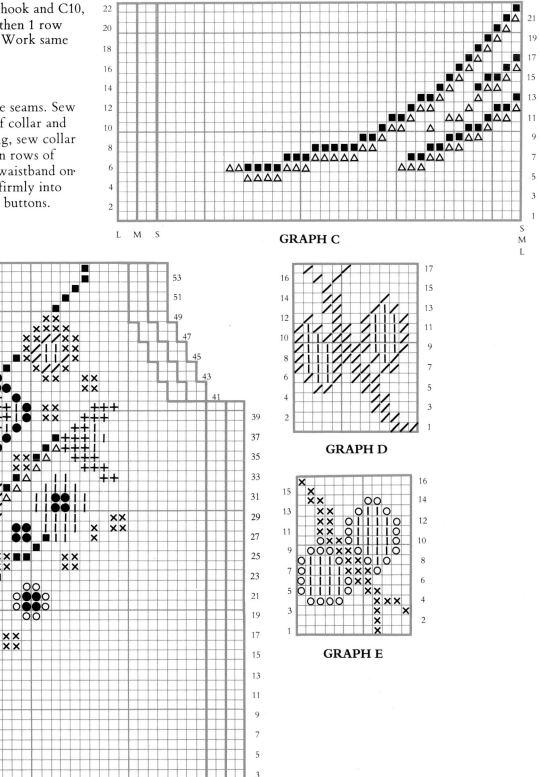

GRAPH C

GRAPH B

GRAPH D

GRAPH E

All on a Summer's Day

CHARLES BLACKMAN

Interpreted by Amy Hamilton

I love the blank, unsmiling faces of Alice, who has obviously seen visions and seems to have no control of what is happening to her; the teapots, cups and saucers, seemingly with minds of their own; the irreverent white rabbit and the wonderfully expressive flowers in the pot.

 When asked to choose an artist whose work I would like to represent in a knitted garment, my first thought was that I would prefer to use my own paintings, instead of someone else's work. I decided that the best way to tackle this project therefore would be to reproduce the chosen painting as closely as possible, thereby making the garment a practical, because wearable, way of showing my appreciation of the painting.

I chose Charles Blackman's *All on a Summer's Day* because Blackman is one of my favourite contemporary artists. I think he is one of the most original painters. His paintings are obviously highly personal but they also invoke strong feelings from the observer.

I particularly like his *Alice in Wonderland* pictures, which are spectacular paintings based on one of my favourite children's stories (although I didn't really appreciate them fully until recently).

Nadine Amadio, in her book on Charles Blackman, *The Lost Domains*, described Blackman's Alice paintings as 'a collective image that is famous and as much a part of Australian painting legend as Sidney Nolan's Ned Kelly'.
Dr Gertrude Langer, commenting in the *Courier Mail* echoed her sentiments:

These paintings will live when much that is now fashionable is forgotten. The impression this exhibition as a whole makes is overwhelming. The intensity and articulatedness of Blackman's poetical feeling and imagination are matched indeed by his resources as a painter. *The bold, as well as sensitive and expressive structure of his works, the luminosity and intensity of his colours and their rare juxtapositions and harmonies, all this is admirable.*

Everything looks spontaneous and just born of inspiration, yet analysis reveals a fine wisdom of picture painting.

I love these paintings, the blank, unsmiling faces of Alice, who has obviously seen visions and seems to have no control of what is happening to her and around her; the teapots, cups and saucers, seemingly with minds of their own; the irreverent white rabbit and the wonderfully expressive flowers in the pot.

I have designed the jumper as if the wearer is actually wearing a representation of the painting—with one side (the half with Alice) on the front—and the painting wraps around the wearer with the rabbit on the back. Because some of the flowers had to be lost in the practicalities of making a garment, I decided to add extra detail here by adding three dimensional pieces—the flowers seem to reach out from the right shoulder as they do in the painting.

I have tried to keep the colours as close to those in the painting, although naturally this was not possible in every case.

Lorraine, one of my trusty band of knitters, found that this jumper was not too difficult to knit and she completed it within a fortnight. It is a one-size-fits-all garment, meant to be comfortable and easy to wear. It would look wonderful on a man—men's chests are flatter and wider and much better for showing off picture knits.

Impressions of an Artist

Behind a large pear tree in the small village of Hahndorf in the Adelaide Hills, Amy Hamilton works full-time in her studio. Her small two-year-old, Alice, keeps her company. Tucking bears into bed, reading to herself and offering the occasional painting, Alice seems happily involved in the environment around her.

In the large shed that acts as a studio, Amy paints, knits and is currently producing metres of hand-patterned silk to be plasticised for raincoats. Under the 6-metre-long work trestle are baskets of wool and an assortment of finished garments. One of her lovely jumpers is draped over the back of a chair. A fox knitted into the back of it appears to be chasing chickens on the front. Amy says the scene is drawn from real life. The local fox not only ate the chickens, but boots, newspapers, wool or anything else that was left lying around outside the house.

Amy gathers her subjects from the life around her: 'I love to paint people showing human behaviour—the bad side usually. The strong feelings always arouse my interest. Exploring the emotions of hate, anger, sadness, jealousy and fear in paint, is very challenging. I often include myself in these efforts.' Rather like her own daughter Alice, Amy has a role model in a mother who seems always to have painted, and even continues to do so with rheumatoid arthritis.

Born in Scotland of an American mother and a South African father, Amy came to Australia in 1969. She studied art at Bedford Park Teachers' College and was particularly inspired by one of her teachers, Tom Gleghorn. She qualified as a teacher in Science, History, English and Art, gaining her Bachelor and Diploma of Education. She lectured in art at Sturt College, but left to take up a position as a gallery attendant at the Old Clarendon Art Gallery, owned by David Driden. After a few years she became David's partner and it was here that her interest in art began to mature. Exposed continually to the works of such artists as Charles Blackman, John Olsen and Frank Hodgkinson, she began to approach her own work more seriously, expressing herself in varying media.

Amy was taught to knit in Scotland and

during the quiet periods at the Old Clarendon Gallery she began to knit again:

I first attempted picture knitting when I bought a whole lot of wool at a sale—and it was all different colours. I had then to design a jumper which would incorporate about 20 different shades. I designed one with big happy faces all over it and on completion added three dimensional parts, noses sticking out, tongues, hair, etc. Kids love it. My mother was ill at the time and I gave it to her to cheer her up.

This garment launched Amy into commercial hand knitting. After ordering a jumper for himself, her partner David recognised the marketing potential of her work and encouraged Amy to hold her first knitting exhibition. Her clients now include Barry Humphries, who ordered as one of his several purchases a jumper featuring gladioli. The artist Jeffrey Smart wanted a jumper that was a compilation of several of his paintings. Amy found that as her skills became known and orders increased, the work could only be completed in a given time by contracting out to other hand

knitters. This works, she says, as long as she keeps strict control over the designs and the quality. She now regularly supplies boutiques such as Dorian Scott at The Rocks in Sydney.

But like other art knitters, Amy sees herself as an artist first and foremost: 'I left Old Clarendon Gallery about six years ago and now see my serious work as painting. I have more time to give to it though I still earn a living knitting, painting silk and decorating pots.'

Amy says she only paints the things she knows:

That's why I don't paint men very often— except in relation to a woman . . . While I was pregnant I tried to paint that feeling—so complicated—and I changed the painting several times as the nine months wore on, but didn't get the chance to finish it. Now I can't because I don't remember properly the feelings and slight craziness—I guess I'll just have to get pregnant again.

Hung haphazardly around the walls of her studio are a number of strong impressionistic paintings awaiting a venue at a gallery. Their expressive and contorted faces grimace while listening to our conversation. Amy is presently working on a painting about the Great Eastern Steeplechase held locally at Oakbank. She saw it on television and taped it because she had a wager on one of the horses. Two horses fell during the race and one, a local hero named River Amos, was destroyed. Amy was devastated:

I feel terrible, guilty that I had been one to encourage such a race by gambling on it, and so helpless because two such beautiful creatures could be so destroyed. I have had nightmares picturing the looks of fear and bewilderment in

those horses' faces. I'm going to use images of old unused carousel horses with broken-off wooden limbs intertwined with flashes of the real event. I feel it is the only way to work it out of my mind.

It is the expression of the darker side of life that attracts Amy in painting. But it is probably the joy she feels in her daughter Alice, which led her to choose Charles Blackman's painting *All on a Summer's Day* to interpret in *The Art of Knitting*. Alice in the boat with the rabbit is Alice in the studio with the teddy bear.

Amy, her partner Rod and Alice live in a cottage in the Adelaide Hills not far from the studio. Surrounded by a large, untamed garden, they have only wildlife for company. Amy's parents live nearby and Alice regularly visits the donkeys, geese, horses, wallabies and cockatoos, which they have on their farm.

Amy says of her lifestyle: 'I enjoy very much the way I'm living. I particularly like being my own boss and doing what feels right at the time. My aim now is to be accepted as a visual artist. Several male artists have suggested that I should "stick to the decorative arts, luv", but I intend to try. My paintings are beginning to sell.'

Amy is warm and serious and appears to be on the threshold of a promising career. Still in her early thirties, she has the talent and the commitment to achieve much.

Amy's knitwear was part of the touring *Art Knits* exhibition curated by Jane de Teliga at the Art Gallery of New South Wales. Her garments have also been exhibited at the *South Australian Regional Art Exhibition* at the Adelaide Festival Centre, May/June 1990. She has had an exhibition at Kensington Gallery in Adelaide in 1989, and one of her hand-painted silk/satin coats has been purchased by the Art Gallery of South Australia.

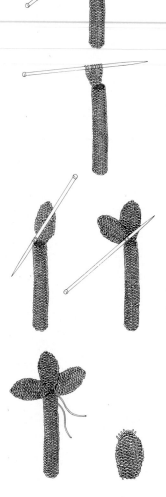

3D FLOWERS
6 sts
20 rows
sew up side seams
pick up stitches from loops on top
knit petal as instructed, cast off
pick up next 2 sts work as before
knit 3rd petal as before
using a crochet hook tie in ends
stitch to garment

LEAVES
stitch to garment slightly at an
angle, stitch about 1/2 inch from
point of leaf on one side with only
a couple of stitches on the other
side

Measurements

	Small	Medium	Large
Actual Garment Measures (*approx*):	114	121	128 cm
Length (*approx*):	66	67	68 cm
Sleeve Seam (*approx*):	44	44	44 cm

Materials

CLECKHEATON 8 PLY MACHINEWASH (*50g balls*)

	Small	Medium	Large
Main Colour (MC) Mid Blue	6	7	8 balls
Contrast 1 (C1) Light Blue	8	9	10 balls
Contrast 2 (C2) White	4	5	6 balls
Contrast 3 (C3) Yellow	1	2	2 ball/s
Contrast 4 (C4) Navy Blue	1	1	1 ball
Contrast 5 (C5) Black	1	2	2 ball/s
Contrast 6 (C6) Dark Green	1	1	1 ball
Contrast 7 (C7) Light Green	1	1	1 ball
Contrast 8 (C8) Grey	1	2	2 ball/s
Contrast 9 (C9) Brown	1	1	1 ball
Contrast 10 (C10) Camel	1	1	1 ball
Contrast 11 (C11) Red	1	1	1 ball
Contrast 12 (C12) Rust	1	1	1 ball

One pair each 3.25mm (No 10) and 4.00mm (No 8), 4.50mm (No 7) (optional for flowers) knitting needles; 2 stitch holders; knitters needle for sewing seams and embroidery (if desired).

Tension

21 sts and 30 rows to 10cm over patt, using 4.00mm needles.

Back

Using 3.25mm needles and MC, cast on 113 (121–127) sts.
Work 20 rows K1, P1 rib, inc 9 sts evenly across last row . . . 122 (130–136) sts.
Change to 4.00mm needles. **

Work in patt as shown on Graph A until row 176 (178–180) has been completed.

SHAPE NECK:
Next Row: Patt 41 (43–44), turn.
Cont on these 41 (43–44) sts.
Work 1 row patt.

SHAPE SHOULDER:
Keeping patt correct from Graph, cast off 14 (14–15) sts at beg of next row and foll alt row, then 13 (15–14) sts at beg of foll alt row.
Slip next 40 (44–48) sts onto a stitch holder and leave. With right side facing, join yarn to rem sts and work to correspond with other side, reversing shaping.

Front

Work as for Back to **
Work in patt as shown on Graph B until row 170 has been completed.

SHAPE NECK:
Next Row: Patt 46 (48–49), turn.
Cont on these 46 (48–49) sts.
Keeping patt correct, dec one st at neck edge in alt rows 3 (4–5) times . . . 43 (44–44) sts.
Work 1 row patt.

SHAPE SHOULDER:
Keeping patt correct from Graph, cast off 14 (14–15) sts at beg of next row and foll alt row, then 13 (15–14) sts at beg of foll alt row, AT SAME TIME dec one st at neck edge in foll alt rows from previous dec 2 (1–0) time/s.
Slip next 30 (34–38) sts onto stitch holder and leave. With right side facing join yarn to rem sts and work to correspond with other side, reversing shaping.

Right Sleeve

Using 3.25mm needles and MC, cast on 53 sts.
Work 20 rows K1, P1 rib, inc once in centre of last row . . . 54 sts.
Change to 4.00mm needles.
Work in patt as shown on Graph C, inc one st at each end of 5th and foll 4th rows until there are 98 (102–106) sts.
Work 25 (17–9) rows patt without

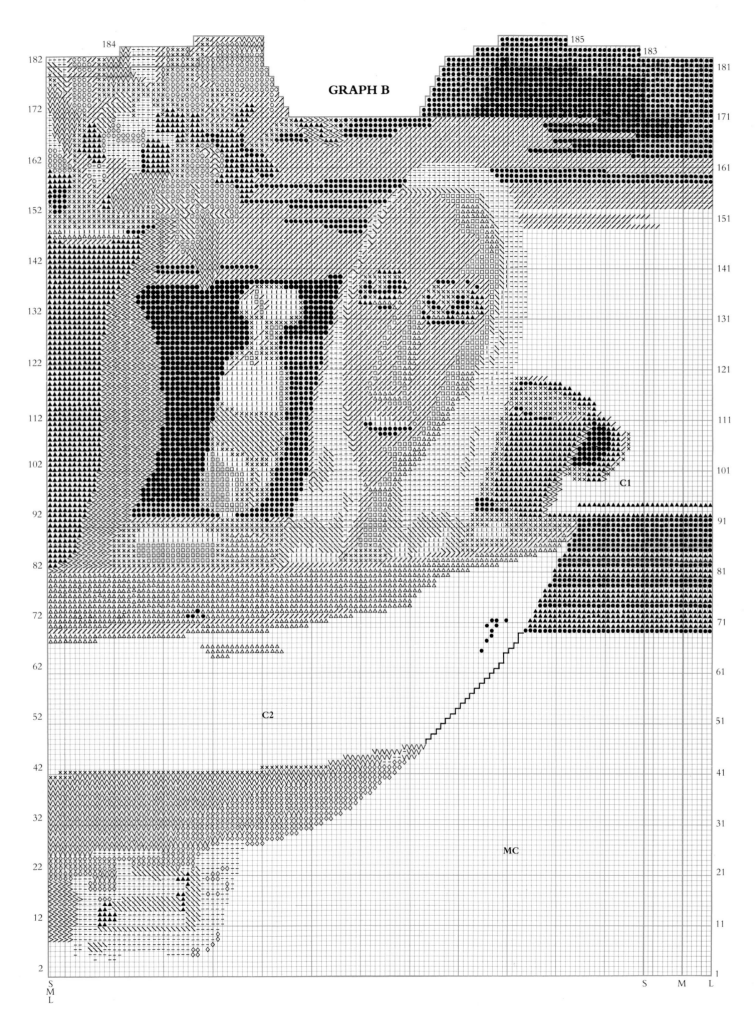

GRAPH B

KEY

MC	=	▲
C1	=	●
C2	=	╱
C3	=	─
C4	=	➤
C5	=	✘
C6	=	V
C7	=	◇
C8	=	△
C9	=		
C10	=	□
C11	=	○
C12	=	╲

shaping. (Row 114 completed)
Cast off loosely.

Left Sleeve

Work as for Right Sleeve, but working
C1 in place of flowers from row 79
onwards as indicated on Graph C.

Neckband

Join right shoulder seam. With right side
facing, using 3.25mm needles and C1, knit
up 97 (109–121) sts evenly around neck,
incl sts from stitch holders and dec once in
centre of back neck stitch holder.
Work 21 rows K1, P1 rib.
Cast off loosely in rib.

Trimming (Optional)

FLOWERS (make 7 in colours to match flowers
knitted in to garment)

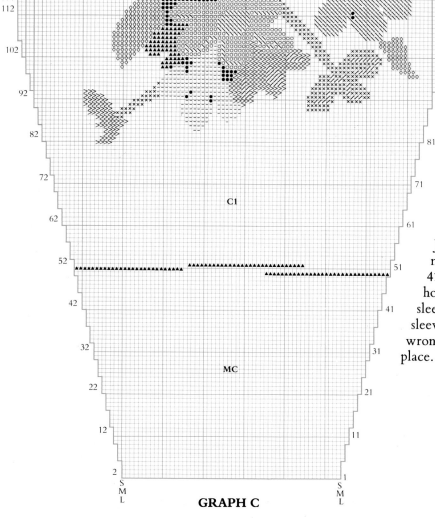

GRAPH C

Petals (make 4 in each colour): Using 4.50mm
needles, cast on 6 sts.
Work 16 rows stocking st, inc one st at
each end of 2nd and 3rd rows and dec one
st at each end of 13th and 14th rows . . . 6
sts.
Cast off.
Stitch petals to garment on right shoulder
as illustrated, on a flower of the same
colour.

STEMMED FLOWERS (make 4 in colours to match
flowers knitted in to garment) (see diagrams)
Stem: Using 4.50mm needles and C5 or C6,
cast on 6 sts.
Work 20 rows stocking st.
Cast off. With right sides together, join
side seam.
Petals (Knit up 4 in same colour): With
right side facing and using 4.50mm
needles, knit up 2 sts from top of stem.
Work 6 rows stocking st, inc one st at
each end of 2nd row and dec one st at
each end of 5th row . . . 2 sts.
Cast off.
Stitch end of stem to garment.

LEAVES (make 3 in C6) (see diagrams)

Using 4.50mm needles, cast on 3 sts.
Knit 10 rows garter st, inc one st at each
end of first 3 rows and dec one st at each
end of last 3 rows . . . 3 sts.
Cast off. Stitch leaves to garment as
instructed on diagram.

Making Up

Join left shoulder seam. Tie a coloured
marker on each side of Back and Front
41 cm up from lower edge to mark armholes. Sew in sleeves, placing centre of
sleeve to shoulder seam. Join side and
sleeve seams. Fold neckband in half onto
wrong side and slip stitch loosely into
place.

Sunlit Hydrangeas

WILLIAM HARDY WILSON

Interpreted by Amy Hamilton

Grecian pillars, hydrangeas and leghorns were some of Wilson's favourite subjects and he managed to combine them all in Sunlit Hydrangeas *in a memorable fashion.*

 William Hardy Wilson was a draughtsman, architect, antiquarian, historian and writer as well as a painter. In fact he is better known for his architectural drawings than for his paintings. Grecian pillars, hydrangeas and leghorns were some of Wilson's favourite subjects and he managed to combine them all in *Sunlit Hydrangeas* in a memorable fashion.

William Hardy Wilson was born in 1881 at Campbelltown, New South Wales to affluent parents. He was educated at Newington College, Sydney and attained a British Architectural degree in London in 1909. He studied town planning in Vienna and submitted a design for the forthcoming national capital, Canberra. Travelling widely in the United States, Wilson was inspired by the old colonial buildings he saw in Boston, New York, Baltimore, Washington and Philadelphia. He loved the Doric columns, the Windsor chairs on rockers, and the wooden walls dappled by shaded trees. Wilson felt that architecture in Australia could be improved by adopting and adapting the American style and its influence can be clearly seen in *Sunlit Hydrangeas*.

Wilson, a collector and man of wide interests, returned to Australia in 1910 with a connoisseur's consignment of antique furniture, pictures, china and glass, some of which was donated to the National Gallery of Victoria in 1914 as part of the Connell Collection in Sydney. He practised

architecture and *Purulia* (his own home) in Warrawee, Sydney, and *Eryldene* built for Professor Waterhouse at Gordon, Sydney, are testimonies to his abilities in this field. Both houses are surrounded by beautifully planned and planted gardens, and the design for *Purulia* was adopted as an architectural prototype throughout Sydney's North Shore a generation later.

Wilson's search for architectural truth took him back to Europe between 1923 and 1927, during which time he did a splendid folio of drawings of classical Greek ruins detailing Doric and Ionic columns. Combining architecture and nature in Barcelona he painted a scene of two snow-white geese in a tranquil pool outside the cathedral. *The Little White Brethren of Barcelona* became his wife's favourite painting. Wilson had always been fond of birds as he found them to be very ornamental in paintings, and along from the Barcelona Art Gallery he found a bird market with beautiful fowls of every kind. These fowls and others from the Royal Easter Show became an element in his drawings, paintings and architectural ornamentation.

I selected *Sunlit Hydrangeas* for the pictorial elements within it.

The composition and the tonal qualities lend themselves very well to interpretation in knitting.

I also empathise with Wilson's subject matter. Hydrangeas are one of my favourite flowers, because of their marvellous range of colours during the varying stages of flowering. Like Wilson,

whose first painting was of a young cock, have always painted leghorns and other chickens on my silk jackets and have also knitted them into my garments.

Wilson's watercolour also appealed because I could envisage the design in a very romantic soft cardigan. I thought that mohair and angora would combine well to make a luxurious garment, which women would love to wear. The design is such that it could also be transposed onto a jumper if the knitter so desired. I designed a feature collar, because I think a beautiful collar acts as a frame around the face. But the collar is also optional for the knitter, as the bands with the button holes can finish off the garment.

KEY

MC =	□
C1 =	✕
C2 =	■
C3 =	●
C4 =	▲
C5 =	○
C6 =	+
C7 =	*
C8 =	▷
C9 =	◁
C10 =	△
C11 =	·
C12 =	◻
C13 =	＼
C14 =	／
C15 =	◇
C16 =	−
C17 =	=
C18 =	V
C19 =	◆

Measurements

	Small	Medium	Large
Actual Garment Measures (*approx*):	108	116	124 cm
Length (*approx*):	64	65	66 cm
Sleeve Seam (*approx*):	46	46	46 cm

Materials

CLECKHEATON MOHAIR 12 PLY (*50g balls*)

	Small	Medium	Large
(MC) White	5	6	7 balls

AND CLECKHEATON MACHINEWASH 8 PLY (*50g balls*)

(C1) Light Brown	2	3	3 balls
(C2) Deep Olive	2	3	3 balls
(C3) Dark Brown	2	2	2 balls
(C4) Cobalt Blue	2	2	2 balls
(C5) Light Blue	2	2	2 balls
(C6) Black	1	1	1 ball
(C7) Pink Fleck	1	1	1 ball
(C8) Mauve	1	1	1 ball
(C9) Lilac	1	1	1 ball
(C10) Orange	1	1	1 ball
(C11) Brick Red	1	1	1 ball
(C12) Lemon	1	1	1 ball

AND CLECKHEATON MOHAIR CLASSIQUE 12 PLY (*50g balls*)

(C13) Camel	1	1	1 ball
(C14) Pale Blue	1	1	1 ball
(C15) Pale Pink	1	1	1 ball

AND CLECKHEATON ANGORA SUPREME 8 PLY (*50g balls*)

(C16) Olive	1	1	1 ball

(C17) Violet	1	1	1 ball

AND CLECKHEATON NATURAL 8 PLY (*50g balls*)

(C18) Beige	1	1	1 ball

AND HIGHLAND 8 PLY (*50g balls*)

(C19) Grey Fleck	1	1	1 ball

One pair each 3.25mm (No 10) and 4.00mm (No 8) knitting needles; one 3.25mm circular needle . . . (80cm long); knitting-in elastic; knitters needle for sewing seams; 2 large buttons.

Tension

23 sts and 29 rows to 10cm over patt using 4.00mm needles.

Back

Using 3.25mm needles, MC and knitting-in elastic tog, cast on 105 (115–125) sts. Work 30 rows K1, P1 rib, inc 9 sts evenly across last row . . . 114 (124–134) sts. Break off knitting-in elastic. Change to 4.00mm needles.
Work in patt as shown on Graph A, inc one st at each end of 11th and foll 10th rows 6 times in all . . . 126 (136–146) sts. Cont without shaping until row 158 (160–162) has been completed.

SHAPE NECK:
Patt 44 (49–54), cast off next 38 sts, patt to end.
Cont on these last 44 (49–54) sts and work

Cont on these last 44 (49–54) sts and work 3 rows, thus completing Graph.
Cast off loosely.
With wrong side facing, rejoin yarn to rem 44 (49–54) sts.
Work 3 rows patt. Cast off loosely.

Left Front

Using 3.25 mm needles, MC and knitting-in elastic tog, cast on 45 (49–55) sts.
Work 30 rows K1, P1 rib, inc 4 (5–4) sts evenly across last row . . . 49 (54–59) sts.
Break off knitting-in elastic. Change to 4.00mm needles.
Work in patt as shown on Graph A, inc one st at beg of 11th and foll 10th rows 5 times in all . . . 54 (59–64) sts.
Work 3 rows patt without shaping, thus completing row 54.

SHAPE FRONT EDGE:

Cont in patt from Graph, dec one st at end (front edge) of next and foll 10th rows 11 times in all, AT SAME TIME inc one

st at side edge in foll 10th row from previous inc . . . 44 (49–54) sts.
Work 7 (9–11) rows without shaping, thus completing Graph.
Cast off loosely.

Right Front

Work to correspond with Left Front, reversing shaping and working as indicated for Right Front on Graph A.

Sleeves

Using 3.25mm needles, MC and knitting-in elastic tog, cast on 45 (49–53) sts.
Work 20 rows K1, P1 rib, inc 5 sts evenly across last row . . . 50 (54–58) sts.
Break off knitting-in elastic. Change to 4.00mm needles.
Work in patt as shown on Graph B, inc one st at each end of 5th and foll 4th rows 16 times in all, then in alt rows 10 times . . . 102 (106–110) sts.
Cont without shaping until row 104 has been completed.
Cast off loosely.

Front Band

Join shoulder seams. With right side facing, using circular needle and MC only, and beg at last dec on right front, knit up 8 (10–12) sts along right front, 4 sts down right side of back neck, 38 sts across back neck, 4 sts up left side of back neck and 8 (10–12) sts along left front to last dec . . . 62 (66–70) sts. Work in K1, P1 rib, knitting up 10 sts along frong edges at end of each row 20 times, then 54 sts (to cast-on edge of fronts) at end of next 2 rows . . . 370 (374–378) sts.
Work 9 rows rib.
Next Row: Rib 10, cast off 2 sts, rib 30, cast off 2 sts, rib to end.
Next Row: Rib to last 40 sts, cast on 2 sts, rib 30, cast on 2 sts, rib 10 . . .
2 buttonholes.
Work a further 10 rows rib.
Cast off loosely in rib.

Making Up

Tie a coloured marker 23 (24–25) cm down from shoulder seam on side edges of Back and Fronts to mark armholes. Sew in sleeves between markers, placing centre of sleeve to shoulder seam. Join side and sleeve seams. Sew buttons in place.

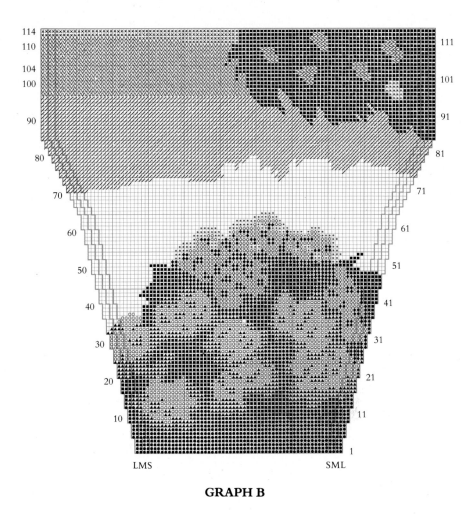

GRAPH B

161
151
141
131
121
111
101
91
81
71
61
51
41
31
21
11
1

L   M   S   S   M   L

Superknit 6

ROBERT ROONEY

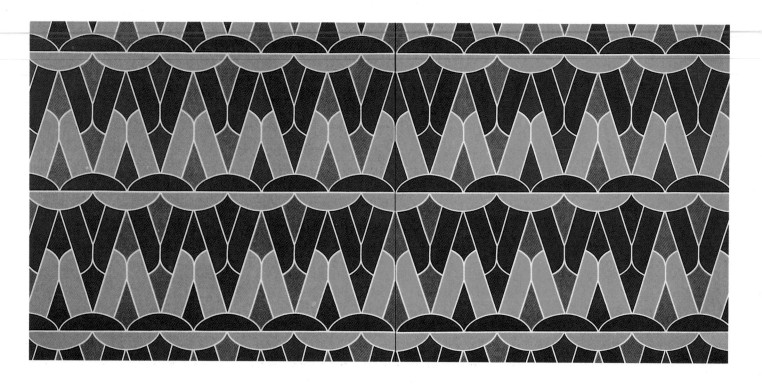

Interpreted by Ken Killeen

I thought that by transforming Superknit 6 *into a jumper I was creating a double metaphor, a visual pun. He had taken the banal, repetitive pattern of knitting stitches and elevated it to the status of art.*
I thought it would be fantastic fun to turn that painting back into knitting.

 When I was approached to design a jumper based on an Australian painting, I thought initially of the painters whose work I find closest in spirit to my own drawing, such as Tim Storrier and John Wolsey. However, my drawing is very different to my knitting, which is mostly geometric and Fair Isle.

I was very excited about the whole concept of the book and flattered to be included in it, but I couldn't decide what painting to use. In a flash of inspiration I remembered Robert Rooney's *Superknit 6*, a painting of knitting. It was perfect.

From what I knew of Robert Rooney, I was not sure how he would feel about his painting being used for a jumper design. Robert Rooney is a highly respected art critic as well as an artist, and he approaches both with uncompromising professionalism and a scathing wit; I hoped he would not find my idea insulting. Not only was he agreeable, he was enthusiastic about the project; he felt as I did that it was entirely appropriate for his painting to become a jumper.

It is difficult to align Robert Rooney with any major art movement—perhaps he is closest to pop art in his intentions. He is an intellectual and philosophical artist who takes commonplace, banal subject matter and uses it to document the everyday aspects of life. The *Superknit* series of paintings from 1970 were the last paintings he did before concentrating totally on photography as his means of visual expression. There is almost a black humour in his work where he looks at the repetitive patterns of human existence; knitting stitches are a symbolic metaphor for this.

Two of the photographic works that illuminate this symbolism and contain the black humour are *Garments 3 Dec. 1972–19 Mar. 1973*, 107 photographs of his clothes folded after each day's wear, and *A.M.–P.M.*, 176 photographs of his bed made and unmade over a period of three months.

I thought that by transforming *Superknit 6* into a jumper I was creating a double metaphor, a visual pun. He had taken the banal, repetitive pattern of knitting stitches (the reverse side of stocking stitch) and elevated it to the status of art. I thought it would be fantastic fun to turn that painting back into knitting.

Designing the actual jumper was not as easy as I had anticipated. After pulling it out and redesigning the pattern three times, I am reasonably pleased with the result. I designed it in 12 ply, because I wanted to see clearly each individual stitch. I would have liked somehow to have a panel of reverse stocking stitch to help make sense of the design; perhaps the bands could be knitted like that.

The design is not instantly recognisable as knitting stitches, but I like the fact it has layers of meaning, which for me gives it some magic. It can be read as simply shapes and colours but on closer observation the

stitch pattern emerges. As the green background colour is the same as the foreground colour, it makes the design a little obscure. If you wanted it clearer, it could be knitted in different colours, even just a different shade of green would be enough.

Finally, a hint on knitting this garment. If you carry your yarn across the back or knit it in as you go, or use separate balls of wool, each will drastically affect the tension and consequently the size of the jumper. I did a little of both, with some wool being carried across the back and knitted in every few stitches and some separate balls of wool, and I had problems with variations in tension. If you are like me and don't like knitting tension squares, I would strongly recommend that you do so for this jumper.

A Knitting Obsession

Castlemaine, Victoria, the home of Ken Killeen is a former gold-mining town. Today the main employment is found in the wool mills. Set in an Australian bush landscape, the small town boasts a good collection of early Australian paintings in its regional art gallery. The local gallery run by Peter Wallace, a superb craftsman in leather, is also impressive with its eclectic array of paintings, pottery and sculpture. Someone around here has a good eye. The pieces are original, professional and with regard to the sculpture, amusing.

Up the hill from the gallery, Ken Killeen lives in a small house close by Buda, a former local mansion, now designated a Heritage House. Buda, from Budapest, was the retreat of a wealthy Hungarian family

who were very involved in the arts. A grand piano testifies to soirees and many fine woodcuts by Margaret Preston and other artists hang on the walls. Castlemaine seems to have encouraged the fine arts in its short history.

Ken says that today there is a small renaissance happening again in the area; across the road in a sculptress's garden a reclining woman, à la Henry Moore, awaits transport to a Bendigo gallery for exhibition. Ken estimates that there are about 60 practising artists in the immediate neighbourhood. Ken is the current President of Castlemaine Artists Incorporated, a mutually supportive group of local artistic talent. As an art teacher at the local college, he is constantly interacting with the artistic aspirations of the community.

Sitting knitting in his comfortable living room, one small metallic spider dropping on a filament of web from one ear, Ken discusses the town and the life he lives here. Around the walls of the room, both on the floor and on plate racks above, are a medley of objects. The collection of Australiana, such as kookaburras and koalas, were gathered from second-hand shops in his teens, and are now mascots from his past. But the many varied feathers he has assembled are a source of on-going fascination for Ken. He's been collecting these since he was a child and the image has been seminal in his artistic development.

Ken began drawing at secondary school. Never keen on sport, he always opted for art classes. He started his Diploma of Fine Arts at Bendigo in 1975 when he was 17, and became the youngest student ever to receive the diploma when he graduated three years later.

Bonded to the Education Department, he was expected to gain two years experience in the commercial world in an area related to his degree. Finding this almost impossible, Ken started work in a wholesale plant nursery in the Grampian Mountains: 'I didn't pick up a pencil or a paintbrush all

the time I was there, but I took lots of photographs. I watched the seasons change and it was great for the soul.'

Following this he began working three days a week at another nursery in Bendigo, Peppergreen Farm, which specialised in herbs. This allowed him four days a week to practise drawing, an area he felt had been neglected in his training because he had graduated in an era when conceptual art was popular: 'People could get their diploma by jumping into buckets of paint.'

Ken set out to redress the balance: 'I concentrated on things I had lying around the house, leaves and feathers and doing abstract things with them, making patterns—nothing illustrative'.

His self-education in drawing continued full time for a further year at the end of which Ken had his first exhibition in tandem with Gary Bish, the potter. Officials from the Department of Education were invited along and obviously impressed, bought a couple of Ken's drawings.

In late 1980 in another collaborative show with Gary Bish at the Jam Factory in Adelaide, Ken used his collection of feathers for reference and inscribed Gary's bisque pots with abstracted feathers. The pots were a sell-out success.

In 1981, Ken began teaching art at a technical school at Mooroolbark: 'It was the worst year of my life. I was extremely nervous and the boys sensed it. Besides I wasn't sure I wanted to or could teach.'

The following year, the Department of Education transferred Ken to Hamilton, where he actually began to enjoy teaching among a very supportive school staff. Becoming more settled and confident, he searched out a venue in Melbourne in which to stage another exhibition. Here at the Christine Abrahams Gallery, Artbank began to buy some of his drawings and Patrick McCaughey also purchased one for the National Gallery of Victoria.

Ken continued to teach and practise drawing and was invited to show in the Ansett Award Exhibition in Hamilton in 1986. Though he missed out on the Acquisitive Drawing Prize, some of his work was purchased by the Hamilton Gallery. Ken enters the Faber Castell Drawing Prize each year and Artbank continue to purchase some of his entries.

Ken began knitting as a child, long before he began painting. He says his mother was a hopeless knitter, but when she was hospitalised for a year, Ken's grandmother taught both he and his sister to knit: 'We used to sit around the fire on cosy winter evenings, all knitting together. One of my bachelor uncles has always knitted so it wasn't a problem for me that boys should knit.'

Ken became a regular knitter in his late teens. Centred in a thriving wool area, Ken purchased a kit spinning wheel and found himself with a large stockpile of homespun wool. The means were to hand but his skills were limited. A friend showed him how to interpret a pattern: 'Before that a jumper was a mystery to me. Then I realised how easy it all was.'

Now with three young sons, Ken has had reason to knit ever since. Once he begins a garment, he is an obsessive knitter, and must see it finished as soon as possible. He also finds that knitting is a form of meditation—an alternative way of using his artistic sensibility.

Limited by time, Ken knits for family and friends but has not been commercially productive. He exhibited a garment in the exhibition sponsored by the Wool Corporation, *Men Knitting*, in 1988. His jumper, *Superknit 6* is only his second entry in a book or catalogue for public display.

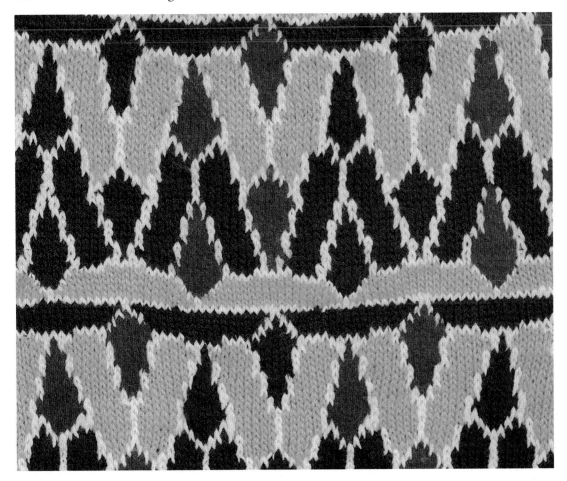

Measurements

	Small	Medium	Large
Actual Garment			
Measures (*approx*):	112	124	135 cm
Length (*approx*):	76	77	78 cm
Sleeve Seam			
(*approx*):	46	46	46 cm

Materials

CLECKHEATON 12 PLY MACHINE WASH (*50g balls*)
Main Colour (MC)

Dark green	6	7	7 balls
Contrast 1 (C1)			
Yellow	5	6	6 balls
Contrast 2 (C2)			
Red	3	4	5 balls
Contrast 3 (C3)			
White (5)	2	3	4 balls

One pair each 4.50mm (No 7) and 6.00mm (No 4) knitting needles; 2 stitch holders; knitters needle for sewing seams.

Tension

17.5 sts and 18 rows to 10cm over patt, using 6.00mm needles.

Back

Using 4.50mm needles and MC, cast on 81 (87–97) sts.
Work 15 rows K1, P1 rib in stripes of 1 row each MC and C1.
Using C1, *16th Row*: Rib 12 (8–14), * inc in next st, rib 2, rep from * to last 9 (7–11) sts, rib 9 (7–11) . . . 101 (111–121) sts.
Change to 6.00mm needles.
Work 70 rows patt as shown on Graph.

KEY

MC	=	☐
C1	=	╱
C2	=	●
C3	=	✕

SHAPE ARMHOLES:
Keeping patt correct, cast off 10 sts at beg of next 2 rows . . . 81 (91–101) sts.**
Work 48 (50–52) rows patt.

SHAPE NECK:
Next Row: Patt 26 (30–33), turn.
Cont on these 26 (30–33) sts.
Keeping patt correct, dec one st at neck edge in next 3 rows . . . 23 (27–30) sts.
Work 2 rows patt.
Cast off loosely.
Slip next 29 (31–35) sts onto a stitch holder and leave. With right side facing, join yarn to rem sts and work to correspond with other side, reversing shaping.

Front

Work as for Back to **
Work 34 rows patt.

SHAPE NECK:
Next Row: Patt 31 (35–38), turn.
Cont on these 31 (35–38) sts.
Keeping patt correct, dec one st at neck edge in next 4 rows, then in foll alt rows 4 times . . . 23 (27–30) sts.
Work 7 (9–11) rows patt.
Cast off loosely.
Slip next 19 (21–25) sts onto stitch holder and leave. With right side facing, join yarn to rem sts and work to correspond with other side, reversing shaping.

Sleeves

Using 4.50mm needles and MC, cast on 41 (41–43) sts.
Work 15 rows, K1, P1 rib in stripes as for Back.
Using C1, *16th Row*: Rib 6, * inc in next st, rib 2 (2–3), rep from * to last 5 sts, rib 5 . . . 51 sts.
Change to 6.00mm needles.
Work in patt as placed on Graph for Sleeves and noting to work extra sts into patt, inc one st at each end of 3rd (row 23 of graph) and alt rows until there are 115 (117–121) sts.
Work 7 (5–1) row/s patt without shaping.
Tie a coloured marker at each end of last row to mark end of sleeve seam.
Work a further 10 rows patt to sew to sts cast off at armholes on Back and Front.
Cast off loosely.

Neckband

Join right shoulder seam. With right side facing, using 4.50mm needles and MC, knit up 89 (97–109) sts evenly around neck, incl sts from stitch holders and dec once in centre of back neck stitch holder.
Work 19 rows K1, P1 rib (beg with a 2nd row) in stripes as for Back.
Cast off loosely in rib.

Making Up

Join left shoulder, side and sleeve seams to markers. Sew in sleeves, placing rows above markers to sts cast off at armholes.
Fold neckband in half onto wrong side and slip stitch loosely into place.

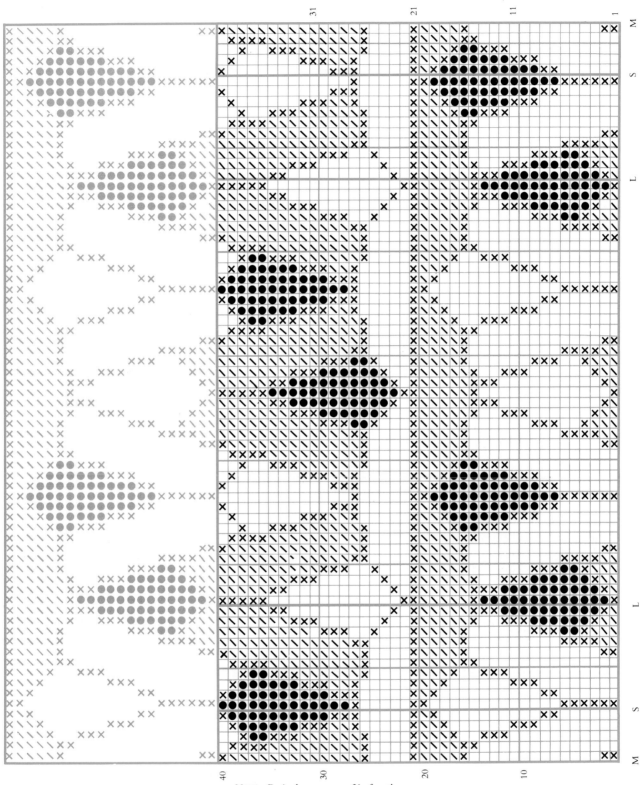

NOTE – Begin sleeves on row 21 of graph.
Extra inc not shown on graph

65

The Bathers

SIDNEY NOLAN

Interpreted by Meredith Russell

Nolan's ability to draw from memory, experience and his own poetic vision gives his work a haunting, timeless presence, which reaches beyond the restraints of ordinary life.

 Sidney Nolan's work has always captivated and intrigued me, but when I saw his retrospective exhibition, *Landscapes and Legends* in Perth in November 1987, I really felt the full power and evolution of his work.

Nolan's ability to draw from memory, experience and his own poetic vision gives his work a haunting, timeless presence, which reaches beyond the restraints of ordinary life. I love his ability to tell stories through his painting and to express and expose innermost feelings in a way that is spontaneous, new and echoes a truth in the viewer. Nolan has travelled widely and is able to portray the unique nature of each landscape, myth, legend and figure, which gives his work a world consciousness.

As a painter myself, I admire Nolan's enthusiasm for expressing his own inner world to the outer world, his inexhaustible visual appetite and the range in which pigment is pushed, pulled, scumbled vigorously and directly on to the canvas or board. Nolan has a wonderful curiosity, a passionate love for the painting process, which is evident in his paintings, and is constantly striving for artistic invention. His creativity has expanded to writing poetry, printmaking, designing for the stage (particularly opera), and involvement with films and computers.

As Nolan says:

I like to change the medium every now and again so that I can work against it, so that I am not proficient in it—because, in some way, I'm always worried by proficiency. It has so

many dangers, especially as there is a certain kind of satisfaction in automatic response. But this could keep out more serious messages . . . You do end up with certain kinds of mannerisms. You handle paint a certain way, you flick it this way and that way, and often this steals in unawares . . .

You see, even the muscles learn tricks . . .

Yes, you must fight against it because I suppose if a painting is worth anything it is supposed to come from some place inside yourself that you cannot get to through any other means.

Throughout the 1940s, Nolan started to use the image of the outsider within the context of the landscape. The Kelly series portrayed the rebel against society, engaging folkish and primitive elements against the conventional taste and propriety of the time. Kelly is armoured against society, but also against the Australian landscape, into which he eventually disappears, becoming a legend. Nolan's next painting followed the tragic story of the doomed explorers Burke and Wills. They were seen as exemplary heroes of society who became famous in history as outsiders who, upon dying, dissolved into the landscape and became part of it. The third images of the outsider used by Nolan are those of Mrs Frazer and her rescuer, the escaped convict, Bracefell.

The St Kilda Bather's series of the 1940s was painted from memory while Nolan was stationed at Wimmera. As Nolan says: 'Memory is I am sure, one of the main factors in my particular way of looking at things. In some ways it seems to sharpen the magic in a way that cannot be achieved by direct means.'

The figures are flatly composed, picturing light, heat and atmosphere. The series is a celebration of the Australian sun and sea, and Nolan's memories of St Kilda, where he spent much of his youth.

As an art student, I also painted beach scenes and became fascinated by the ritual of sunning and bathing and the isolated quality that people at the seaside seem to possess, despite their exposure to the elements and to each other. I chose *The Bathers, 1946* because of this empathy with Nolan's vision and because it has bold and striking spacial patterning and particularly Australian colours, which makes it suitable to translate into knitting terms. I have attempted to retain the bold flattened areas, colours and patterning of Nolan's painting, giving contrast in texture and colour where possible, by using cottons, mohair, wool and angora. I am interested in the painterly, textural qualities that can be achieved in knitting, even though knitting itself is a rigid stitch by stitch process, which progresses in a grid-like manner. There is great freedom within the boundaries of an art form and the possibilities of expression are endless.

An Imaginative Store

 In literature, knitting has often been used as a synonym for time; Shakespeare's 'ravelled sleeve', for example. Meredith Russell sits unravelling the past, recalling her childhood:

My mother was an excellent cook, a very fine knitter, dressmaker, cake decorator and embroiderer. She made our clothes and jumpers and I can remember being stopped often while on errands as a child so that other knitters could admire my patterned Fair Isle jumpers.

I grew up with my brother in an outer suburb of Adelaide, which I remember as a playground of olive and almond groves, vineyards and open fields. There were ducks and chooks and plenty of sleepy lizards around. I was very proud of my first set of oil paints and painted tiny landscapes and Nan's cocky, and had many commissions whilst at primary school to draw pictures and cards as presents for parents.

Alice Miller, a German psychoanalyst says that when you inquire about a person's childhood you are asking about their soul. From Meredith's description, the warmth and joy of her early years reflect a soul rich in an infinite variety of ways.

Meredith learnt to knit as a child, but did not study art at high school because the IQ grading system at the time relegated the art option to those with a lower intelligence level. Her art studies began when she left high school at 16 and joined the advertising department at John Martin's large department store in Adelaide. For four years Meredith learnt fashion drawing and layouts for newspapers and brochures. During the evening she attended classes at the South Australian School of Art.

In 1975 Meredith left John Martin's and became Head of Department and Fashion Coordinator with Golden Breed sportswear designers and manufacturers. For the next two years she concentrated on silkscreening, posters, brochures, label design coordination and finished art work. In her spare time she studied oil painting.

While working for Golden Breed, Meredith met Mandy Martin, today one of Australia's leading women artists. Mandy encouraged Meredith to forgo commerce and study art full time. At 23, Meredith started a four-year degree course at the South Australian School of Art. She remembers the years spent there as ones of both personal and professional growth. Aside from her studies, in the process of self-searching, Meredith developed interests in conservation, yoga, meditation and alternative ways of healing. She felt these were a natural flow-on from the social and spiritual aspects of art.

Restless to experience first-hand the paintings and culture she was exposed to in visual art theory, Meredith and a friend decided to leave art school at the end of third year and travel abroad. To cover expenses Meredith designed a range of children's clothing for an Adelaide company, and waitressed at Cafe des Arts during the Adelaide Festival of 1980.

Introductions from Alistair Livingstone, an English set and costume designer whom Meredith had met in Adelaide, smoothed their way into London's art world. In London Meredith shared a flat with a talented machine knitter who made complex one-off garments for rock stars and television personalities. One of her creations was the 'Thomas the Tank Engine' jerseys for Ringo Starr. As well as this original, creative influence under her own roof, Meredith was exposed to a wide, artistic cross-section of London life.

Meredith travelled through Europe with a friend, camping and hitchhiking on the way. In Paris they met an Algerian photographer, Ali, who encouraged them to travel to the Atlas Mountains in North Africa and meet his people, the Kabylie. Here, says Meredith:

We were welcomed by a people, proud and open, wearing their souls like shining garments. We were shown through the houses which they shared with their animals, their clay pots and their weaving. The women taught us so much about being women. They were so strong, creative, yet essentially feminine, expressing themselves through colour, decoration, jewellery, singing, dance and music.

Meredith moved further south into the Sahara and camped in the desert with the Bedouins. She visited the village bazaars where all manner of rugs, fabrics and precious objects were bartered. As she says: 'The visual imagery and experiences from this time were so rich and powerful that they affected my work and attitude to life completely.'

Returning to Australia in 1983 with Alistair Livingstone as her companion, Meredith began to interpret her experiences in book form, using linocuts and narrative. She also became interested in paper making and was encouraged in this by an Adelaide artisan, Dion Channer.

Meredith and Alistair accepted the invitation of a friend working on the Balgo Mission Station in the western Australian desert to visit and experience Aboriginal culture. Meredith says:

We were immediately accepted and shown many powerful sites, told Dreamtime tales, taken hunting for bush-tucker and to favourite swimming holes. The realisation that even the rock formations, waters and trees were alive and had spirits and a reason for being and could speak, and that people could develop different powers of perception had great impact on me. After this trip I painted and drew from my imagination and memory, rather than from real life, and a whole new personal world flowed for me.

In 1981, Meredith and Alistair returned to England to live for a year and settled in a sixteenth-century farmhouse in Devon, awaiting the birth of their first child, Raphael. After Raphael's birth, Meredith designed a range of hand-knitted garments, which were marketed in Australia. Then, deciding to proceed with her experiments in paper making, Meredith and her family returned to Adelaide to enable her to work once again with Dion Channer.

In Adelaide, Alistair worked on several set and costume projects for the Australian Ballet, the South Australian Opera and the South Australian Film Corporation, and Meredith assisted in the work. As well she employed knitters to help produce her first Australian range of knitwear. She also completed her Fine Arts degree. Between projects she finished the limited edition of hand-bound books on the women of the Atlas Mountains, *The Sun is in My Heart*.

Enlarging the range of her artistic scope, Meredith designed the sets and costumes for an Australian Dance Theatre piece choreographed by Julia Blaikey. This was to be the first of several similar productions. Meredith said that she 'loved the work and the way dance emerges from an idea combined with music, costume, lighting and set.'

Between times Meredith designed and knitted, exhibited and sold garments, preferring individual commissions through which she could express her painterly qualities and own personal imagery. Between 1984 and 1988 she exhibited in *Knitting up a Storm* in Adelaide in 1985; the yearly Australian Wool Board promotions; a *Winter Colours* exhibition in Melbourne; the Bicentenary *Art Knits* exhibition at the Art Gallery of New South Wales, 1988; and *The Knitterarti* in Adelaide in 1989.

A second child, Jasmin, was born in 1987, and in 1988 the family moved to Perth where Meredith worked with an American choreographer, John McLaughlin, designing sets for the West Australian Ballet Company.

Separating from Alistair, Meredith returned to Adelaide with her two children. Here the sudden death of her father, to whom she was very close, compounded the grief she had felt at the separation from Alistair:

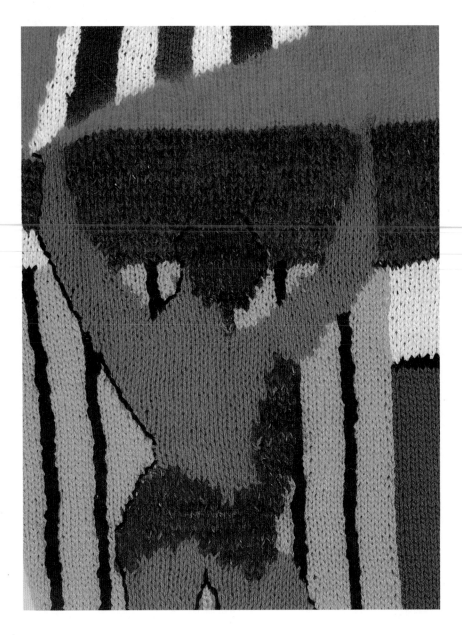

Losing the two most important men in my life caused great distress and much soul searching. Throughout this period I worked on a visual journey, creative in a quest for knowledge and freedom from self-imposed boundaries. This resolved itself in a dance piece called Learning to Fly, *which with a grant from the Australia Council, was staged in December 1989.*

Meredith visited Rajasthan in India with Rob Crocker, an English writer, whom she married in early 1990, and once again the wealth of colour and decoration employed there in the arts, the spectacular harsh beauty and the deep spirituality of the country, have left their mark on her.

Meredith will continue studying for her Diploma in Education, teaching general drawing at the North Adelaide School of Art and giving workshops to ceramic students at the South Australian College of Advanced Education. She and Rob are also restoring a wonderful old house on the beachfront in the Adelaide suburb of Grange.

Measurements

	Small	Medium	Large
Actual Garment			
Measures (*approx*):	90	100	110 cm
Length (*approx*):	108	110	112 cm
Sleeve Fits:	43	43	43 cm

Materials

CLECKHEATON 8 PLY MACHINE WASH (*50 g balls*)

Main Colour (MC)			
Royal blue	8	10	12 balls
Contrast 1 (C1)			
Yellow	9	11	13 balls

CLECKHEATON 8 PLY ANGORA SUPREME (*40 g balls*)

Contrast 2 (C2)			
Pale blue	5	5	5 balls

CLECKHEATON 8 PLY COTTON (*50 g balls*)

Contrast 3 (C3)			
Orange	1	1	1 ball
Contrast 4 (C4)			
Black	1	1	1 ball
Contrast 5 (C5)			
White	1	1	1 ball
Contrast 6 (C6)			
Red	1	1	1 ball
Contrast 7 (C7)			
Cream	1	1	1 ball

CLECKHEATON SENSATION 12 PLY (*50g balls*)

Contrast 8 (C8)			
Blue fleck	2	2	2 balls
Contrast 9 (C9)			
Red fleck	1	1	1 ball

One pair each 3.25mm (No 10) and 5.00mm (No 6) knitting needles; one set of 3.25mm needles; knitters needle for sewing seams and embroidery.

Tension

21 sts and 26 rows to 10cm over stocking st, using 5.00mm needles and MC.

Dress (*Worked in one piece, beg and ending at lower edge*)

Using 3.25mm needles and MC, cast on 96 (106–116) sts.
Work 28 rows K1, P1 rib.
Change to 5.00mm needles.
Work in patt as shown on Graph for *Front* of Dress, beg at row 13 (7–1), until row 152 has been completed.

SHAPE FOR SLEEVES:

Keeping patt correct from Graph, inc one st at each end of next and foll 4th rows 5 times in all, then in alt rows 9 times . . . 124 (134–144) sts.
Work 1 row.
Cast on 2 sts at beg of next 20 (18–16) rows, 7 sts at beg of next 2 rows, 8 (9–10) sts at beg of next 4 rows, then 10 sts at beg of foll 2 rows . . . 230 (240–250) sts, row 216 (214–212) completed.

NOTE: *A circular needle might be easier to use at this point.*

Cont in patt without shaping until row 270 has been completed.

NECK OPENING:

Next Row: Patt 86 (91–96), keeping colours correct as for Graph cast off next 58 sts for neck opening, patt to end.
Next Row: Patt 86 (91–96), turn and keeping colours correct as for Graph cast on 58 sts, turn and patt to end of row . . . 230 (240–250) sts.
Cont in patt as shown on Graph for *Back* of Dress until row 326 (328–330) has been completed.

SHAPE FOR BODY:

Keeping patt correct from Graph, cast off 10 sts at beg of next 2 rows, 8 (9–10) sts at beg of next 4 rows, 7 sts at beg of next 2 rows, then 2 sts at beg of foll 20 (18–16) rows . . . 124 (134–144) sts.
Dec one st at each end of next and alt

rows 9 times in all, then in foll 4th rows 5 times . . . 96 (106–116) sts, row 391 completed.
Cont without shaping until row 530 (536–542) has been completed, thus completing Graph.
Change to 3.25 mm needles and MC only and work 28 rows K1, P1 rib.
Cast off loosely.

Neckband

With right side facing, using set of 3.25mm needles and MC, C5 and C6, knit up 116 sts evenly around neck opening, matching these 3 colours to same colours around neckline (so that stripes follow up).
Work 3 rows K1, P1 rib.
Keeping colours correct, cast off loosely in rib.

Left Cuff

With right side facing, using 3.25mm needles and MC, C5 and C6 in that order, knit up 56 (60–64) sts evenly around left sleeve edge, knitting up 4 sts in each colour all around.
Keeping 4 st stripes correct, work 24 rows K1, P1 rib.
Keeping colours correct, cast off loosely purlways.

Right Cuff

With right side facing, using 3.25mm needles and C6, knit up 56 (60–64) sts evenly around right sleeve edge.
** Work 3 rows K1, P1 rib.
Using C5, knit 1 row.
Work 2 rows rib.
Using C6, purl 1 row.
Work 3 rows rib. **
Using C5, purl 1 row.
Work 2 rows rib.
Using C6, knit 1 row.
Rep from ** to ** once.
Using C6, cast off loosely purlways.

Making Up

Using C4 and stem stitch outline features as indicated on Graph.
Join side and sleeve seams.

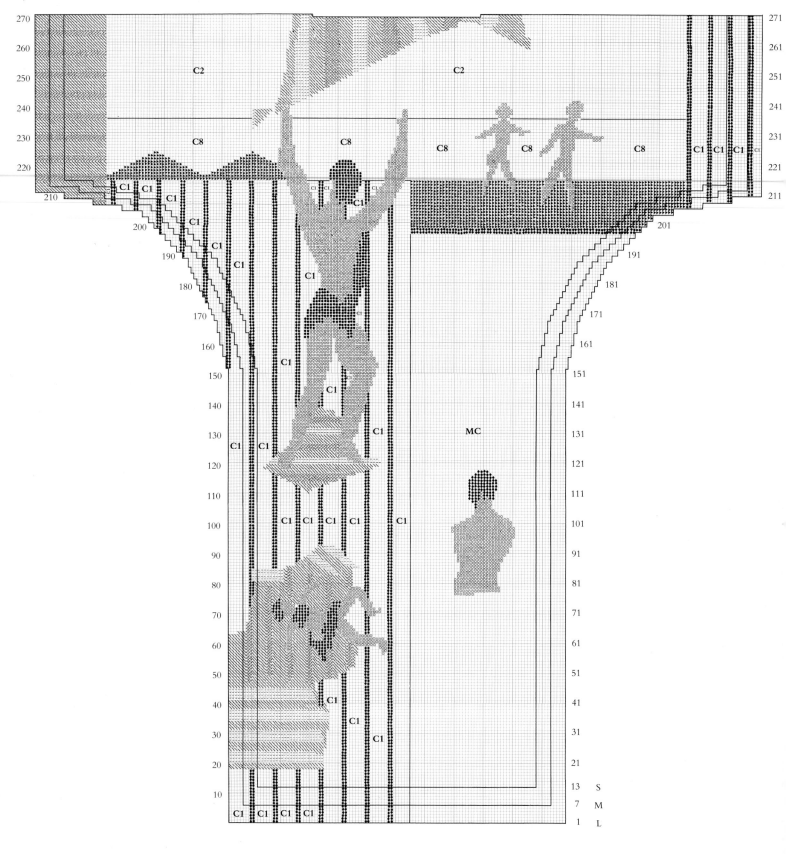

FRONT

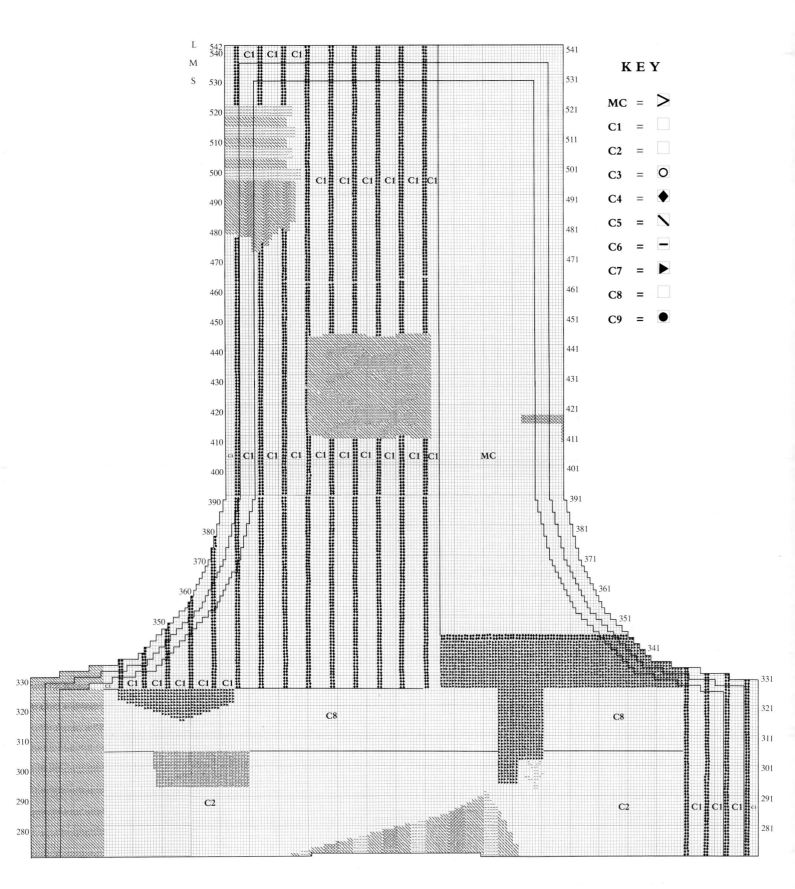

KEY

MC =

C1 =

C2 =

C3 =

C4 =

C5 =

C6 =

C7 =

C8 =

C9 =

BACK

Man Absorbed
in Landscape

JOHN OLSEN

Interpreted by Robyn Malcolm

I am delighted by his brush strokes, his pattern making and his colour use. It seems

to have a gentle humour that mocks the obsessive order in our daily lives.

 John Olsen's paintings affect me in such a mysterious and intangible way that I find it difficult to describe in words. In *Man Absorbed in Landscape*, I respond to Olsen's naive and childish representation of nature, which is free and abandoned. The painting is refreshingly loose in appearance and yet delicately balanced. I am delighted by his brush strokes, his pattern making and his colour use. It seems to have a gentle humour that mocks the obsessive order in our daily lives. I don't think you would find work like this in any other country in the world. Kandinsky and Klee affect me in nearly the same way, but they have an underlying restraint that is barely discernable.

I found it difficult to interpret the painting on to a garment shape, because it was hard to decide what to leave out—I wanted to include it all. But it was also easy, because I was totally inspired by the work and drew endlessly. I could have made 20 different garments from this one lovely painting. It was hard to limit myself and make just two.

It was difficult to work in a limited colour range as my colour choice is usually bold and I love strong contrasts, but I did enjoy the subdued tones in this painting. The colours are rich and warm. There are many browns, reds and ochres—it was a challenge to create an exciting garment using a small range of colours. You will notice when you look closely at the garment that there are small dots of green,

which intensify the red. The black shapes also intensify the colours. The overall richness is again accentuated by the bone background.

It was also challenging to place the design upon the garment shape, and make a pattern that was 'knittable'. Placing the design upon the garment is an art in itself. It takes many attempts to get it right and once it is, you think 'of course—it couldn't be anywhere else.' I moved the whole design about six centimetres to the left after the first sample was knitted, because the initial placement was wrong. I assure

you that this is 'knittable' and I think you'll find it enjoyably challenging to knit. At one stage you will have more than 20 different colours in a row. Incidentally, I always work from separate balls of wool for each colour to produce a smoother fabric, as carrying the wool behind makes the surface uneven.

John Olsen's work to me is essentially Australian in both approach and subject matter. I hope that I have captured the spirit of this painting in these garments.

Fashion Knits for the Avant-Garde

In her Fremantle studio, Robyn Malcolm discusses both the therapeutic and obsessional aspects of knitting and the innovative techniques employed by others to satisfy them:

During the war the father of a friend of mine, a confirmed knitter, was under fire in the trenches. His reaction to the possibility of death on one hand and hours of boredom on the other, was to knit. He'd unravel the hessian used in sandbags and knit it up on pieces of wire. As soon as he finished he'd unpick it and start knitting again.

Robyn identifies with both the compulsion and the innovation in this story. She began knitting when she was eight, and often being impatient with the process, she would innovate and make up patterns and stitches as she went along.

Not only did Robyn's knitting skills improve at college but her basic groundwork in art was also implemented there. The two necessary adjuncts to her future career in art knits fell into place as she trained to become a teacher. After she finished her studies at the Tasmanian College of Advanced Education in 1979, by completing an art major in painting, she taught for four years at a primary school.

In 1984 Robyn took a year's leave from teaching, without pay, and travelled to Papua New Guinea, the United States and Europe. While in Paris she attended a short course in design at the Paris–American Academy. As part of the training she visited a designer's studio, Alain Lalou, and showed him her drawings. He was sufficiently impressed to invite her to work with him on his 1985 *Spring–Summer Collection*. Robyn jumped at the chance and spent the next three months both absorbing and contributing to the work.

The experience was a seminal one as Robyn describes: 'It was a turning point. It made me decide to give up teaching and do this full time. I came back to Australia, applied for and received a grant of $10 000 from the Australia Council.' Robyn's partner lived in Western Australia, so she left Hobart, where she was living at the time, and moved to Perth.

Here, she made and exhibited startlingly original, avant-garde fashion knits, which as she admits were often impracticable in a wearable sense. Her designs were included in the 1986 *Australian Art Clothes* exhibition sent to Edinburgh as part of the Commonwealth Arts Festival there. In the same year the Australian Wool Corporation exhibited her garments in the *Designer Showcase* exhibition in Melbourne, and she took part in a number of other exhibitions in Western Australia.

Robyn's design and colour sense ensured her inclusion in the Bicentenary *Art knits* exhibition in 1988 and the *Contemporary Art of Dress* exhibition at the Victoria and Albert Museum in London in 1989.

Robyn's latest range of knitted coats was inspired by West Australian wildflowers and plants. She values the unique beauty of

KEY

C1 = ☐
C2 = +
C3 = =
C4 = ✕
C5 = ╲
C6 = ●
C7 = ○
C8 = ╱
C9 = −
C10 = |
C11 = <
C12 = >
C13 = ■

the flora and fauna around her. She also values the isolation of Western Australia and the effect this has on her work: Robyn employs a number of piece-work knitters to fulfil her contracts. A garment takes about 70 hours to knit and both Robyn and the knitter share the creative process: 'My knitters are wonderful. They know much more about technique than I do. We consult and they often advise and make suggestions to me on how the design can be improved.'

Ambitious for the future, Robyn will circumvent whatever obstacles hinder her ultimate goal, which is to be recognised as one of the leading knitwear designers in the world: 'I want beautiful knitwear to be synonymous with my name.' Robyn is well on the way.

Jumper

Measurements

Actual Garment	Small	Medium	Large
Measures (approx):	113	118	123 cm
Length (approx):	66	67	68 cm
Sleeve Seam:	43	43	43 cm

Materials

CLECKHEATON 8 PLY MACHINE WASH (50g balls)

	Small	Medium	Large
Colour 1 (C1) Natural	3	3	4 balls
Colour 2 (C2) Tan	2	2	2 balls
Colour 3 (C3) Rust	1	1	1 ball
Colour 4 (C4) Black	1	1	1 ball
Colour 5 (C5) Mid Brown	1	1	1 ball
Colour 6 (C6) Bright Red	1	1	1 ball
Colour 7 (C7) Dark Red	1	1	1 ball
Colour 8 (C8) Mid Green	1	1	1 ball
Colour 9 (C9) Dark Green	1	1	1 ball
Colour 10 (C10) Beige	1	1	1 ball
Colour 11 (C11) Gold	1	1	1 ball
Colour 12 (C12) Dark Brick	1	1	1 ball
Colour 13 (C13) Chocolate Brown	1	1	1 ball

One pair each 4.00mm (No 8) and 3.25mm (No 10) knitting needles; 2 stitch holders; knitters needle for sewing seams.

Tension

22 sts and 30 rows to 10cm over stocking st using 4.00mm needles.

Back

Using 3.25mm needles, cast on 66 (69–72) sts C1, 10 sts C5, 5 sts C6, 20 sts C3, 5 sts C6, then 20 (23–26) sts C1 . . . 126 (132–138) sts.
Work 18 rows K1, P1 rib in colours as placed.
Change to 4.00mm needles.
Work in patt as shown on Graph A until row 110 has been completed.

SHAPE ARMHOLES:
Keeping patt correct from Graph, cast off 9 sts at beg of next 2 rows, then dec one st at each end of next and alt rows 6 times in all 96 . . . (102–108) sts.
Cont in patt as shown on Graph until row 180 (182–186) has been completed.

SHAPE SHOULDERS:
Cast off 16 (17–18) sts at beg of next 4 rows.
Leave rem 32 (34–36) sts on a stitch holder.

Front

Using 3.25mm needles, cast on 20 (23–26) sts C1, 5 sts C6, 20 sts C3, 5 sts C6, 10 sts C5, then 66 (69–72) sts C1 . . . 126 (132–138) sts. Cont as for Back, noting to reverse colours as indicated on Graph A, until row 158 has been completed.

SHAPE NECK:
Next Row: Patt 40 (43–46) sts, turn.
Cont on these 40 (43–46) sts.
Keeping patt correct from Graph, dec one st at neck edge in alt rows 8 (9–10) times . . . 32 (34–36) sts.
Work 5 (5–7) rows (row 180 (182–186) completed from Graph).

SHAPE SHOULDER:
Cast off 16 (17–18) sts at beg of next row and foll alt row.

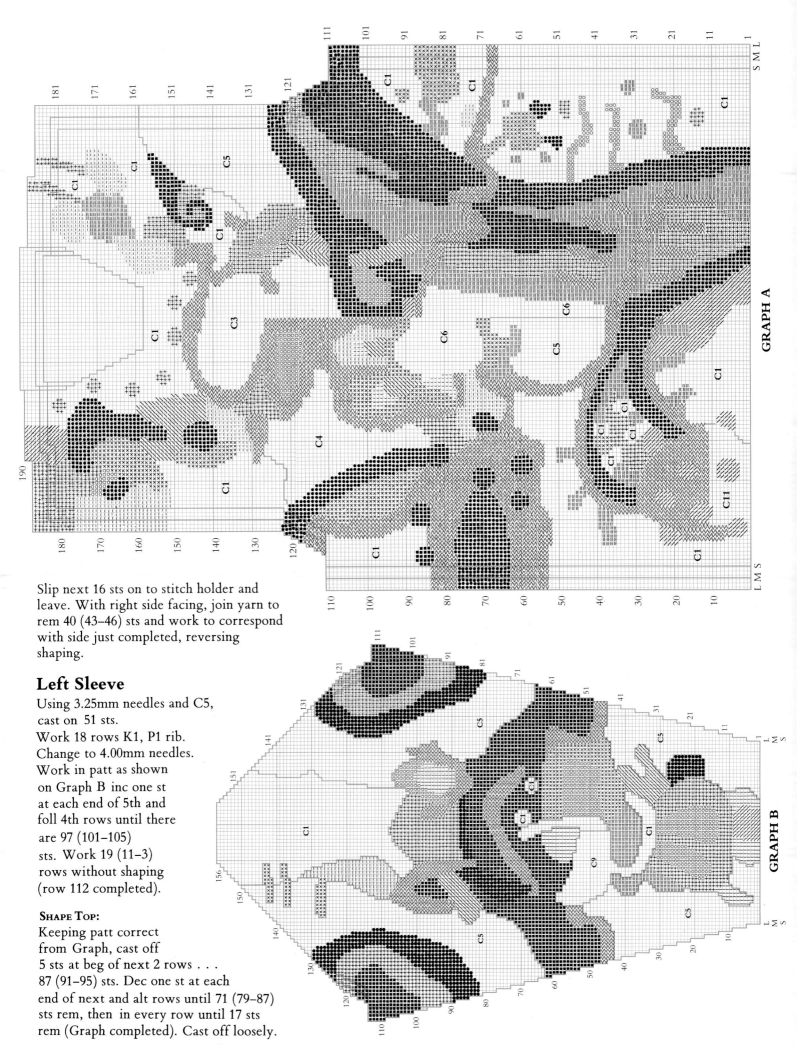

Slip next 16 sts on to stitch holder and
leave. With right side facing, join yarn to
rem 40 (43–46) sts and work to correspond
with side just completed, reversing
shaping.

Left Sleeve

Using 3.25mm needles and C5,
cast on 51 sts.
Work 18 rows K1, P1 rib.
Change to 4.00mm needles.
Work in patt as shown
on Graph B inc one st
at each end of 5th and
foll 4th rows until there
are 97 (101–105)
sts. Work 19 (11–3)
rows without shaping
(row 112 completed).

Shape Top:

Keeping patt correct
from Graph, cast off
5 sts at beg of next 2 rows . . .
87 (91–95) sts. Dec one st at each
end of next and alt rows until 71 (79–87)
sts rem, then in every row until 17 sts
rem (Graph completed). Cast off loosely.

GRAPH A

GRAPH B

81

Right Sleeve

Work as for Left Sleeve, noting to work cuff in C1 instead of C5 and to work from Graph C instead of Graph B.

Neckband

Join right shoulder seam. With right side facing, using 3.25mm needles and C1, knit up 90 (96–106) sts evenly around neck, incl sts from stitch holders.

Cardigan

Measurements

	Small	Medium	Large
Actual Garment Measures (*approx*):	113	118	123 cm
Length (*approx*):	66	67	68 cm
Sleeve Seam (*approx*):	43	43	43 cm

Materials

CLECKHEATON 8 PLY MACHINE WASH (*50g balls*)

	Small	Medium	Large
Colour 1 (C1) Natural	3	3	4 balls
Colour 2 (C2) Tan	2	2	2 balls
Colour 3 (C3) Rust	1	1	1 ball
Colour 4 (C4) Black	1	1	1 ball
Colour 5 (C5) Dark Grey	1	1	1 ball
Colour 6 (C6) Bright Red	1	1	1 ball
Colour 7 (C7) Dark Red	1	1	1 ball
Colour 8 (C8) Mid Green	1	1	1 ball
Colour 9 (C9) Dark Green	1	1	1 ball
Colour 10 (C10) Beige	2	2	2 balls
Colour 11 (C11) Gold	1	1	1 ball
Colour 12 (C12) Orange	1	1	1 ball
Colour 13 (C13) Brown	1	1	1 ball

One pair each 4.00mm (No 8) and 3.25mm (No 10) knitting needles; 3 stitch holders; knitters needle for sewing seams; 7 large buttons; shoulder pads.

Tension

22 sts and 30 rows to 10 cm over stocking st using 4.00mm needles.

Next Row: * K1, P1, rep from * to end.
Rep last row 20 times.
Cast off loosely in rib.

Making Up

Join left shoulder, side and sleeve seams. Sew in sleeves. Fold neckband in half on to wrong side and slip stitch loosely in position.

Back

Using 3.25mm needles and C1, cast on 127 (133–139) sts.
Work 26 rows K1, P1 rib.
Change to 4.00mm needles.
Work in patt as shown on Graph A until row 110 has been completed.

SHAPE ARMHOLES:
Keeping patt correct from Graph, cast off 9 sts at beg of next 2 rows, then dec one st at each end of next and alt rows 6 times in all . . . 97 (103–109) sts.
Cont in patt as shown on Graph until row 180 (182–186) has been completed.

SHAPE SHOULDERS:
Cast off 16 (17–18) sts at beg of next 4 rows.
Leave rem 33 (35–37) sts on a stitch holder.

Left Front

Using 3.25mm needles and C1, cast on 79 (81–85) sts.
Work 25 rows K1, P1 rib.
Next Row: Rib 16 sts and slip these onto a stitch holder for front band, rib to end, *Size Medium only*—inc once in centre of row.
All Sizes: 63 (66–69) sts.
Change to 4.00mm needles.
Work in patt as shown on Graph A until row 110 has been completed.

SHAPE ARMHOLE:
Keeping patt correct from Graph, cast off 9 sts at beg of next row, then dec one st at beg of alt rows 6 times . . . 48 (51–54) sts.
Cont in patt as shown on Graph until row 159 has been completed.

SHAPE NECK:
Keeping patt correct from Graph, cast off 8 sts at beg of next row, then dec one st at

neck edge in next and alt rows 8 (9–10) times in all . . . 32 (34–36) sts. Cont without shaping until row 180 (182–186) has been completed.

SHAPE SHOULDER:
Cast off 16 (17–18) sts at beg of next row and foll alt row.

Right Front

Using 3.25mm needles and C1, cast on 79 (81–85) sts.
Work 4 rows K1, P1 rib.
Next Row: Rib 5, cast off 5 sts, rib to end.
Next Row: Rib to last 5 sts, cast on 5 sts, rib 5 . . . one buttonhole.
Work 19 rows rib.
Next Row: Rib to last 16 sts (*Size Medium only*—inc once in centre of row), slip last 16 sts on to stitch holder for front band.
All Sizes—63 (66–69) sts.
Cont as for Left Front, reversing shaping, and working as indicated on Graph A for Right Front.

Left Sleeve

Using 3.25mm needles and C2, cast on 51 sts.
Work 18 rows K1, P1 rib.
Change to 4.00mm needles.
Work in patt as shown on Graph B inc one st at each end of 5th and foll 4th rows until there are 101 (103–105) sts. Work 11 (7–3) rows without shaping (row 112 completed).

SHAPE TOP:
Keeping patt correct from Graph, cast off 9 sts at beg of next 2 rows . . . 83 (85–87) sts.
Dec one st at each end of next and alt rows until 61 (61–57) sts rem, then in every row until 19 sts rem (Graph completed).
Cast off loosely.

Right Sleeve

Work as for Left Sleeve, noting to work cuff in C1 instead of C2 and to work from Graph C instead of Graph B.

Right Front Band

With wrong side facing and using 3.25mm needles and C1, rib across 16 sts left on stitch holder on Right Front. Cont in rib, matching band colours to body and working a buttonhole (as before) in 11th and 12th rows and foll 31st and 32nd rows

from previous buttonhole until there are 6 buttonholes in all. Work 19 rows rib, ending in C1. Do not break off yarn. Leave sts on needle. Sew band in position.

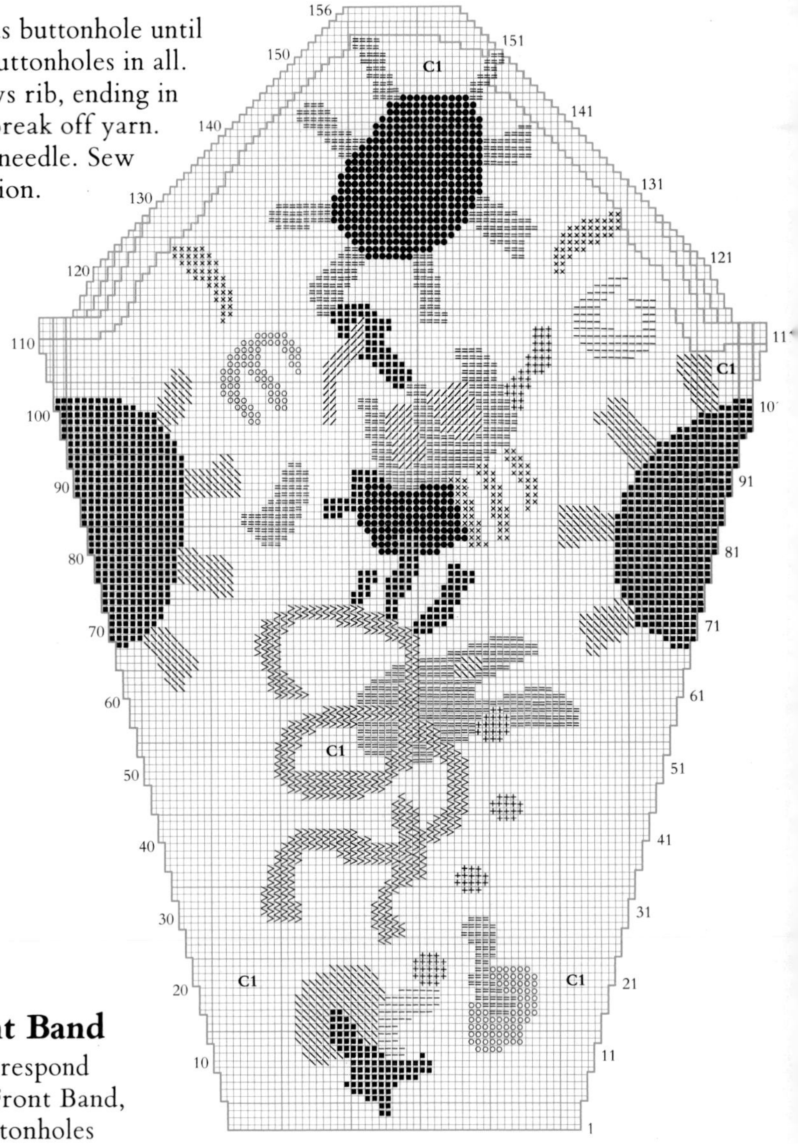

Left Front Band

Work to correspond with Right Front Band, omitting buttonholes and matching band colours to body, and noting to work 1 row less in C1 at top. Break off yarn. Leave sts on a stitch holder. Sew band in position.

Neckband

Join shoulder seams. With right side facing and using 3.25mm needle holding right front band sts and C1, knit up 99 (105–115) sts evenly around neck then rib across left front band sts . . . 131 (137–147) sts.
Work 15 rows K1, P1 rib, working a buttonhole (as before) in 10th and 11th rows.
Cast off loosely in rib.

Making Up

Join side and sleeve seams. Sew in sleeves. Sew buttons in place. Insert shoulder pads.

GRAPH C

Aboriginal Design
with Sturt's Desert Pea

MARGARET PRESTON

Interpreted by Liz Gemmell

In her extremely truthful depiction of stiff gum leaves, prickly banksias, glossy desert peas and waxy Christmas bells, Margaret Preston captures the innate beauty of these survivors of a stringent environment.

Three significant periods incorporate Margaret Preston's mature paintings: still life, colour paintings from 1915 to 1928; a geometric phase 1927–28; and an Aboriginal phase from 1940 to 1945.

Margaret Preston became interested in Aboriginal art and culture in the early 1920s when she was searching for a truly 'national' art form. In 1924 she decided that such a style should incorporate the hard black outlines featured in her wood-block printing at that time, as well as the Aboriginal boomerang shape, concentric circles and the gum-leaf shape. Her proposed colours were red, yellow ochre and blue. Her idea was to promote national forms and colours for the design of domestic items and textiles for furnishings. Preston felt that Aboriginal art was more reflective of national design than the indigenous flora and fauna, which she herself offered in her very popular flower-paintings of the time.

While living at Berowra Waters, 40 kilometres from Sydney, from 1932 to 1939, Margaret Preston and her husband discovered many Aboriginal rock engravings in the surrounding bushland. A close friend, Fred McCarthy, was Curator of Anthropology at the Australian Museum during these years and he encouraged and advised the Prestons with their research and interest in Aboriginal culture.

Preston's growing respect for the art of the Aborigines culminated in her wartime Aboriginal paintings of 1940–1945, one of which was *Aboriginal Design with Sturt's Desert Pea*. Some critics see these paintings as the pinnacle of her career.

Margaret Preston's insight into Aboriginal culture and the Australian bush has always impressed me. Her bush flora is not gentle and soft, but often leathery and glossy with brilliant short-lived blossoms seemingly designed to cope with harsh conditions. In her extremely truthful depiction of stiff gum leaves, prickly banksias, glossy desert peas and waxy Christmas bells, Margaret Preston captures the innate beauty

of these survivors of a stringent environment. They are not mere subjects or parts of a still life, they are given their own life through her perception and love of nature.

Aboriginal Design with Sturt's Desert Pea is a masonite cut. The texture of the masonite is an integral part of the colour. The bold white lines move in an abstract fashion over the print, leaving an area to be filled with the vibrant red desert peas. These peas have no need to be abstracted—nature has already seen to that.

I have used woven colour stranding as the main technique for interpreting the print into a knitted garment. White is carried across each row and is woven in at the back into every stitch. This allows the white to show through the solid areas of brown and black, just as the masonite texture shows on the print. The peas were knitted separately and sewn on, in order to evoke a three-dimensional effect, a spontaneity, and a realistic appearance.

The Finesse of Technique

 The knitting of a carpet was part of a journeyman's test of his skills in the era when knitting guilds were strong in Europe in the sixteenth and seventeenth centuries.

A prime example of the art resides in the Victoria and Albert Museum in London. The intricacy of pattern and the level of expertise astound and intimidate any latter day knitter.

When Liz Gemmell was researching a lecture she was giving at a craft seminar, she discovered the art of carpet knitting. Needing a challenge and a larger palette on which to exercise her skills, she decided to knit a carpet. When I visited her cottage at

Balmain in Sydney, Liz was knitting her fifth carpet. Developing the original idea further, Liz is now preparing to publish a book on knitted carpets. A true professional, this will be the fifth book on knitting to be published by Liz in the past ten years.

Liz was taught to cast on stitches and knit by a neighbour. Later when she was old enough to decipher a knitting book another neighbour taught her to cast off. Between times she knitted many scarves. She was well into her teens before she began knitting consistently.

Born in Germany of Russian émigré parents, Liz came to live in Newcastle when she was four years old. Her grandmother and mother, who were both teachers, were strong, affirmative influences in her life. They had to acquire innovative skills to survive in a new country. Both learnt to sew and so did Liz. Liz also followed their professional role model and became a teacher. Married at 20 and eager for adventure, she and her teacher husband, Leigh, travelled in the United Kingdom and United States and finally settled in Canada for three years, where their two sons were born a year apart.

Returning to Newcastle and settling near Lake Macquarie in mid-1972, Liz and Leigh built their first house. After 18 months of

settling in, Liz enrolled in a part-time Fine Arts course at Newcastle Technical College, three nights a week, for five years. She recalls:

It was wonderful. The course covered ceramics, painting and drawing and the majority of us were mature age students. The Star Hotel was opposite the tech and of course after class we'd all cross the road for a few drinks and a chat. Both socially and educationally they were good years.

I was fully extended because I was also teaching craft part-time to a class of retarded children. My husband was a teacher at the school at the time. We found that our children were happier and better adjusted when we were fulfilling our own potential and were not frustrated. Aware of this, when we decided to radically change our lifestyle after I finished my art course, we didn't hesitate. We sold our house and bought a boat. We hadn't sailed much before but were prepared to learn.

For two years the family lived on the boat. Liz says of this period: 'Because of the close living conditions on board we got to know one another a lot better and a close rapport was established between us. . . . We all got to like one another. The kids were always present at discussions and helped make decisions.' And says Liz, 'we got it right. We didn't lose a bucket or a kid overboard.' Though both their parents were teachers neither child wanted to take formal lessons from them. Liz and Leigh maintain that the practical skills the children absorbed living on board a boat more than compensated for classroom learning. They learnt to read navigation charts, almanacs and newspapers, how to light a kerosene stove and operate the radio on board.

After two years of the mariner's life the family decided to return to the mainstream once again. Berthed at a marina in Sydney Harbour for a year, Liz began knitting a jumper a week for a boutique. Capitalising on the popularity of Jenny Kee's picture knits, Liz designed a range of garments and published her first book. It was a huge success, selling around 40 000 copies. She contends that part of its success was the clear and simple instructions she included: 'As I was knitting the jumpers myself while writing the book, I was aware of all the problems the knitters themselves would find. It was a learning experience for me too.'

Liz's progression into creating picture knits extended both her expertise and her reputation. The Wool Corporation recruited her for workshops, and since 1980 Liz has participated in their seminars or shows a couple of times annually. The Wool Corporation's ability to successfully promote knitters with their touring exhibitions is acknowledged by professional knitters such as Liz.

Liz continues to combine her art training and her knitting skills to further extend the boundaries of what she can create with a pair of knitting needles: 'My picture knits, in retrospect, were very basic. Then I was discovering pattern and technique, now I'm exploring colour. A painter mixes colours together and that's what I'm doing in wool, using 50 or 60 different colours together.'

Though the mediums are different, Liz contends that both need finesse of technique and an original vision to become a work of art: 'Both have a craft to them and with a lot of knitting as well as painting, neither get past the craft stage. Because it's utilitarian, on the craft level, a jumper, unlike a painting, is valid, but it must reach a higher level before it becomes art. And that for me is the challenge.'

Kaffe Fassett has been a liberating mentor for Liz:

Picture knits for me was like opening the first door to a new library, but it was Fassett's approach to knitting which held the key to the rest of the volumes. Seeing his work was as revelatory to me as seeing my first Van Gogh painting. Suddenly I realised what knitting could be all about, its potential for design, technique and colour. Cutting the wool into small pieces and tying them together allows a knitter a similar freedom to a painter with dozens of tubes of paint. Fassett's broken the egg, so to speak, for all time now and knitting is free to go anywhere it likes. There are few boundaries now.

Putting into practice her new insight, Liz began her carpet knitting. Frustrated by the limitations of garment knitting, the tyranny of the armhole and the demands of fashion, Liz experimented first with a small rug then quickly moved to a 6' × 7' size. Though her reference points, the carpets of the seventeenth century, were knitted on frames, Liz quickly evolved a much easier technique. Now she is finding the rugs a pleasure to knit and neither physically nor mentally demanding.

Contributing considerably to Liz's success is the empirical approach to her work and the knowledge she acquired charting unfamiliar knitting terrain. An explorer with the knitting needle, today Liz is knitting not only rugs, but bedthrows, upholstery and curtains. Although she intends concentrating on rugs in the immediate future, exploring further boundaries is on her agenda.

Liz's personal and professional satisfaction in her work peaked with the inclusion of her knitted ensemble in the *Art knits* exhibition, curated by Jane de Teliga for the Art Gallery of New South Wales in 1988. As Newcastle was one of the places it toured, Liz felt that her talents had come full circle and had finally been brought home.

KEY

MC = ☐

C1 = O

C2 = V

C3 = ＼

Measurements

	Small	Medium	Large
Actual Garment Measures:	110	122	134 cm
Length (*approx*):	75	75	75 cm
Sleeve Fits (*approx*):	43	43	43 cm

Materials

CLECKHEATON NATURAL 12 PLY (*50g balls*)

	Small	Medium	Large
Main Colour (MC) Brown	11	13	15 balls
Contrast 1 (C1) White	8	10	12 balls
Contrast 2 (C2) Red	3	3	4 balls

CLECKHEATON 12 PLY MACHINE WASH (*50g balls*)

	Small	Medium	Large
Contrast 3 (C3) Black	9	9	10 balls

One each 4.00mm (No 8) and 5.50mm (No 5) circular knitting needles (80cm long); one pair 4.00 mm knitting needles; one set 4.00mm knitting needles; 3 stitch holders; 6 buttons; small quantity of polyester fibre filling; knitters needle for sewing seams and embroidery.

Tension

17 sts and 18 rows to 10 cm over patt, using 5.50mm needles.

NOTE: *C1 (white) should be carried across the back of your work from edge to edge and woven in at every st when not in use, regardless of other colour in use. This technique enhances the appearance of this particular jacket and should be used for the entire garment. Always carry MC and C1 to ends of rows and always carry MC above other colours. When not in use, MC should be woven in at every 5th st. When using C2 and C3, do not carry across width of work but use a separate ball of yarn for each section of colour. When changing to or from C2 or C3 in the middle of a row, twist the colour to be used (on wrong side) underneath and to the right of the colour just used, remembering at all times to cont to carry C1 across back as explained above.*

Back

Using 4.00mm circular needle and C3, cast on 87 (97–107) sts.

NOTE: *Do not break off C3 or MC but carry loosely along sides of work.*

1st Row: Using MC, K2, * P1, K1, rep from * to last st, K1.

Do not turn, slide sts to other end of needle.

2nd Row: Using C3, complete as for 1st Row, turn.

3rd Row: Using MC, K1, * P1, K1 rep from * to end.

Do not turn, slide sts to other end of needle.

4th Row: Using C3, complete as for 3rd Row, turn.

These 4 rows form Rib Patt.

Cont in rib patt until work measures approx 8cm from beg, ending with a 4th patt row and inc 9 sts evenly across this row . . . 96 (106–116) sts.

Change to 5.50mm circular needle.

Work in patt as shown on Graph until row 56 has been completed.

SHAPE FOR SLEEVES:

Keeping patt correct from Graph, inc one st at each end of next and alt rows 4 (5–3) times in all, then in every row 9 (3–3) times . . . 122 (122–128) sts.

Cast on 5 sts at beg of next 10 rows, then 14 (19–21) sts at beg of foll 2 rows . . . 200 (210–220) sts.

Cont in patt from Graph on these sts until row 120 has been completed.

SHAPE FOR NECK AND SHOULDERS:

Patt 85 (87–92), turn.

NOTE: *When turning on shoulders, bring yarn to front of work, slip next st on to right hand needle, yarn back, then slip st back on to left hand needle, then turn and proceed as instructed. This avoids holes in work.*

Next Row: P2tog, patt 43 (40–40), turn.
Next Row: Patt to last 2 sts, K2tog.
Next Row: Patt 23 (20–20), turn.
Next Row: Patt to end.
Leave these rem 83 (85–90) sts on a spare needle or thread.
Slip next (centre) 30 (36–36) sts onto a stitch holder and leave.
With right side facing, join yarn to rem 85 (87–92) sts and patt to end.
Next Row: Patt to last 2 sts, P2tog.
Next Row: K2tog, patt 42 (39–39), turn.
Next Row: Patt to end.
Next Row: Patt 23 (20–20), turn.
Next Row: Patt to end.
Leave these rem 83 (85–90) sts on a spare needle or thread.

Left Pocket Lining

Using 5.50mm circular needle and MC, cast on 22 sts.

Work 20 rows stocking st.
Work rows 21 and 22 between pocket markers as indicated on Graph for Left Front.
Leave these sts on a stitch holder.

Right Pocket Lining

Work as for Left Pocket Lining, working rows 21 and 22 between pocket markers as indicated on Graph for Right Front.

Left Front

Using 4.00mm circular needle and C3, cast on 43 (49–53) sts.
Work in rib patt as for Back lower band, working same number of rows and inc 5 (4–5) sts evenly across last row . . . 48 (53–58) sts.
Change to 5.50mm circular needle.
Work in patt as shown on Graph for Left Front, until row 22 has been completed. **
23rd Row: Patt 8 (13–18) sts from Graph, patt across Left Pocket Lining sts, slip next 22 sts onto stitch holder and leave, patt rem 18 sts.
Cont in patt from Graph until row 56 has been completed.

SHAPE FOR SLEEVES AND FRONT SLOPE:
Keeping patt correct from Graph, inc one st at beg of next and alt rows 4 (5–3) times in all, then at same edge in every row 9 (3–3) times, AT SAME TIME dec one st at front edge in foll 3rd rows (beg with row 59) 5 (4–2) times . . . 56 (57–62) sts.
Cast on 5 sts at beg of next row and foll alt rows 5 times in all, then 14 (19–21) sts at beg of foll alt row, AT SAME TIME dec one st at front edge in foll 3rd rows from previous dec 12 (16–18) times . . . 83 (85–90) sts rem.
Work without shaping until row 121 of Graph has been completed.

SHAPE SHOULDER:
Next Row: Patt 43 (40–40), turn.
Next Row: Patt to end.
Next Row: Patt 23 (20–20), turn.
Next Row: Patt to end.
Leave these 83 (85–90) sts on a spare needle or thread.

Right Front

Work as for Left Front to **, working patt from Graph as indicated for Right Front.

23rd Row: Patt 18 sts from Graph, patt across Right Pocket Lining sts, slip next 22 sts onto stitch holder and leave, patt rem 8 (13–18) sts.
Cont in patt from Graph and work to correspond with Left Front, reversing all shaping.

Shoulder Rouleau

With wrong side of Left Front facing corresponding wrong side of Back, and using 5.50mm circular needle and C3, * knit one st from each needle tog, rep from * to end . . . 83 (85–90) sts.
Do not turn, slide sts to other end of needle.
Next Row: Using MC, knit to end, turn.
Next Row: Using C3, purl to end.
Do not turn, slide sts to other end of needle.
Next Row: Using MC, purl to end, turn.
Next Row: Using C3, knit to end.
Do not turn, slide sts to other end of needle.
Cast off loosely knitways, using MC.
Fold rouleau in half to Back and slip-stitch in place, filling lightly with filling as you go.
Work same rouleau on right shoulder.

NOTE: *At this point, press work lightly on wrong side, using a warm iron over a damp cloth.*

Right Front Band

Using 4.00mm circular needle and C3, knit up 155 (157–157) sts evenly along Right Front and around back neck to centre of stitch holder, noting to inc one st in last st.
Work 4 rows rib patt as for Back lower band, beg with a 2nd row.
Next Row: Using C3, rib 2, (yfwd, K2tog, rib 12) 5 times, yfwd, K2tog, rib to end . . . 6 buttonholes.
Work a further 4 rows rib patt.
Cast off loosely in rib, using both MC and C3 tog.

Left Front Band

Work to correspond with Right Front Band, omitting buttonholes. Join front bands at centre back neck.

Collar

With right side facing, using 5.50mm circular needle and C3, beg and ending at first dec of front slope shaping, knit up

161 (167–167) sts evenly around neck, inside front bands.

1st Row: P1 C3, * P1 MC, P1 C3, rep from * to end.

2nd row: K1 MC, * K1 C3, K1 MC, rep from * to end.

Last 2 rows form collar patt.

Work 1 row patt.

Keeping patt correct, dec one st at each end of every row until 101 (107–107) sts rem.

Cast off 5 sts at beg of next 2 rows . . . 91 (97–97) sts.

Leave these sts on a spare needle or thread.

Collar Rouleau

With right side of collar facing, using 5.50mm circular needle and C3, knit up 32 sts along shaped edge of collar, knit across sts left on needle, then knit up 32 sts along other side of collar . . . 155 (161–161) sts.

Complete as for shoulder rouleau.

Fold rouleau in half to underside of collar and slip-stitch in position, filling lightly with filling as you go.

Pocket Facings

With right side facing and using MC, *purl* across 22 sts left on stitch holder for pocket.

Work 6 rows stocking st, beg with a purl row.

Cast off loosely.

Cuffs

Join side and sleeve seams. With right side facing, using set of 4.00mm needles and C3, knit up 49 (51–53) sts evenly around sleeve edge, beg at lower sleeve seam.

1st Round: Using MC (K1, P1) 0 (1–2) time/s, * (K1, P1) twice, K2 tog, P1, rep from * to end . . . 42 (44–46) sts.

2nd Round: Using C3, K1, * P1, K1, rep from * to end.

3rd Round: Using MC, K1, * P1, K1, rep from * to end.

Rep 2nd and 3rd Rounds until cuff measures 12cm.

Cast off loosely in rib.

Desert Peas

These are worked in 2 half pieces with a separate bobble sewn to centre.

1st Piece:

Using 4.00mm needles and C2, cast on 3 sts.

1st Row (wrong side): (K1, P1, K1, P1, K1) into first st, P1, (K1, P1, K1, P1, K1) into last st . . . 11 sts.

2nd Row: K5, P1, K5.

3rd and Alt Rows: Knit all knit sts and purl all purl sts as they appear.

4th Row: K3, K2tog, P1, K2tog tbl, K3 . . . 9 sts.

6th Row: K4, P1, K4.

8th Row: K2, K2tog, P1, K2tog tbl, K2 . . . 7 sts.

10th Row: K3, P1, K3.

12th Row: K1, K2tog, P1, K2tog, tbl, K1 . . . 5 sts.

14th Row: K2, P1, K2.

16th Row: K2tog, P1, K2tog tbl . . . 3 sts.

18th Row: K1, P1, K1.

19th Row: P2tog, P1.

Pass first st over second st. Fasten off.

2nd Piece:

With right side facing, using 4.00mm needles and C2, knit up 3 sts along cast-on edge of first piece.

1st Row (wrong side): As 1st row of 1st Piece.

Complete as for 1st Piece.

Length of pea may be varied by omitting or repeating rows 6, 10 or 14 as required.

CENTRE PIECE:

Using 4.00mm needles and C3, and leaving 30cm end place slip knot on needle. Work (K1, P1, K1, P1, K1) into slip knot . . . 5 sts.

Work 4 rows stocking st.

Do not turn. Slip 2nd st from needle point over 1st, then 3rd and 4th sts in same way. Fasten off, leaving a 30cm end.

Attach centre piece to centre of pea, pulling long ends through to wrong side.

Make 25 desert peas in total, of varying length, in this way.

Attach 18 peas to Back only as indicated on Graph. Adjust as desired. These may be stitched on curve.

Using chain stitch and C3 end, stitch along centre of pea, along purl st. Tips of pea may be left unsewn to allow them to curl. In this case, cont chain st embroidery to tip.

Attach 7 peas to collar, as illustrated.

Making Up

Fold pocket facings to inside along purl ridge and slip-stitch in place. Slip-stitch pocket linings to fronts. Sew buttons in place. Fold cuffs back.

Centre Landscape

TREVOR NICKOLLS

Interpreted by Liz Gemmell

The Rock has always fascinated my imagination. When I saw Trevor Nickolls' Centre Landscape, *I was struck with its power. There was the 'Rock' of my imagination—bold, stark, powerful, full of glaring sun and unequivocally stating its presence.*

 Trevor Nickolls, an artist of Aboriginal descent, was born in Port Adelaide in 1949. He began art lessons when he was eight and in 1967 enrolled in Fine Art studies at the South Australian School of Art, where he gained a Fine Arts diploma. After further studies in South Australia and Canberra he became an art teacher. He gained a post-graduate diploma in painting from the Victorian College of Arts and was subsequently awarded a creative arts fellowship at the Australian National University.

In 1979, Trevor Nickolls met Dinny Nolan, a Papunya painter. This was his first contact with a traditional artist and a catalyst in his approach to his art; he now began to view Australian art as being drawn from both white and Aboriginal cultures. Based in Darwin after he finished his studies, Nickolls became more involved in outlying Aboriginal communities, resulting in his growing awareness of desert art techniques and the religious aspects of the landscape.

The relation of humanity to twentieth-century cityscape and landscape is central to much of Trevor Nickolls' work. 'Machinetime' and 'Dreamtime' are two constant themes, the former relating to the aggression and alienation of industrialised urban life and the latter to the depth of meaning in traditional Aboriginal life.

The Rock has always fascinated my imagination. When I saw Trevor Nickolls' *Centre Landscape*, I was struck with its power. There was the 'Rock' of my imagination—bold, stark, powerful, full of glaring sun and unequivocally stating its presence.

The composition of the painting is simple, yet the uncompromising colours have been streaked, swirled, dotted and cross-hatched, stating all the intricacy and mythology that is the Rock and its environs.

I felt the challenge was to interpret the colours of the painting in wools, to keep the composition in the garment simple, and to try to include all the colour patterns of the three primary areas, namely rock, land and sky.

To achieve this colour and patterning, I have used a combination of knitting techniques. The colour stranding of each area has its own pattern of alternating colours to get as much vibrancy and movement of colour as Trevor Nickolls has in his composition.

The child's jumper is a facsimile of the painting while the adult's jumper depicts the painting framed in the simplest and boldest of frames—black and white.

Adult's Jumper

Measurements

	Small	Medium	Large
Actual Garment Measures (approx):	114	119	124 cm
Length (approx):	58	59	60 cm
Sleeve Seam:	47	47	47 cm

Materials

CLECKHEATON 8 PLY MACHINE WASH (50g balls)

Main Colour (MC) White	9	9	10 balls
Contrast 1 (C1) Black	4	5	5 balls
Contrast 2 (C2) Bright Red	1	1	1 ball
Contrast 3 (C3) Dark Red	1	1	1 ball
Contrast 4 (C4) Gold	1	1	1 ball
Contrast 5 (C5) Rust	1	1	1 ball
Contrast 6 (C6) Pale Blue	1	1	1 ball
Contrast 7 (C7) Royal	1	1	1 ball
Contrast 8 (C8) Dark Green	1	1	1 ball

AND CLECKHEATON MERINO 8 PLY (50g balls)

Contrast 9 (C9) Violet	1	1	1 ball
Contrast 10 (C10) Maroon	1	1	1 ball
Contrast 11 (C11) Light Green	1	1	1 ball

One pair each 3.25mm (No 10) and 4.00mm (No 8) knitting needles; 2 stitch holders; knitters needle for sewing seams and embroidery.

Tension

22 sts and 30 rows to 10cm over stocking st, using 4.00mm needles.

NOTE: *When using contrast colours (except when C1 is worked at sides of work), do not carry across width of work but use a separate ball of yarn for each section of patt. When changing patt blocks in the middle of a row and to or from MC or C1 at sides of rows, twist the colour to be used (on wrong side) underneath and to the right of the colour just used.*

Back

Using 3.25mm needles and C1, cast on 122 (128–134) sts.
Work 20 rows K1, P1 rib, inc 11 sts evenly across last row . . . 133 (139–145) sts.
Change to 4.00mm needles.**
Work 70 rows stocking st.
Work 3 rows stocking st in stripes of 1 row each C3, C9 and C7.
Using MC for rem, work 57 (61–63) rows stocking st, beg with a purl row.

SHAPE SHOULDERS AND NECK:
Next Row: Cast off 14 (14–15) sts, K30 (32–33), turn.
Cont on these 30 (32–33) sts.
Dec one st at neck edge in next 3 rows, AT SAME TIME cast off 14 (14–15) sts at beg of 2nd row.
Cast off rem 13 (15–15) sts.
Slip next 45 (47–49) sts on to a stitch holder and leave. With right side facing, join yarn to rem 44 (46–48) sts and work to correspond with side just completed, reversing shaping.

Front

Work as for Back to **
Work 30 rows stocking st.
Next Row: K20 (23–26) C1, patt 93 sts from 1st row of Graph A, K20 (23–26) C1.
Next Row: P20 (23–26) C1, patt 93 sts from 2nd row of Graph A, P20 (23–26) C1.
Keeping 20 (23–26) C1 sts at side edges correct, cont in patt as shown on Graph A *as placed* in last 2 rows, until Row 39 has been completed.
Work 2 rows stocking st (beg with a purl row) in stripes of 1 row each C1 then C3.
Next Row: P20 (23–26) C9, patt 93 sts from 1st row of Graph B, P20 (23–26) C9.

KEY

MC	=	✖
C1	=	●
C2	=	.
C3	=	✳
C4	=	╲
C5	=	＊
C6	=	❙
C7	=	▬
C8	=	╱
C9	=	○
C10	=	■
C11	=	‖

L MS **GRAPH A** SL M

Next Row: K20 (23–26) C7, patt 93 sts from 2nd row of Graph B, K20 (23–26) C7.
Next Row: P20 (23–26) MC, patt 93 sts from 3rd row of Graph B, P20 (23–26) MC.
Keeping 20 (23–26) sts at side edges correct in MC for rem, cont in patt as shown on Graph B *as placed* in last 3 rows, until Row 39 has been completed.
Keeping side edges correct in MC and working centre 93 sts in sky patt (as placed in last 8 rows), work a further 18 rows.
Next Row: K20 (23–26) MC, K93 C7, K20 (23–26) MC.
Next Row: P20 (23–26) MC, P93 C9, P20 (23–26) MC.
Working rem in MC, work 8 rows stocking st.

SHAPE NECK:

Next Row: K54 (57–60), turn.
Cont on these 54 (57–60) sts.
Dec one st at neck edge in every row until 41 (43–45) sts rem.
Work 0 (1–2) row/s stocking st.

SHAPE SHOULDER:

Cast off 14 (14–15) sts at beg of next row and foll alt row.
Work 1 row. Cast off rem 13 (15–15) sts.
Slip next 25 sts on to stitch holder and

leave. With right side facing, join yarn to rem 54 (57–60) sts and work to correspond with side just completed, reversing shaping.

Sleeves

Using 3.25mm needles and MC, cast on 46 (46–48) sts.
Work 20 rows K1, P1 rib, inc 13 (15–15) sts evenly across last row . . . 59 (61–63) sts.
Change to 4.00mm needles.
Work in stocking st, inc one st at each end of 5th and alt rows until there are 73 (79–85) sts, then in foll 4th rows until there are 119 (123–127) sts.
Cont straight until work measures 47 cm (or length desired) from beg, ending with a purl row.

SHAPE TOP:

Cast off 13 (13–14) sts at beg of next 8 rows.
Cast off rem 15 (19–15) sts loosely.

Back Collar

With right side facing, using 4.00mm needles and MC, knit up 4 sts evenly down right side of neck, knit across sts on stitch holder then knit up 4 sts evenly up left side of neck . . . 53 (55–57) sts.
1st Row: Knit.
2nd Row: K2, purl to last 2 sts, K2.

Rep last 2 rows until work measures 20 cm from beg, ending with a 1st Row. Cast off loosely.

Front Collar

With right side facing, using 4.00mm needles and MC, knit up 16 (20–22) sts evenly down left side of neck, knit across sts on stitch holder then knit up 16 (20–22) sts evenly up right side of neck . . . 57 (65–69) sts.
Complete as for Back Collar.

Making Up

Using knitting stitch and colours as indicated on Graph, embroider trees (Graphs C, D and E) on land section and Sun (Graph F) on sky section as illustrated. Join shoulder seams. Using a flat seam, join sides of collar. Tie a coloured marker 26 (27–28) cm down from beg of shoulder shaping on side edges of Back and Front to mark armholes. Sew in sleeves between markers, placing centre of sleeve to shoulder seam. Join side and sleeve seams.

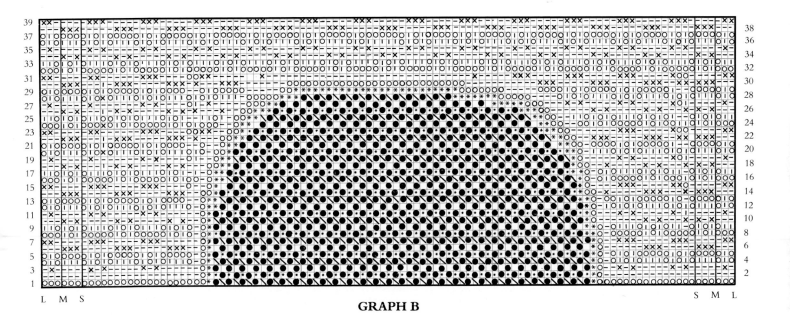

GRAPH B

Child's Jumper

Measurements

	Small	Medium	Large
Actual Garment			
Measures (approx):	79	84	89 cm
Length (approx):	53	57	61 cm
Sleeve Seam:	35	40	42 cm

Materials

CLECKHEATON 8 PLY MACHINE WASH (50g balls)

	Small	Medium	Large
Main Colour (MC) White	2	2	2 balls
Contrast 1 (C1) Black	2	2	3 balls
Contrast 2 (C2) Bright Red	2	2	2 balls
Contrast 3 (C3) Dark Red	1	1	1 ball/s
Contrast 4 (C4) Gold	2	2	2 balls
Contrast 5 (C5) Rust	1	1	2 ball/s
Contrast 6 (C6) Pale Blue	2	2	3 balls
Contrast 7 (C7) Royal	2	3	3 balls
Contrast 8 (C8) Dark Green	1	1	1 ball/s

AND CLECKHEATON MERINO 8 PLY (50g balls)

	Small	Medium	Large
Contrast 9 (C9) Violet	2	3	3 balls
Contrast 10 (C10) Maroon	1	1	1 ball/s
Contrast 11 (C11) Light Green	1	1	1 ball/s

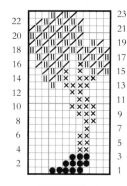

GRAPH C

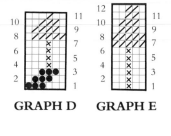

GRAPH D   **GRAPH E**

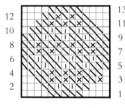

GRAPH F

(*For child's jumper - use C7 instead*
of MC and C9 instead of C6)

L ᔆ **GRAPH G** ᔆ L
  ᴹ   ᴹ

One pair each 3.25mm (No 10) and
4.00mm (No 8) knitting needles; a stitch
holder; knitters needle for sewing seams
and embroidery; 2 buttons.

Tension

22 sts and 30 rows to 10cm over stocking
st, using 4.00mm needles.

NOTE: *When working Fair Isle, carry colours not in
use loosely across back of work. Always carry
colours to ends of rows (except when working from
Graph B) and always carry MC or C1 above
contrasts. When changing patt blocks in the middle of
a row, twist the colour to be used (on wrong side)
underneath and to the right of the colour just used.*

Back

Using 3.25mm needles and C1, cast on 88
(94–100) sts.
Work 18 rows K1, P1 rib in stripes of 1
row each C4, C2 and C1, inc 5 sts evenly
across last row . . .93 (99–105) sts.
Change to 4.00mm needles.
Work in patt as shown on Graph A until
Row 12 has been completed, then work
rows 1 to 39 incl.
Work 2 rows stocking st (beg with a purl
row) in stripes of 1 row each C1 then C3.
Work in patt as shown on Graph B until
Row 39 has been completed. Rep last 8
rows throughout for sky patt until work

measures 52 (56–61) cm from beg, working
last row on wrong side.

SHAPE SHOULDERS:
Keeping patt correct, cast off 15 (16–17)
sts at beg of next 2 rows, then 14 (16–17)
sts at beg of foll 2 rows.
Break off yarns. Leave sts on stitch
holder.
With right side facing, using 3.25mm
needles and C7, knit up 93 (99–105) sts
evenly across shoulders and back neck,
incl sts from stitch holder.
Work 3 rows K1, P1 in stripes of 1 row
C7 and 2 rows C9. Cast off loosely in rib.

Front

Work as for Back until there are 12 rows
less than Back to shoulder shaping.

SHAPE NECK:
Next Row: Patt 39 (42–45), turn.
Cont on these 39 (42–45) sts.
Dec one st at neck edge in every row until
29 (32–34) sts rem.
Work 1 (1–0) row/s patt.

SHAPE SHOULDER:
Cast off 15 (16–17) sts at beg of next row.
Work 1 row. Cast off rem 14 (16–17) sts.
Slip next 15 sts on to stitch holder and
leave. With right side facing, join yarn to
rem 39 (42–45) sts and work to correspond

with side just completed, reversing shaping.
With right side facing, using 3.25 mm
needles and C7, knit up 29 (32–34) sts
evenly across top of left shoulder.
Work 3 rows K1, P1 rib in stripes of 1
row C7 and 2 rows C9. Cast off loosely in
rib.
Rep across top of right shoulder.

Sleeves

Using 3.25mm needles and C9, cast on 40
(40–44) sts.
Work 19 rows K1, P1 rib in stripes of 1
row each C9, C7 and C6.
Using C7, *20th Row*: Rib 2 (2–4), * inc in
next st, rib 1, rep from * to last 0 (0–2) sts,
rib 0 (0–2) . . . 59 (59–63) sts.
Change to 4.00mm needles.
Work in patt as shown on Graph G and
noting to work extra sts into patt, inc
one st at each end of 5th and foll alt rows
until there are 77 (81–85) sts, then in
foll 4th rows until there are 97
(105–111) sts.
Cont straight until work measures 35
(40–42) cm (or length desired) from beg,
working last row on wrong side.

SHAPE TOP:
Cast off 14 (15–16) sts at beg of next 6
rows.
Cast off rem 13 (15–15) sts loosely.

Front Neckband

Lap front shoulders over back for 1cm and
catch in position for half width of
shoulder. Slip stitch underlap in position.
With right side facing, using 3.25mm
needles and C7 knit up 15 sts evenly down
left side of neck, knit across sts on stitch
holder, then knit up 15 sts evenly up right
side of neck . . . 45 sts.
Work 1 row K1, P1 rib.
Using C9, *Next Row*: Rib 3, y fwd, work 2
tog, rib to last 5 sts, work 2 tog, yfwd, rib
3 . . . 2 buttonholes.
Work 1 row K1, P1 rib.
Cast off loosely in rib.

Making Up

Using knitting stitch and colours as
indicated on Graph, embroider trees
(Graphs C, D and E for Adult Jumper)
on land section and Sun (Graph F
for Adult Jumper) on sky section as
illustrated. Tie a coloured marker 22
(24–25) cm down from shoulder
on side edges of Back and Front to mark
armholes. Sew in sleeves between
markers, placing centre of sleeve to
shoulder seam. Join side and sleeve seams.
Sew buttons in position on back neck.

Emus–Broken Hill Area

HUGH SCHULZ

Interpreted by Libby Peacock

I love the subtlety of colour in the painting, the wonderful 'blue' of the saltbush and sky, and the way the emus disappear into the background.

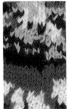

Except for five years spent overseas in the army from 1941 to 1946, Hugh Schulz has lived in the outback of Australia all his life. Before the war he worked in the goldmines in Kalgoorlie, and prospected for gold from the south to the north of Western Australia. Postwar, he settled in Broken Hill, a remote mining town in western New South Wales.

Hugh began painting when his daughters and their high school friends encouraged him to illustrate their history, geography and social studies textbooks. Starting with coloured pencils, he progressed to water colours and as his technique improved, he won several local and interstate art prizes. Hugh joined a group called 'The Brushmen of the Bush', formed by a local artist Eric Minchin, and for 16 years they painted and donated the proceeds, more than a million dollars, to charity.

For the past fourteen years Hugh Schulz has been painting full time and his love of the outback and the indigenous flora and fauna is most evident in his paintings. I chose *Emus—Broken Hill Area* to interpret in knitting because I love his work and identify strongly with the passion he feels for the unique beauty of the outback. He paints 'to make people aware of the treasure they possess and of the responsibility that is part of such an inheritance'.

For some time now I have been considering designing knitwear inspired by the Australian bush. Its colours and stark

beauty fascinate me, so the opportunity to interpret Hugh Schulz was both exciting and challenging. I felt strongly the need to interpret his painting in a way of which he would approve—I often felt he was looking over my shoulder as I matched his colour tones in wool and embroidered the emus. I love the subtlety of colour in the painting, the wonderful 'blue' of the saltbush and

sky, and the way the emus disappear into the background.

I would like to think that my garment does justice both to Hugh's painting and to the outback of Australia and that it is not too difficult for a competent craftsperson to knit.

A Family Affair

 As a child Libby Peacock experienced the joy of growing up on a property in the wheatbelt area of Quairading in Western Australia. A unique feature of the farm was the rabbit-proof fence, which formed one of the boundaries and helped maintain the prosperity that contributed to a secure and happy childhood.

Speaking of those early days Libby says:

My first memories are of sheep, crops of wheat, dams, bush and wildflowers. I was a very happy little girl. In 1953 when I was about eight years of age we moved to Brookton, 70 miles south-east of Perth to a lovely property called 'Dale Park' with huge mounds of granite outcrop and the Dale River, a tributary of the Avon, running through it. I spent endless happy hours wandering along the river and over the rocks, dreaming, picking wildflowers and drawing.

Libby continues: 'My mother taught me to knit when I was about ten. My efforts were limited at this stage to scarves and dolls' clothes and mostly knitted to kill hours of bus travel going to and from school.'

In 1958 Libby was sent to Kobeelia, a boarding school in Katanning. There were 82 other boarders at Kobeelia, mostly farmers' and station-owners' daughters, who usually attended school with their horses! The arts were encouraged at Kobeelia and Libby was exposed to art classes, speech and drama classes and musical appreciation evenings. Libby knitted her first jumper here, 'a ghastly iridescent orange which took forever to knit and which I never wore.'

Libby's final year was spent at John Curtin High School in Fremantle, where an art teacher, Henry Froudist, inspired her creativity. Libby consequently topped the state in art for her Leaving Certificate.

Libby met her future husband, Tom a student from New South Wales, during her final year at school and her life revolved around him for the next few years. She was engaged at 18 and their first daughter, Fenella, was born two years later.

From early 1967 to 1973, Libby and her husband lived mainly in Dunedin, New Zealand, where Tom studied dentistry. Libby's 18-year-old brother was killed in an accident during this time and she returned to Western Australia for 18 months to be with her parents.

Libby's other two daughters, Ashe and Georgia, were born in New Zealand, and as her family grew in size, Libby continued to draw, paint, design, screen print and make various craft-orientated objects, which she sold to local shops to help supplement their income.

The family returned to Western Australia in 1973, and settled in Narrogin. In 1975 they moved to Perth where Tom commenced his own dentistry practice in Palmyra. Libby had little free time for creative pursuits in the next couple of years but in 1977, when she and Tom separated, Libby needed to earn an income of her own.

With her daughters, Libby moved to Fremantle where she began producing a range of children's and women's clothes. In 1980, when Libby moved to a cottage in Cottesloe, her career prospects brightened:

I was fascinated to see beautiful imported hand knits appearing in various boutiques. No-one seemed to have any local hand knits however. So I saw the opportunity to satisfy my need to create while simultaneously earning a living by

combining my two greatest loves, art and fashion, into wearable art knits. An added bonus was that I'd be able to work from home and be with my daughters while they were growing up.

Libby continues:

I had to teach myself to picture knit, as it was an unheard of art in Western Australia at that time. My first effort, a very long jumper for Fenella, covered with Australian flora and fauna, was such a sensation at Perth Technical College (which as the youngest graphic art student ever accepted, Fenella was attending) that Libby Peacock Designs were immediately launched.

In the early days Libby's jumpers kept to a simple shape with plain back and sleeves and a picture on the front. She knitted the fronts while her mother and aunt knitted the backs and the sleeves. Often they knitted one jumper a day between them. Libby's main outlet at that time was a boutique in Claremont and as demand grew, Libby's mother and aunt graduated to fronts and a contract knitter was employed for the backs and sleeves of the garments.

In 1981 Libby entered two outfits in the West Australian Designer Awards and was delighted to make the finals. One of her outfits, 'Mrs Jiddicks' was featured in the *West Australian* newspaper.

As demand grew Libby found herself employing more and more knitters. Libby and her mother had to teach all of them to picture knit.

By 1982 Libby was supplying various Australian shops and boutiques with a variety of garments, from bright colourful Australiana wool jumpers, leg warmers, dresses and caps for winter, to bright natural cottons in bare midriff singlet tops with matching skirts and shorts for summer.

Libby began to consider the market in the Eastern States in 1984 and was gratified to be offered the chance, with several other designers, of a West Australian Government sponsored promotional tour of Sydney and Melbourne. Libby succeeded in establishing several outlets in both cities, and gaining an 'agent' who subsequently disappeared with a full range of her samples! This was a devastating blow to her small business at the time.

By 1985, Libby's house was bursting at the seams and she decided to move into a studio a short walk away from her home. Her teenage daughters had become both her greatest fans and her greatest critics and were perfect for modelling her garments. Fenella began working with her mother and together they employed 50 knitters. They also began to attract considerable media coverage for their garments.

Extending the concept of picture knits in 1985, Libby added Pop Art to the range of her images with her favourite comic strip character, The Phantom. She obtained Australia-wide rights for five years and throughout Australia attracted a lot of media coverage as shop windows featured the image in knits. Libby says: 'My greatest thrill came when Lee Falk, the creator of Mandrake and The Phantom ordered eight phantom jumpers for family and friends, one of whom was Randolph Hearst.'

With the advent of the America's Cup in Fremantle in 1986, Libby moved to a studio there, which she shared with Fenella and Brett Wilson (they had recently launched their own designer label 'Empire Line'). The Wool Corporation commissioned Libby to design and knit a series of jumpers based on the theme of the America's Cup to be used in promotional parades and exhibitions throughout the year.

Towards the end of 1986, Libby took part in an Australian promotion at the Nieman Marcus store, in Dallas, Texas, where the American coordinator of the promotion chose one of Libby's pieces as a gift of thanks from Australia.

The 1988 Bicentennial year was very busy for Libby. She employed more than 120 knitters, and hoping to rationalise her operation, entered into a business partnership with a West Australian businessman. Unfortunately, it was a move she regretted and she terminated it after a year's trial.

Libby had long felt the lure of the Eastern States, and in 1989 the family ventured to live in Sydney. Within a short time they became disillusioned with the lifestyle and returned to Perth. Libby is now content to work from there and dedicate her future to the creation of beautiful and unique hand knits.

KEY

MC =	☐
C1 =	●
C2 =	○
C3 =	☐
C4 =	=
C5 =	+
C6 =	−
C7 =	⌐

Measurements

	Small	Medium	Large
Actual Garment			
Measures (*approx*):	98	108	118 cm
Length (*approx*):	84	86	88 cm
Sleeve Seam:	43	43	43 cm

Materials

CLECKHEATON MACHINEWASH 8 PLY (*50g balls*)

Main Colour			
(MC) Pale Blue	8	10	12 balls
Contrast 1			
(C1) Brick	4	4	5 balls
Contrast 2			
(C2) Brown	2	3	3 balls
Contrast 3			
(C3) White	2	3	3 balls
Contrast 4			
(C4) Cobalt Blue	1	1	1 ball
Contrast 5			
(C5) Pale Green	1	2	2 ball/s
Contrast 6			
(C6) Olive	1	1	1 ball
Contrast 7			
(C7) Light Brown	1	2	2 ball/s

One pair each 4.00mm (No 8) and 5.00mm (No 6) knitting needles; 3 stitch holders; small quantity of bouclé yarn (olive) for tree embroidery; 12 buttons; selection of small beads for eyes of emus; knitters needle for sewing seams and embroidery.

Tension

20 sts and 24 rows to 10cm over patt, using 5.00mm needles.

NOTE: *This garment has been designed at a looser tension than normally recommended.*

Back

Using 5.00mm needles and C1, cast on 100 (110–120) sts.
Work 14 rows K1, P1 rib.
Work in patt as shown on Graph A until row 190 (194–198) has been completed.

SHAPE SHOULDERS:
Cast off 34 (39–44) sts, K32, cast off last 34 (39–44) sts. Leave rem 32 sts on a stitch holder.

Left Front

Using 5.00mm needles and C1, cast on 60 (64–70) sts.
Work 14 rows K1, P1 rib, inc 0 (1–0) st/s in centre of last row . . . 60 (65–70) sts.

NOTE: *The Front Bands of this jacket are worked tog with the Fronts. The Graph does not show these extra sts. The colours used for the front bands correspond with the main colour in use on the front piece at the time. These being C1 for first 83 rows, then C4 for next 5 rows, then the rem in MC.*

Keeping rib and colours correct on last 10 sts for Front Band, work in patt on rem 50 (55–60) sts as shown on Graph B until row 172 has been completed.

GRAPH A

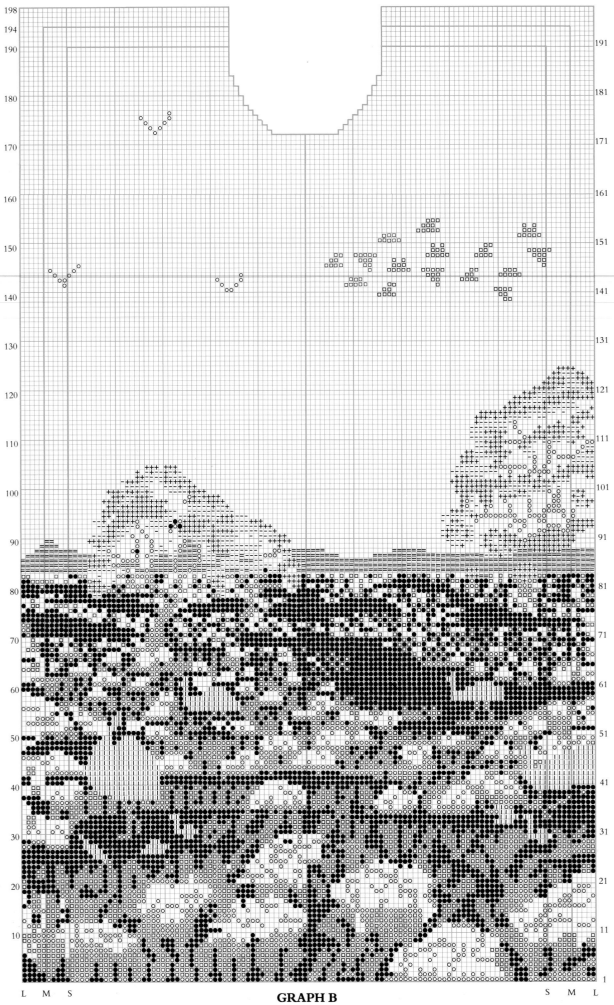

GRAPH B

SHAPE NECK:
Next Row: Knit to last 17 sts, slip these last 17 sts onto a stitch holder and leave.
Cont on rem 43 (48–53) sts and dec one st at neck edge in every row until 37 (42–47) sts rem, then in alt rows until 34 (39–44) sts rem.
Work 5 (9–13) rows without shaping, thus completing Graph.
Cast off rem sts loosely.

Right Front

Using 5.00mm needles and C1, cast on 60 (64–70) sts.
Work 2 rows K1, P1 rib.
3rd Row: Rib 4, K2tog, yfwd, rib to end . . . buttonhole.
Work 7 rows rib.
11th Row: As 3rd row.
Work 3 rows rib, inc 0 (1–0) st/s in centre of last row . . . 60 (65–70) sts.

NOTE: *Further buttonholes are worked in 25th, 33rd, 61st, 69th, 97th, 105th, 133rd, 141st and 169th rows of Graph . . . 11 buttonholes in all from beg.*

Keeping rib, colours and buttonholes correct on first 10 sts, work in patt on rem 50 (55–60) sts as shown on Graph B and complete to correspond with Left Front, reversing shaping and noting that 173rd row will read thus: Slip first 17 sts onto a stitch holder and leave (do not break off yarn), rejoin another ball of MC to rem sts and patt to end.

Left Sleeve

Using 4.00mm needles and MC, cast on 42 (46–50) sts.
Work 18 rows K1, P1 rib, inc 10 sts evenly across last row . . . 52 (56–60) sts.
Change to 5.00mm needles.
Work in stocking st, inc one st at each end of 3rd and foll 4th rows until there are 78 (82–86) sts.
Work 1 row. **

PLACE PATT:
1st Row: K29 (31–33) MC, K5 C3, K44 (46–48) MC.
2nd Row: P45 (47–49) MC, P3 C3, P30 (32–34) MC.
Keeping patt correct as shown on Graph C , as *placed* in last 2 rows, until row 19 has been completed (beg with 3rd row), then working rem in MC, AT SAME TIME inc one st at each end of next and foll

4th rows until there are 94 (98–102) sts.
Cont without shaping until work measures 43cm (or length desired) from beg, ending with a purl row.
Cast off loosely.

Right Sleeve

Work as for Left Sleeve to **.

PLACE PATT:
1st Row: K28 (30–32) MC, K2 C2, K48 (50–52) MC.
2nd Row: P47 (49–51) MC, P1 C2, P2 MC, P1 C2, P27 (29–31) MC.
Keeping patt correct as shown on Graph D, as *placed* in last 2 rows, until row 23 has been completed (beg with 3rd row), then working rem in MC, complete to correspond with Left Sleeve.

Neckband

Join shoulder seams. With right side facing, using 5.00mm needles and MC, patt across 17 sts left on Right Front stitch holder, knit up 16 (20–24) sts evenly along Right Front neck edge, knit across 32 sts left on Back stitch holder, knit up 16 (20–24) sts evenly along Left Front neck edge, then patt across 17 sts left on Left Front stitch holder . . . 98 (106–114) sts.
Work 7 rows rib, working a buttonhole (as before) in 4th row . . . 12 buttonholes in all.
Cast off loosely in rib.

Making Up

Using C7 outlines as a guide, embroider feather detail to all adult emus and chicks, using stem stitch and C2 and C7. Using C2, outline adult emus' heads and necks and using satin stitch and MC, fill this area. Using C7, outline chick body adding beak and feet features using C2.
Sew beads in position for eyes.
Using bouclé yarn and a large horizontal stitch, add foliage detail to trees. Sew beads in position of C3 birds on top sections of Left Front, Back and Left Sleeve, outlining if desired in stem stitch in same colour. Tie a coloured marker 23 (24–25) cm down from shoulder seam on side edges of Back and Fronts to mark armholes. Sew in sleeves, placing centre of sleeve to shoulder seam. Join side and sleeve seams. Sew buttons in position.

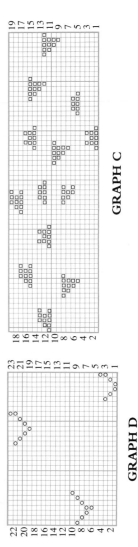

GRAPH C

GRAPH D

Anxious Angels

SALLY MORGAN

River Picture

Sally Morgan creatively crosses the black/white divide without losing her authenticity or her integrity. Her language is lyrical, poetic and heartfelt. She uses traditions of both black and white cultures and amalgamates them into sensitive, universal myths for all people to share.

Interpreted by Rosella Paletti

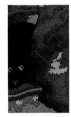

Are not painting and colour inspired by love? Is not painting merely the reflection of our inner self, whereby even one's skill with a brush is surpassed? It has nothing to do with it. Colour with its lines contains our character and our message.

If all life moves inevitably towards its end, we should during ours paint it with our colours of love and hope. In this love lies the social logic of life and the essential part of each religion. For me perfection in art and life stems from this bibilical source.

I read these words of Marc Chagall over and over again. As I look at Sally Morgan's work, I see a similar message expressed in her paintings. Ever since I first saw Sally Morgan's work, I have loved and admired it. I identify with it so closely that I feel it

has come out of me also, from some inner shared source of being.

I relate to Sally's symbolism, her storytelling and the way in which she makes a strong statement in a beautiful and poetic way. Her paintings have the feeling

of a new age and growth and although at times sad political issues are raised in her work, the overall feeling is one of great optimism.

I found it very difficult to draw up a pattern from her work, because my own imagery and what I had to say was ever present. I had to respect and empathise with her integrity, but at the same time add a dimension of my own. I didn't want to reproduce Sally's work per se; I aspired towards a harmonious combination of her vision and my interpretation. Her celebratory use of colour, which is full of intense, joyous life echoes my own approach to life and art.

Politically I am aligned and in sympathy with Sally Morgan and the way in which the Aboriginal people are viewed in the white community today. Reading *My Place*, I was shocked to think that the Aboriginal people living now had been subjected to such discriminatory and racist legislation and attitudes.

Soon after reading *My Place* I went to Oodnadatta, a small, isolated black/white community in the north of South Australia, where I worked as an artist in residence. I was with Aboriginal people who could have stepped out of Sally's book—adults who as children had been taken away from their parents and sent to white institutions in faraway towns to be 'educated'.

These adults were now in limbo. They had not been taught their Aboriginality as children so were separated from their 'Dreaming' in the black community. Their 'white' education precluded them from stepping easily into the Aboriginal community, but their Aboriginality excluded them from the white community.

Subsequently, I read Sally Morgan's second book, *Wanamurraganya*, about her Uncle, Jack McPhee. This was another

warm, compassionate story of a person who
against all odds, still had an integral belief
in the goodness of human nature.
This optimism is a
wonderful, driving
force in Sally's
writing and painting.

In an interview in *Artlink*
in 1990, Sally reaffirms her point
of view: 'My work is basically
optimistic because even though we have
had a terrible history in Australia, I think if
you haven't got hope you may as
well give up—if you haven't got hope that
things will change.'

Sally Morgan is pioneering a new
language for both black and white
Australians. She has combined the spiritual
beliefs of the Aboriginal Dreaming, with
the obsessive and often preclusive
individuality of the white Australian.

She explains her position: 'I don't know
if there's something that makes my work
look particularly Aboriginal although
people tend to relate to it that way. People
do have an expectation when they look at it
and they say, "why haven't you used
traditional colours?" I don't like to be

bound by those kind of constraints.'

Sally Morgan creatively crosses the
black/white divide without losing her
authenticity or her integrity. Her language
is lyrical, poetic and heartfelt. She uses
traditions of both black and white cultures
and amalgamates them into sensitive,
universal myths for all people to share. This
is why I have chosen to interpret her work.

A Spiritual Catalyst

Parts of the Adelaide Hills in
South Australia can evoke
memories of Tuscany.
Mellow old stone farmhouses
are dotted throughout the
landscape among orchards
of olives, grapes, apples, stonefruit and
citrus. Other parts are more reminiscent of
an English landscape, particularly in
autumn when there is a wealth of glowing
leaves refracting in the sunlight. There are
interesting galleries and some fine
restaurants in the area as well. The

ambience is such that it attracts those with
an artistic sensibility, such as Rosella
Paletti.

Rosella's predisposition towards reality is
intimated by her front fence. All the tall
pickets have turned into grinning, writhing
snakes waiting to usher you in to Rosella's
very private Garden of Eden. Myth has it
that Eve knitted the pattern on the
serpent's back in the garden, and Rosella
may have had this in mind when she
transformed her front boundary. There are
improbable creatures sculptured or made

from found objects, and grinning cheshire-type cats. There are 'discoveries', such as nooks and altars and wayward paths. It is quite an adventure to arrive at the front door. And within the four walls the same unique vision sweeps through the house and knits its way into all of her garments. Nothing is compartmentalised in Rosella's life, it all flows together.

Like most other art knitters, Rosella started knitting at a young age, when she was about eight. Her grandmother and godmother hand knitted jumpers for the six children in the family, but it was Rosella's mother who taught her to knit. Rosella flirted with knitting at high school but it was a premature romance. She had learnt to sketch as a child with her father, but did not take lessons in art until she attended college at 17 and trained as an art teacher. Like other bonded students, she taught for three years in South Australia and when free, in 1977, travelled overseas for the next two years.

While visiting a gallery in Cornwall she saw a piece of original knitting that inspired her. Part of a machine-knitted exhibition from Germany, the garment was three-dimensional and with the use of textural and luminescent fibres, depicted an underwater scene with angel fish floating

around. In terms of personal expression, the concept gave her a new perspective on knitting.

Returning to Australia, Rosella took a position as a part-time teacher to support herself and moved into a 'garret' in the Adelaide Hills. Here she began to explore the spiritual and psychic side of her nature, recording her dreams and writing poetry. She also began to knit obsessively to express the changes she was undergoing. The designs were free-form and evolved as she knitted them. As an ad-lib knitter, Rosella admits at times the shapes tended towards eccentricity with arms far too long or necks rather askew.

In the early 1980s, Rosella exhibited in various exhibitions, organised a fashion extravaganza and became involved in community arts projects. In 1983 traumatic events in Rosella's life reinforced her spiritual approach to life. Her mother found she had terminal cancer when Rosella was seven-and-a-half months pregnant. The day after Rosella was told of this, she visited her mother to comfort her. It was Ash Wednesday and while Rosella was absent, her house and all her possessions were burnt to cinders.

After the birth of her daughter, Ptiika, and the death of her mother in 1984, Rosella continued to knit and exhibited three pieces in *More Than Gumtrees and Galahs*. A group of mutually supportive South Australian knitters, collaborated together in 1985, hired a gallery and mounted the *Knitting up a Storm* exhibition. Rosella sold all her exhibits and received orders for more.

Rosella began employing other knitters to help fulfil the demand and at this time she learnt to transpose her ideas onto a graph so that others could interpret her designs. Gradually Rosella began to embellish her pieces more with detailed embroidery and beautiful handmade buttons from Jo Clark. Dorian Scott at The Rocks in Sydney marketed the pieces for Rosella.

In 1986 Rosella's garments were included in the Australian Arts Clothing exhibition, part of the Australian contribution to 'Software', an all Commonwealth Countries exhibition in Edinburgh. She was invited to show in the Wool Corporation's exhibition *On the Sheep's Back*, held in Adelaide, and *Winter Exhibition* at the Beaver Galleries in Canberra. Her ability was acknowledged by the Craft Board with a Professional Development Grant, which allowed her to experiment with the many ideas flowing from her fertile imagination.

Rosella is very conscious of the constructive symbiotic relationship between knitting and art in her career and life: 'Knitting gave me really good professional opportunities as an artist. It was an area of craft where personal expression had not been overtly emphasised. It was an opportunity to develop and make your mark during the 1980s.'

Rosella found that even small production lines of hand knits employing five or six knitters restricted artistic expression:

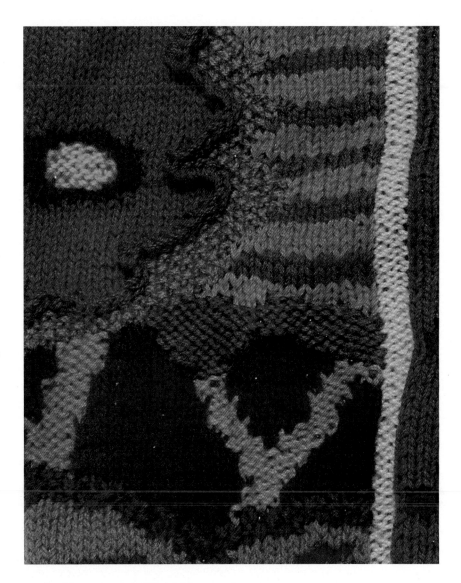

Knitwear in any quantity must often conform to current fashions. I found that aspect fickle and trendy and not what I wanted to do. I preferred to concentrate on parenting and developing my artistic side in a more individualistic and meaningful way. To maintain some artistic integrity and independence I elected to wash dishes in a restaurant.

Rosella concentrated on one-off pieces for a variety of exhibitions in the next couple of years. Her garments were included in the two most important benchmarks in Australian textile exhibitions, the travelling *Art knits* originating at the Art Gallery of New South Wales in 1988 and Australian Fashion—the Contemporary Art

at the Victoria and Albert Museum in London in 1989.

The philosophical and spiritual content in Rosella's designs runs deep. She has always been attracted to pattern and decoration but wanted to use it in knitting as a symbol of greater significance: 'Whenever I do a major piece, I always draw upon a meaningful experience I've had and incorporate my own small repertoire of symbols. The birth of my daughter Ptiika was one such instance and I celebrated her in knitting as a gift of great humanity.'

When Rosella was commissioned to exhibit a piece in *The Art of Knitting* exhibition at the National Gallery of Victoria early in 1990, a close friend had just died of cancer. Taking a creative

approach to death, Rosella depicted her in the knitting rising above the crowd of friends and well-wishers surrounding her, who were happy she was free of pain at last, and were sending her off with spirals of love, affection and thanks.

Rosella recounts a strange phenomenon that occurred as she knitted the piece: 'When I was embroidering it late at night, inside the figure rising at the back of the coat, I unconsciously made a baby inside the dead person rising up. Soon after another friend who was six months pregnant died suddenly. It was a very strange experience.'

Rosella's deep involvement with her own spirituality and the symbols that arise from it, ally her to the works of Sally Morgan, whose paintings she has interpreted for the book. Her practical experience with teaching children in Oodnadatta last year made her even more empathetic with the plight of the Aborigines:

I went initially to give a fabric printing workshop to eight Aboriginal high school students and stayed on to do some relief teaching. I had read Sally's book My Place, *and that gave me a compassionate insight into the nature of Aboriginal families and lifestyle. I was very shocked when I came face to face with the realities of how Aboriginal people live and are discriminated against.*

The experience has politicised Rosella and she would like to both initiate and support a change in the way Aborigines are viewed in the wider community.

For Rosella the interpretation of Sally Morgan's paintings has a threefold dimension: it reflects a spiritual affinity, an artistic empathy and is an act of political sympathy and support.

All parts of Rosella's life flow into her work and her art knits are a spiritual treasurehouse of her psyche.

Anxious Angels

Measurements

	Small	Medium	Large
Actual Garment Measures (*approx*):	109	114	119 cm
Length (*approx*):	78	79	80 cm
Sleeve Seam (*approx*):	45	45	45 cm

Materials

CLECKHEATON 8 PLY MACHINE WASH (*50g balls*)

	Small	Medium	Large
Main Colour (MC) Black	9	9	10 balls
Contrast 1 (C1) Mid Blue	5	5	5 balls
Contrast 2 (C2) Dark Red	1	1	1 ball
Contrast 3 (C3) Bright Red	2	2	2 balls
Contrast 4 (C4) Apricot	1	1	1 ball
Contrast 5 (C5) Mid Green	2	3	3 balls
Contrast 6 (C6) Bright Blue	2	3	3 balls
Contrast 7 (C7) Dark Green	1	1	1 ball
Contrast 8 (C8) Light Green	1	1	1 ball
Contrast 9 (C9) Yellow	2	2	3 balls

NOTE: *Quantities are approximate as they vary between knitters.*

One pair each 4.00mm (No 8) and 3.25mm (No 10) knitting needles; one 3.25mm circular needle (80 cm long); knitters needle for sewing seams and embroidery; red bugle beads and black thread (one strand of MC) for embroidery; 12 buttons.

Tension

22 sts and 30 rows to 10cm over stocking st using 4.00mm needles.

Back

Using 3.25mm needles and C1, cast on 104 (110–116) sts.
Work 20 rows K1, P1 rib.
Change to 4.00mm needles.
Work in patt as shown on Graph A, inc one st at each end of 9th and foll 8th rows 11 times in all . . . 126 (132–138) sts.
Cont without shaping until row 198 (200–204) has been completed, noting to tie a coloured marker at each end of row 98 to mark armholes.

SHAPE SHOULDERS:
Keeping patt correct from graph, cast off 10 sts at beg of next 8 rows, then 9 (11–13) sts at beg of foll 2 rows.
Cast off rem 28 (30–32) sts loosely.

Left Front

Using 3.25mm needles and C1, cast on 52 (55–58) sts.
Work 20 rows K1, P1 rib.
Change to 4.00mm needles.
Work in patt as shown on Graph B, inc one st at beg of 9th and foll 8th rows 11 times in all . . . 63 (66–69) sts.
Work 9 rows patt without shaping, thus completing row 98.
Tie a coloured marker at end of last row to mark armhole.

SHAPE FRONT EDGE:
Cont in patt from graph, dec one st (inside 6 sts) at end (front edge) of next and foll 6th rows 5 (9–13) times in all, then in foll 8th rows 9 (6–3) times, noting that blank section represents decreased sts (knit 6 sts at left edge in with rows) . . . 49 (51–53) sts.
Work 3 (5–9) rows without shaping, thus completing row 198 (200–204).

SHAPE SHOULDER:
Keeping colours correct as placed in last row (noting to work C5 only in angel panel), cast off 10 sts at beg of next and alt rows 4 times in all, then 9 (11–13) sts at beg of foll alt row.

Right Front

Work to correspond with Left Front, reversing shaping and working as indicated for Right Front on Graph B.

Sleeves

Using 3.25mm needles and C1, cast on 49 (49–51) sts.
Work 20 rows K1, P1 rib.
Change to 4.00mm needles.
Work in patt as indicated for Sleeves on Graph A (you may want to draw an outline of your size in red pen), inc one st at each end of 3rd and alt rows 28 times in all . . . 105 (105–107) sts.
Cont in Fair Isle as placed in last 16 rows for rem, inc one st at each end of foll alt

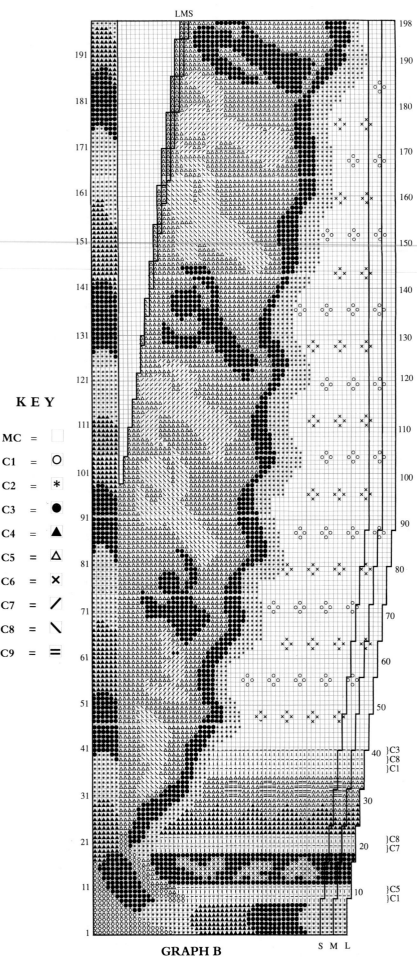

KEY

MC = ☐

C1 = ◯

C2 = ✳

C3 = ●

C4 = ▲

C5 = △

C6 = ✕

C7 = ╱

C8 = ╲

C9 = ═

GRAPH B

rows until there are 141 (149–155) sts, then in foll 4th row/s until there are 149 (153–157) sts.

Cont in patt without shaping until work measures approx 45 cm from beg, working last row on wrong side.

Working rem in MC after completing last star pattern.

SHAPE TOP:

Cast off 30 (30–31) sts at beg of next 4 rows.

Cast off rem 29 (33–33) sts loosely.

Front Band

Join shoulder seams.

Using 3.25mm needles and C1, cast on 47 sts.

Work 4 rows K1, P1 rib.

Next Row: Rib 6, cast off 3 sts, rib 29, cast off 3 sts, rib to end.

Next Row: Rib 6, cast on 3 sts, rib 29, cast on 3 sts, rib to end . . . 2 buttonholes.

Cont in rib, working 2 buttonholes (as before) in foll 21st and 22nd rows 5 times, until work measures length required to fit (slightly stretched) up right front, across back neck and down left front.

Cast off loosely in rib.

Making Up

Sew in sleeves between markers, placing centre of sleeve to shoulder seam. Join side and sleeve seams. Sew front band in position. Sew buttons in place.

| | = purl sts on wrong side/knit sts on right side

─ = purl sts on right side/knit sts on wrong side

✚ = knit sts on right side/knit sts on wrong side in C1

■ = knit sts on right side/knit sts on wrong side in C8

122

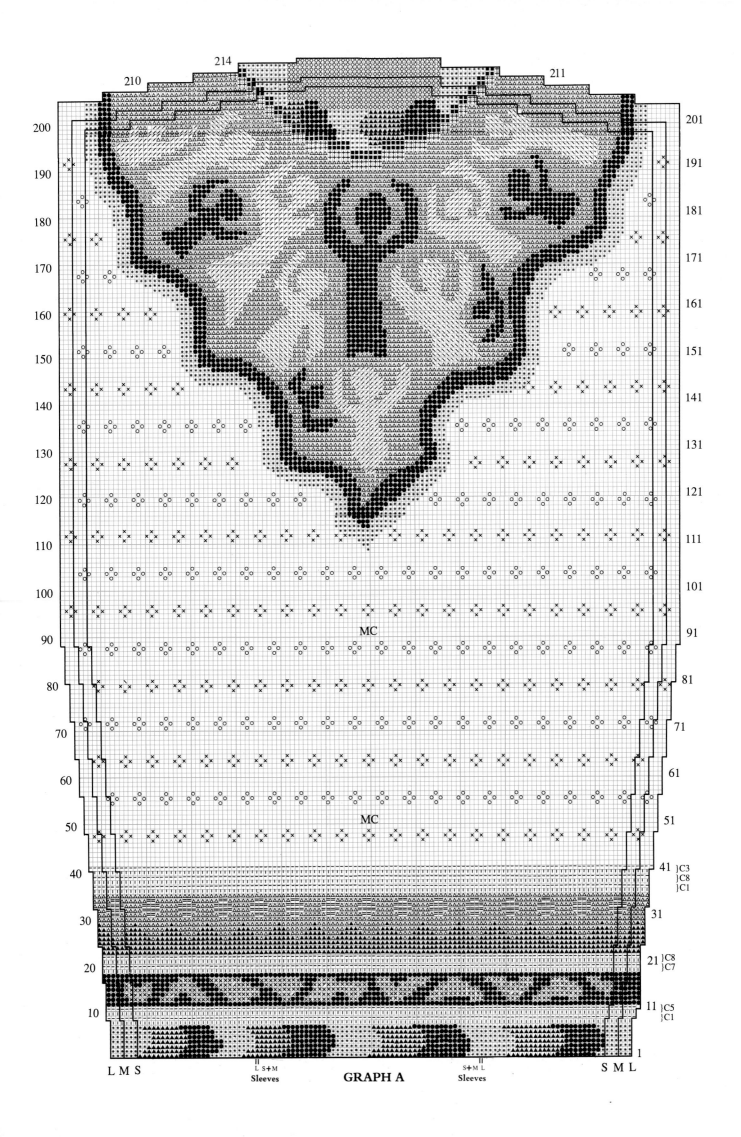

GRAPH A

River Picture

Measurements

	Small	Medium	Large
Actual Garment Measures (approx, at armholes):	116	121	126 cm
Length (approx):	69	70	71 cm
Sleeve Seam (approx):	46	46	46 cm

Materials

Cleckheaton 8 ply Machine Wash (50g balls)

Main Colour			
(MC) Royal Blue	10	10	11 balls
Contrast 1 (C1) Bright Blue	8	8	9 balls
Contrast 2 (C2) Mid Blue	1	1	2 ball/s
Contrast 3 (C3) Bright Red	3	3	4 balls
Contrast 4 (C4) Mid Green	3	3	4 balls
Contrast 5 (C5) Apricot	1	1	1 ball
Contrast 6 (C6) Olive Green	1	1	1 ball
Contrast 7 (C7) Dark Red	1	1	1 ball
Contrast 8 (C8) Light Green	1	1	1 ball
Contrast 9 (C9) Bright Green	1	1	1 ball
Contrast 10 (C10) Dark Green	1	1	1 ball
Contrast 11 (C11) Yellow	1	1	1 ball
Contrast 12 (C12) Black	1	1	1 ball

Note: *Quantities are approximate as they vary between knitters.*

One pair each 4.00mm (No 8) and 3.25mm (No 10) knitting needles; knitters needle for sewing seams and embroidery; 4.00mm (No 8) crochet hook for trimming; 12 buttons.

Tension

22 sts and 30 rows to 10cm over stocking st using 4.00mm needles.

Back

Using 3.25mm needles and MC, cast on 105 (111–117) sts.
Work 14 rows K1, P1 rib, inc one st at

KEY

MC	=	□
C1	=	□
C2	=	□
C3	=	I
C4	=	□
C5	=	O
C6	=	●
C7	=	−
C8	=	⊙
C9	=	✕
C10	=	+
C11	=	■
C12	=	V

each end of last row . . . 107 (113–119) sts.
Change to 4.00mm needles.

Note: *On Graphs,* * = *Moss st worked for this section of colour (K1, P1 alternated every stitch and row).*
Work in patt as shown on Graph A, inc one st at each end of 9th and foll 8th rows 11 times in all . . . 129 (135–141) sts.
Cont without shaping until row 192 (196–198) has been completed.

Shape Shoulders:
Keeping patt correct from graph, cast off 10 sts at beg of next 8 rows, then 10 (12–14) sts at beg of foll 2 rows.
Cast off rem 29 (31–33) sts loosely.

Left Front

Using 3.25mm needles and MC, cast on 38 (40–42) sts.
Work 14 rows K1, P1 rib, inc one st at end of last row . . . 39 (41–43) sts.
Change to 4.00mm needles.
Work in patt as shown on Graph B, inc one st at beg of 9th and foll 8th rows 11 times in all . . . 50 (52–54) sts.
Cont without shaping until row 192 (196–198) has been completed.

Shape Shoulder:
Keeping patt correct from graph, cast off 10 sts at beg of next and alt rows 4 times in all, then 10 (12–14) sts at beg of foll alt row.

Right Front

Work to correspond with Left Front, reversing shaping and working from Graph C instead of Graph B.

Sleeves

Using 3.25mm needles and MC, cast on 46 (50–54) sts.
Work 14 rows K1, P1 rib.
Change to 4.00mm needles.
Work in patt as shown on Graph D, inc on st at each end of 5th and foll 4th rows 11 times in all, then in foll alt rows 33 times . . . 134 (138–142) sts (row 111 completed).
Work 1 row patt, thus completing graph.
Using C1 only for rem, cont in stocking st, inc one st at each end of next and alt rows 8 times in all . . . 150 (154–158) sts.
Work 3 rows straight.

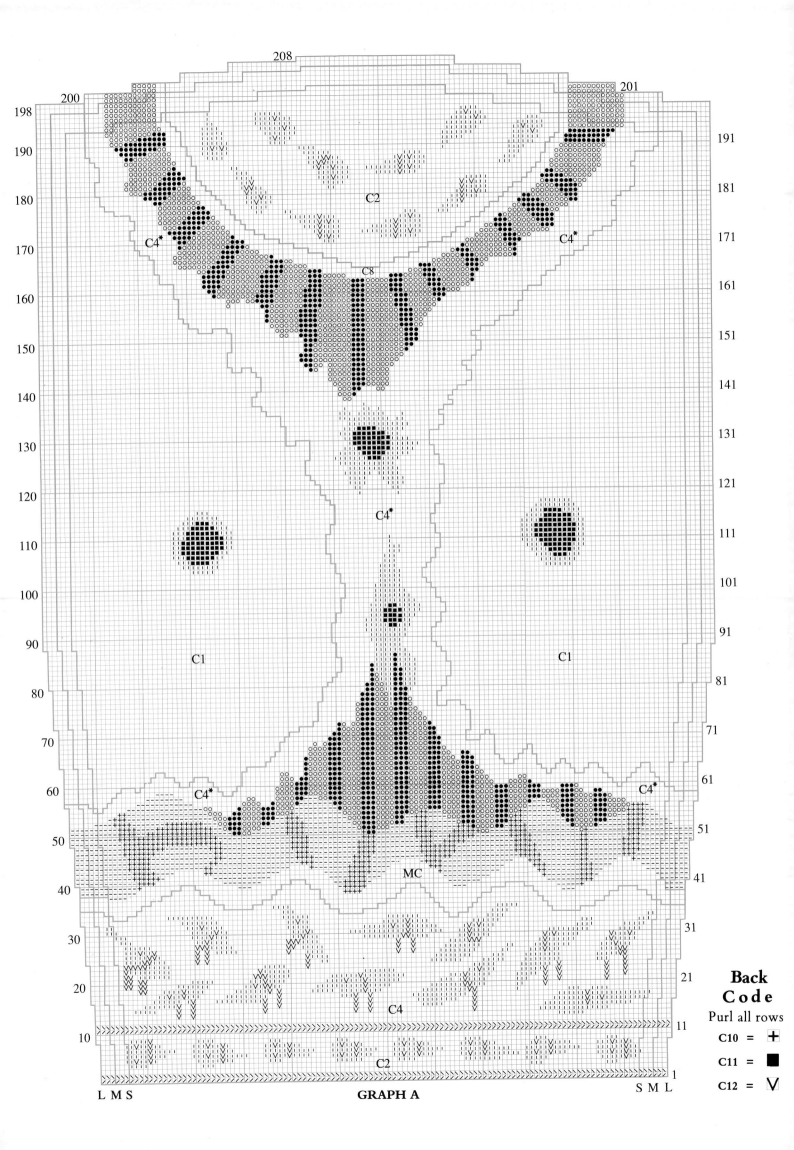

GRAPH A

Back Code

Purl all rows

C10 = +

C11 = ■

C12 = V

Shape Top:
Cast off 22 sts at beg of next 6 rows.
Cast off rem 18 (22–26) sts loosely.

Front Band

Join shoulder seams.
Using 3.25mm needles and MC, cast on 51 sts.
Work 4 rows K1, P1 rib.
Next Row: Rib 8, cast off 3 sts, rib 29, cast off 3 sts, rib to end.
Next Row: Rib 8, cast on 3 sts, rib 29, cast on 3 sts, rib to end . . . 2 buttonholes.
Cont in rib, working 2 buttonholes (as before) in foll 13th and 14th rows, then in foll 21st and 22nd rows 4 times (12 buttonholes in all), until work measures length required to fit (slightly stretched) up right front, across back neck and down left front.
Cast off loosely in rib.

Making Up

Sew in sleeves, placing centre of sleeve to shoulder seam. Join side and sleeve seams. Sew front band in position. Sew buttons in place. Using hook and C2, work 1 row double crochet evenly along outside edge of C4 moss st section on fronts and back as illustrated.

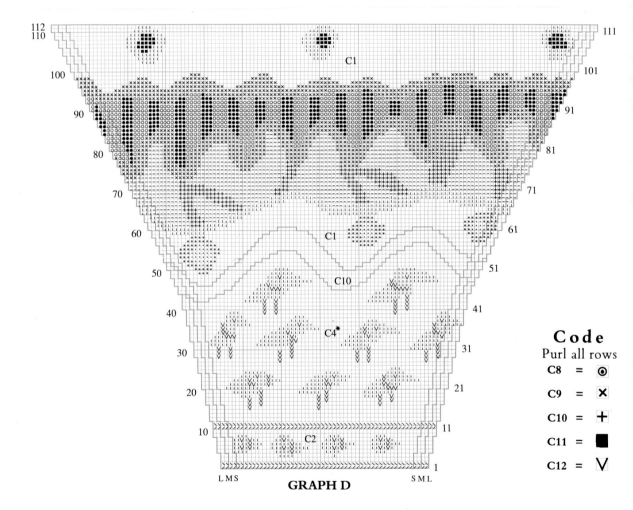

GRAPH D

Code

Purl all rows

C8 = ◉

C9 = ✗

C10 = ✚

C11 = ■

C12 = V

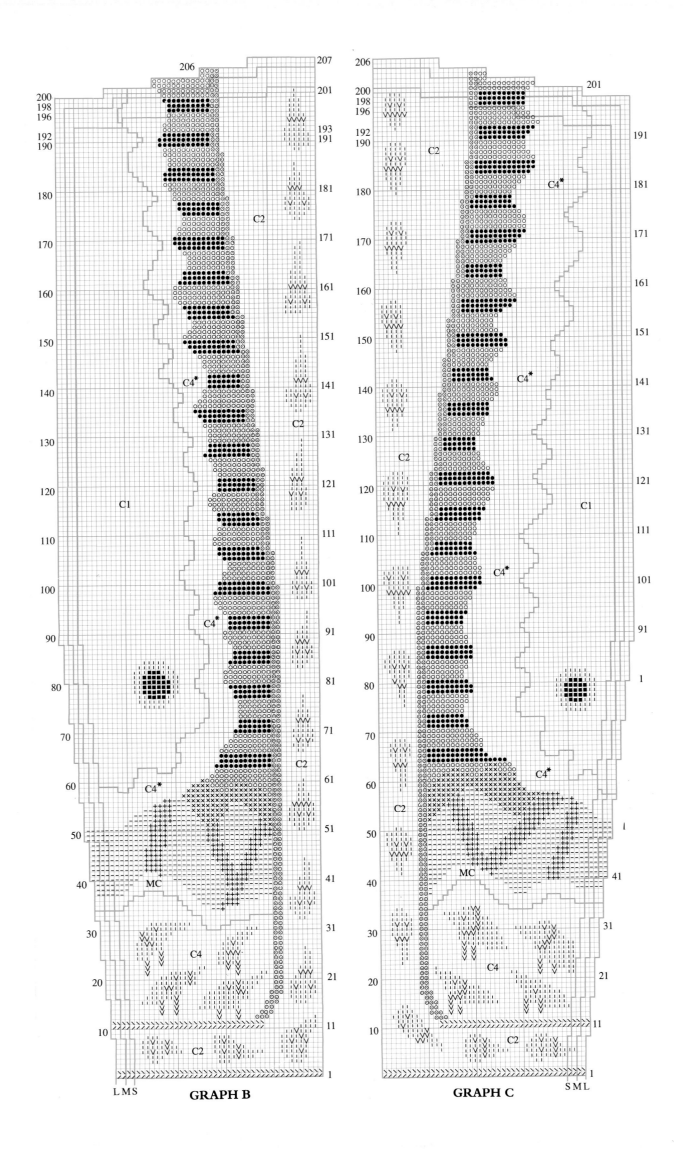

GRAPH B

GRAPH C

Australian
Gum Blossoms

MARGARET PRESTON

Interpreted by Julie Rubenstein

I was attracted by the contrast of the brightly coloured blossoms against the more subtle background and felt that it would readily translate into an interesting knitted garment.

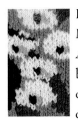 I initially chose to interpret Margaret Preston's work *Australian Gum Blossoms* (1928) because I was attracted by the contrast of the brightly coloured blossoms against the more subtle background and felt that it would readily translate into an interesting knitted garment. The aptness of my choice was further enhanced as I researched the artist's life. Although I had been aware of Margaret Preston's world renowned reputation as an Australian artist of great merit, I was now fascinated to discover how her work and style evolved over time, following a variety of experiences. She was a dynamic personality in her own right as well as being an interior decorator, my current profession.

Margaret Preston was Australia's foremost woman painter between the First and Second World Wars. Many of the best Australian artists at this time were women. They were committed artists, more for pleasure than for the expectation of commercial benefits. Margaret Preston, however, was quite different. She sought tangible recognition for her undoubted talents, as well as enjoyment. She felt that Australia contained a truly indigenous national art, liberated from its English ancestors. Her spirited crusade was partly the expression of her 'broad and bursting personality', as her friend Hal Missingham once put it, and also an outcome of the tenacity bred in her by experience.

Unlike other Australian women artists who received financial support from their families while they indulged in their hobbies, Margaret Preston had a much harder life. She was born in Adelaide, moved to Sydney, then Melbourne and then back to Adelaide after her father died, to help support her widowed mother and younger sister. Preston submitted to the necessity of teaching, rather than compromise her art by painting pictures to suit the general public for a quick sale. As

she wrote in 1927, she wanted to 'paint her pictures as she would, to choose her own subjects and do them in her own way, leaving all thought of selling out of her mind'.

Her determination to see where she stood artistically took her to England and Europe from 1904 to 1907, where her pride in her accomplished realism was shattered by coming face to face with modern European art—an experience she described in 1927 in an article entitled 'From Eggs to Electrolux'.

On returning to South Australia she resumed her teaching and her personal explorations, saving all the while 'to be able to make a dash back to Paris to see if she had moved a little'. This she did in 1912, consolidating her earlier lessons by spending some years in England and Europe. This allowed her to experience the fierce, non-realistic colour and bold, apparently crude draughtsmanship of the Fauvists. Expression of design was now guided by the decorative possibilities of colour, which fascinated Margaret Preston.

In 1919 she married William George Preston in Australia. This late and financially secure marriage released her from the need to earn a living and allowed her full rein in applying her considerable energies and willpower to developing her art and theories.

Settling in Sydney, where local modernism was a stylish watered-down variant of the European revolutionary mode, Preston applied aesthetic values to interior decoration, fabric design and even flower arrangement, in addition to painting and printmaking.

Although the Australia to which she had returned was a far more urban society than the one she had left behind, the landscape and pioneering traditions of the nineteenth century were still the touchstone of Australian visual expression. The bush was still regarded as essentially masculine—a place to escape to from the ladylike refinements of the city. This attitude was a wonderful challenge to Preston, who spent more than 25 years examining the bush ethos and the entrenched traditionalism of Australian art from a totally different perspective.

I have accordingly endeavoured to capture this mood in my own interpretation of *Australian Gum Blossoms*, which is now on view at the Art Gallery of New South Wales. The entire garment, which is certainly wearable, has been shaped like a flower, in particular the peplum, which evokes the petals of a flower.

A Sense of Style

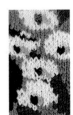 Julie Rubenstein enjoys discussing both the virtues and the limitations of woollen yarns. Adamantly she says:

When you're knitting a garment you've got to recognise that it is a craft, but with skill and imagination it can reach the realms of high fashion. Hand knitting cannot impersonate fabric and you've got to make the most of the properties of the yarn itself. For moulding the body and draping, there is little that is superior.

Julie keeps abreast of international fashion and would like to see more everyday knitters aspire to the originality and sense of style predominant in European fashion houses. The 'Pitti Filati' fashion show held in Florence every year sets the swinging knitwear styles for the world of fashion and Julie is well aware of the heights it is possible to achieve in knitting:

If you're going to spend most of the winter knitting yourself a garment it should be knitted from the best quality yarn available. It should

be sewn together carefully and it should have a sense of style about it. Otherwise you might just as well go and buy a cheap mass-produced garment. To maximise the results of their efforts and to look their best, the average knitter would benefit from adapting and changing published patterns, improvising, innovating and using a graph. This would make the piece they knit far more individual and exciting. The potential for really creative knitting lies in the knitters' hands.

The wardrobe of original garments Julie has made for herself confirms and reflects this philosophy. There are wonderful slinky and sexy silk knits, chic and colourful cotton knits and a glamorous range of woollen items. If Julie has a special social event on the calendar she will design and knit up something eye-catching to wear. She remembers: 'At one party I went to a friend was so insistent about having a replica made of the dress I was wearing, I ended up giving her mine as she had to have it immediately.'

Julie Rubenstein lives with her husband Norman, a solicitor, and her 14-year-old daughter, Sally Anne, in Malvern, Melbourne. An interior decorator, her

charming home attests to her ability in this field. Her clientele come through word-of-mouth among satisfied customers and acquaintances. Like many women she prefers to practise her profession around the needs of the family, who have first priority in her life. She leads a very active social life and is not inclined to place undue emphasis on any particular aspect of her life. She would rather all aspects flowed into each other.

Julie began knitting as a young girl and is self-taught, her first efforts being for her doll. During her formative years she says: 'I was always knitting something and I would spend hours just looking at yarns of different kinds. If I had a special Saturday night date, I'd make up a design with perhaps the front and back made of fabric and the sleeves knitted in. I'd experiment a lot.'

During her teenage years Julie took art lessons privately and when she finished her schooling she did a business course, which landed her a very responsible job at one of Australia's largest mining companies. When her daughter reached kindergarten age, Julie decided to explore the market for hand knits. She employed five knitters on a contract basis to make up one-only garments. Distelfink Gallery in Melbourne exhibited her pieces and a large department store placed a big order. Julie says: 'The buyer was so impressed she became a regular client and was never without one of my pieces.'

Laughingly Julie remembers one special order from a sophisticated female executive at the store who wanted something sensational to wear at a forthcoming social function:

I designed this black, slinky gown with a snake writhing its way from the front around to the back of the dress and its head encrusted with bugle beads, emerald eyes and a black, forked tongue appearing over the right shoulder. The knitter had only one week in which to make it up. She misread my instructions and I received back a beautifully knitted piece but the snake unfortunately was writhing in the wrong direction. The knitter, who had jet-propelled fingers, undid the garment and luckily finished it in time for the function.

One problem that arose with Julie's small but successful creation of hand knits was the sense of isolation it imposed on her:

I was spending too much time at home. I'm not a sociable knitter. I don't knit in public and I don't find knitting therapeutic. In fact I get so revved up knitting that I'll stay up until all hours to finish a garment. My husband doesn't like to see me knitting as he says it reminds him

unfortunately of the guillotine. So in a sense, I'm a closet knitter and this can be very lonely. I decided to forgo knitting for a while and instead took an interior decorating course at the Melbourne College of Decoration in 1986–87. In 1988 I received my first commission helping a friend to decorate her house and since then I've had regular commissions.

These days Julie combines many aspects of her skills in a very busy social life. She draws in charcoal when she can find the time, she will knit up anything that interests her, and she practises her profession of interior decorating. She enjoys knitting for children and gets excited at the prospect of a range of original garments for them. Perhaps this will be the area to attract her next.

Measurements

	Small	Medium	Large
Actual Garment Measures (*approx*):	90	100	110 cm
Length (*approx*):	56	58	60 cm
Sleeve Seam (*approx*):	43	43	43 cm

Materials

CLECKHEATON 8 PLY MERINO (*50g balls*)

Main Colour (MC)			
Taupe	12	14	16 balls

CLECKHEATON 8 PLY COUNTRY (*50g balls*)

Contrast 1 (C1)			
Green	1	1	1 ball

CLECKHEATON 8 PLY MACHINE WASH

Contrast 2 (C2)			
Dark Green	1	1	1 ball
Contrast 3 (C3)			
Maroon	1	1	1 ball
Contrast 4 (C4)			
Brick	1	1	1 ball
Contrast 5 (C5)			
Red	1	1	1 ball
Contrast 6 (C6)			
Brown	1	1	1 ball
Contrast 7 (C7)			
Lemon	1	1	1 ball
Contrast 8 (C8)			

Yellow	1	1	1 ball
Contrast 9 (C9)			
Black	1	1	1 ball

AND CLECKHEATON 8 PLY ANGORA (*50g balls*)

Contrast 10 (C10)			
Bright Pink	1	1	1 ball
Contrast 11 (C11)			
Pale Pink	1	1	1 ball
Contrast 12 (C12)			
Red	1	1	1 ball

One pair each 3.25mm (No 10) and 4.50mm (No 7) knitting needles; 2 stitch holders; knitting-in elastic; 3.50mm crochet hook; knitters needle for sewing seams.

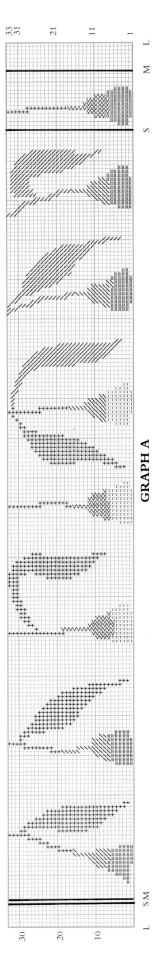

GRAPH A

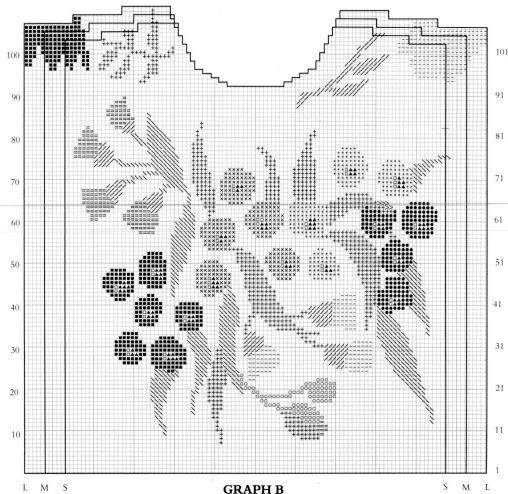

100

90

80

70

60

50

40

30

20

10

L M S   **GRAPH B**   S M L

101

91

81

71

61

51

41

31

21

11

1

Next Row: P4 (6–6), * inc in next st, P7 (5–4), rep from * to end . . . 94 (104–114) sts. **
Work 100 (102–104) rows stocking st, thus ending with a purl row.

SHAPE NECK:
Next Row: K36 (40–44), turn.
Cont on these 36 (40–44) sts.
Next Row: P3tog, purl to end.

SHAPE SHOULDER:
Cast off 9 (11–12) sts at beg of next row and foll alt row, AT SAME TIME work 3 sts tog at neck edge in next 3 rows. Work 1 row. Cast off rem 10 (10–12) sts. Slip next 22 (24–26) sts onto a stitch holder and leave. With right side facing, join yarn to rem sts and work to correspond with side just completed, reversing shaping.

Front

Work as for Back to **, then work in patt as shown on Graph B until row 92 has been completed.

SHAPE NECK
Next Row: Patt 40 (45–50), turn.
Cont on these 40 (45–50) sts.
Keeping patt correct from Graph, work 3 sts tog at neck edge in next 4 rows, then dec one st at neck edge in alt rows 2 (3–4) times . . . 30 (34–38) sts. Work 1 row.

SHAPE SHOULDER:
Cast off 9 (11–12) sts at beg of next row and foll alt row, AT SAME TIME dec one st at neck edge in next and foll alt row. Work 1 row. Cast off rem 10 (10–12) sts. Slip next 14 sts onto stitch holder and leave. With right side facing, join yarn to rem sts and complete to correspond with side just completed, reversing shaping.

Left Sleeve

Using 3.25mm needles and MC, cast on 55 (57–59) sts.
Work 5cm K1, P1 rib, working last row on right side.
Next Row: Rib 8 (6–6), * inc in next st, rib 1, rep from * to last 5 (5–3) sts, rib 5 (5–3) . . . 76 (80–84) sts.
Change to 4.50mm needles.
Work in patt as shown on Graph C, inc one st at each end of 11th and foll 10th rows

K E Y

MC = ☐
C1 = ╲
C2 = +
C3 = ─
C4 = ╱
C5 = ═
C6 = ◄
C7 = ►
C8 = ●
C9 = ○
C10 = ✕
C11 = ✻
C12 = ■

▲ ☐ *use any contrasting colours*

Tension

20.5 sts and 28 rows to 10 cm over stocking st, using 4.50mm needles and MC.

Back

Using 4.50mm needles and MC, cast on 196 (210–224) sts.
Work in stocking st for 3cm, ending with a purl row.
Next Row (right side): Purl.
Work 1 (3–3) row/s stocking st, beg with a purl row.
Work in patt as shown on Graph A until row 33 has been completed.
Using MC only for rem of Back, work 4 (4–6) rows stocking st.
Next Row: * P2tog, P3tog, P2tog, rep from * to end . . . 84 (90–96) sts.
Using knitting-in elastic with yarn, work in stocking st for 5cm on these 84 (90–96) sts, ending with a knit row.
Break off knitting-in elastic.

until there are 96 (100–104) sts.
Work 5 rows patt, thus completing
graph.
Cast off loosely.

Right Sleeve

Work as for Left Sleeve, working patt as
shown on Graph D.

Neckband

Join right shoulder seam. With *wrong* side
facing, using 3.25mm needles and MC, knit
up 82 (86–92) sts evenly around neck,
noting to purl across sts on stitch holders.
Work 5 rows stocking st (beg with a knit
row).
Cast off very loosely purlways.

Making Up

** Fringe all gumnut blossoms as
illustrated, using yarn same shade as
gumnut.
Join left shoulder seam. Tie a coloured
marker 23 (24–25) cm down from beg of
shoulder shaping on each side of back and
front to mark armholes. Sew in sleeves
between markers, placing centre of sleeve
to shoulder seam. Join side and sleeve
seams. Turn peplum hem to inside along
purl ridge and slip-stitch loosely in
position. Roll neck band to outside and
slip-stitch very loosely in place.

Fringing for Gumnuts:

With right side facing, using crochet hook
and single strand of yarn 5cm long, fold
yarn in half and draw a loop through
centre of stitch along edge of colour
change of gumnut (diagram A). Draw
ends through this loop and pull lightly to
form a knot (diagram B). Cont along edge
of colour change, working fringe between
stitches as well as in centres. Trim ends of
fringe as required.

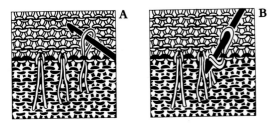

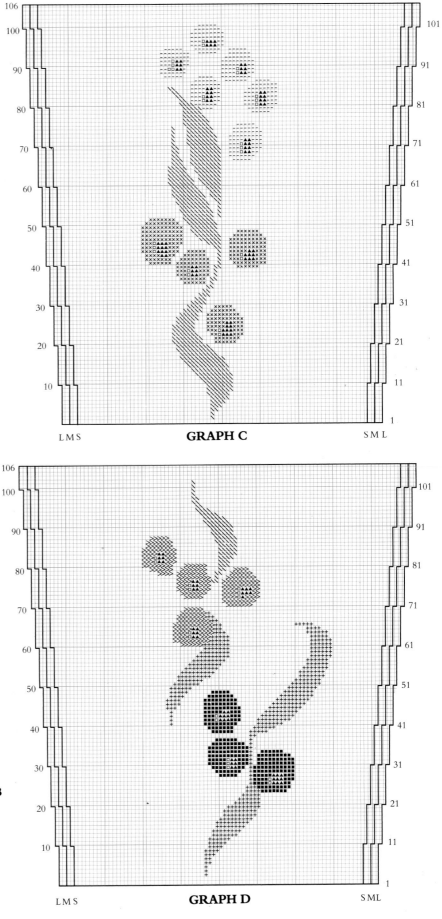

Hardy River, Mount Turner Syncline

FRED WILLIAMS

Interpreted by Maria Galinovic

Williams saw the Australian landscape as 'relentlessly monotonous', with no discernible focal point.
He also saw it as a challenge to his inventiveness.

A few years ago, in the early stages of my knitting career I went through a monochromatic period. Instead of figures and pictures, I used many shades of a particular colour to create 'mood and texture'. Bobbles of different sizes, combined with a variety of stitches gave the impression of a landscape.

'It looks a bit like a Fred Williams' painting,' remarked someone more versed than me in Australian art. I kept that in mind, although, becoming bored with texture, I moved on to 'colour and movement'.

When the opportunity to contribute to this book came along I thought it would be a challenge to actually try and render a Fred Williams' painting into purl and plain.

Fred Williams, who died in 1982 aged 55, was always interested in the translation of a subject from one medium to another. He was similarly aware of the formal possibilities in increasing or reducing the size of a particular image.

He became interested in landscape painting in the 1950s after years of concentrating on figures. As he studied landscapes, he realised there was something he wanted to say and decided to use landscape as he had previously used figures, as the basis for formal artistic invention.

In stark contrast with the European countryside, which was naturally composed and picturesque, Williams saw the Australian landscape as 'relentlessly monotonous', with no discernible focal point.

He also saw it as a challenge to his inventiveness: 'Obviously it was too good a thing for me to pass up the fact that if there is to be no focal point in the landscape then it had to be built into the paint . . . I am basically an artist who sees things in terms of paint.'

Williams mastered the landscape to the extent that the majority of his paintings impart a profound sense of the vast, open nature of the country. Just as we can walk without difficulty through open-treed countryside, so we are able to move through his landscapes—up and across, or down and into gullies, into stands of trees and out again, past hillsides and along creeks. I wanted to create the three-dimensional effect present in his paintings, in wool.

Williams often quoted the sayings of the great French landscape artist Camille Corot (1796–1875) to whom he attributed the observation that the success of the landscape painting depended upon the treatment of the relationship between sky and horizon. Williams was conscious of this relationship throughout his life.

In many of his works, the trunks of trees on distant hills are lost against the sky, and we see only bunches of foliage, transformed into marks of paint of endless variety.

Over the years the pattern of trees on the horizon would be lightened, darkened, touched with bright colours, glazed, scraped and scumbled.

The sky itself was never elaborated. Ignoring clouds as he ignored cast shadows, Williams treated the sky as a band of beautiful paint, making it usually cream,

137

off-white or grey, modulated with a darker tone of paint or glaze.

Hardy River, Mount Turner Syncline appealed to me because it is fairly representative of Williams's work. It also looked relatively easy to knit, without too many colour changes to daunt less adventurous knitters.

The piece also seemed to lend itself to innovation and change—especially in wool. There is no reason why a purple and mauve landscape cannot be changed into different shades of blue, especially if the knitter does not like mauve.

I extended the purple scrub area to elongate the garment, and collected as many shades of Cleckheaton purple as I could find . . . including a bit of 12 ply.

Garter stitch and bobbles of different sizes were used to create texture and depth and like Williams I left the sky alone, knitting it in a flat stocking stitch.

To finish the garment off, I embroidered branches over the purple and knotted in a few pieces of wool to give an unruly effect and separate the foreground from the background.

A Career Chameleon

Maria Galinovic claims that her knitwear design career really began only eight years ago when she gave up smoking. 'It was winter and I suddenly had nothing to do with my hands,' she explains. But her background in knitting has a much longer history.

Maria, who is of Yugoslavian parentage, came to Australia with her family when she was five years old and they settled in Wodonga. In the late 1950s migrants were encouraged to relocate themselves in the area to provide labour for industry, and Maria's parents, former farmers, were absorbed into the local workforce.

Being proficient in cottage crafts was part of the peasant culture in Yugoslavia and before the advent of television, a productive means of using time in the long winter months. As part of that culture, Maria was taught by her mother to knit, sew and embroider at an early age.

At school Maria knitted dolls' clothes, scarves and a few plain jumpers. Fostering creative skills was not a priority at school. Maria says: 'I went to the local Catholic

school until I was 17, but art was not an important part of the curriculum. It was something you were allowed to do on a Friday afternoon, if you were good.'

Maria attended teachers' college in Toorak, Melbourne, between 1971 and 1973 and here she had some elementary art lessons in painting and pottery. She also became more innovative with her knitting, as much out of necessity as pleasure.

Maria explains: 'Living on a pittance, the girls at the hostel for country students would get together and make their own winter clothes and virtually everybody produced a jumper or two during the winter. I found I could deviate from the Patons' patterns and produce something original, although I did not do anything with it until I found myself without a job, after five fairly traumatic years of teaching.'

Maria's years of teaching in Melbourne and Wodonga finished in 1979 when she opted for a different and less-structured lifestyle. She experimented with applique and patchwork and also painted. To support herself she took a series of odd jobs, such as

dishwashing at Myers and acting as cook, part-time manager and jack-of-all-trades in a friend's restaurant.

She resumed her interest in knitting about this time and decided to produce a range of hand knits for commercial production. She advertised for knitters, bought bulk retail wool and as she says, proceeded to lose money: 'It did not occur to me for a while that not all women who answered knitting advertisements could actually knit. Eventually through trial and error and common sense, I refined the process sufficiently to make a few dollars.'

With the birth of her daughter Elizabeth in 1984, Maria preferred to work from home and began to take design and knitting far more seriously. She sold garments to boutiques in Albury and also began to merchandise them through Dorian Scott's boutique at The Rocks, in Sydney.

Between 1984 and 1988, Maria employed a maximum of 15 knitters at one time and extended her range of production. She concentrated on Australiana designs because of the demands of the marketplace. Her more sophisticated, figurative garments, some with elongated Modigliani-type faces appeal to a narrower but more discriminating clientele. She caters successfully to a wide range of tastes.

Maria finds inspiration for her designs from a range of painterly sources. Her Yugoslavian rural background has given her a love of the primitive and naive. Her appreciation of European modern art inclines her towards Modigliani. Her patchwork and appliqued wall hangings also find their way into her knitting.

When Elizabeth approached school age, Maria decided to venture into a new career and at the age of 36, became a reporter on the local newspaper. Her ambition is to attain a good grading in journalism and become a worthwhile writer.

Knitting the two strands of her life together, Maria will continue to produce garments for sale at boutiques and galleries with the ten knitters she employs. As yet she has not been included in any major art knits exhibitions in Australia. With a tongue-in-cheek approach to life and an irreverent attitude towards her knitting skills, Maria hasn't taken her creations too seriously. One feels that if she were inclined to do so there are many prizes within her reach.

Measurements

	Small	Medium	Large
Actual Garment			
Measures (approx):	105	115	125 cm
Length (approx):	71	72	73 cm
Sleeve Seam			
(approx):	45	45	45 cm

Materials

CLECKHEATON NATURAL 8 PLY (*50g balls*)
Colour 1

(C1) Charcoal	2	2	2 balls

CLECKHEATON HIGHLAND 8 PLY (*50g balls*)
Colour 2

(C2) Purple fleck	1	1	1 ball

CLECKHEATON NOSTALGIA (*50g balls*)
Colour 3

(C3) Dark Purple	1	1	1 ball

CLECKHEATON MOHAIR CLASSIQUE 12 PLY (*50g balls*)
Colour 4

(C4) Purple	2	2	2 balls

Colour 5

(C5) Violet	2	2	2 balls

CLECKHEATON NEW CAPRICE 8 PLY (*50g balls*)
Colour 6

(C6) Cornflower	2	2	2 balls

Colour 7

(C7) Mauve	2	2	2 balls

Colour 8

(C8) Red	2	2	2 balls

Colour 9

(C9) Black	1	1	1 ball

Colour 10

(C10) White	1	1	1 ball

Cleckheaton Machine Wash 8 Ply (*50g balls*)

Colour 11			
(C11) Pink	2	2	2 balls
Colour 12			
(C12) Apricot	1	1	1 ball
Colour 13			
(C13) Lemon	1	1	1 ball

Cleckheaton Angora Supreme 8 Ply (*40g balls*)

Colour 14			
(C14) Grey	2	2	3 balls

One pair each 3.75mm (No 9) and 4.50mm (No 7) knitting needles; 2 stitch holders; knitters needle for sewing seams and embroidery.

Tension

20.5 sts and 28 rows to 10cm over patt, using 4.50 needles.

Abbreviations

'*Bobble A*'=Join appropriate colour to loop between last st worked and next st (tie with a slip knot, leaving a 6cm end), (K1, P1, K1) in next st, turn, P3, turn, K3, turn, P3, turn, K3, pass 2nd and 3rd sts over first st. Break off yarn, knot ends and thread through work to secure.

'*Bobble B*' = Join appropriate colour to loop between last st worked and next st (tie with a slip knot, leaving a 6cm end), (K1, P1, K1, P1, K1) in next st, turn, P5, turn, K5, turn, P5, turn, K5, turn, P5, turn, K5, pass 2nd, 3rd, 4th and 5th sts over first st. Break off yarn, knot ends and thread through work to secure.

Front

Using 3.75mm needles and C1, cast on 110 (120–130) sts.
Work 20 rows K1, P1 rib.
Change to 4.50mm needles.
Work in patt as shown on Graph A until row 120 has been completed.

Shape Armholes:

Keeping patt correct from Graph A, cast off 9 (10–11) sts at beg of next 2 rows . . . 92 (100–108) sts.
Dec one st at each end of next and alt rows until 74 (80–86) sts rem. **
Cont in patt from Graph A until row 156 has been completed.

Shape Neck:

Using C14 for rem.
Next Row: K32 (35–38), turn. Cont on these 32 (35–38) sts and dec one st at neck edge in alt rows until 23 (26–29) sts rem.
Work 3 (5–7) rows, thus completing row 178 (180–182) of Graph.

Shape Shoulder:

Cast off 8 (9–10) sts at beg of next row and foll alt row.
Work 1 row. Cast off rem 7 (8–9) sts.
Slip next 10 sts onto a stitch holder and leave. With right side facing, join C14 to rem 32 (35–38) sts and work to correspond with side just completed, reversing shaping.

Back

Work as for Front to **, noting to reverse Graph.
Cont in patt from Graph A until row 178 (180–182) has been completed.

Shape Shoulders:

Cast off 8 (9–10) sts at beg of next 4 rows, then 7 (8–9) sts at beg of foll 2 rows.
Leave rem 28 sts on stitch holder.

Sleeves

Using 3.75mm needles and C1, cast on 48 (50–52) sts.
Work 17 rows K1, P1 rib.
18th Row: Rib 4 (2–6), * inc in next st, rib 3 (3–2), rep from * to last 4 (0–4) sts, rib 4 (0–4) . . . 58 (62–66) sts.
Change to 4.50mm needles.
Work in patt as shown on Graph B, inc one st at each end of 5th and foll 6th rows until there are 68 (72–76) sts, then in foll 8th rows until there are 84 (88–92) sts.
Work 15 rows without shaping, thus completing row 108 of Graph.

Shape Top:

Keeping patt correct from Graph B, cast off 5 sts at beg of next 2 rows . . . 74 (78–82) sts.
Dec one st at each end of next and alt rows until 56 (60–64) sts rem, then in every row until 10 sts rem, thus completing Graph.
Cast off rem sts.

Neckband

Join right shoulder seam. With right side facing, using 3.75mm needles and C14,

KEY

C9	= ✕
C10	= ■
C13	= ●

BOBBLES

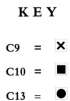

C6	= <
C8	= \
C9	= ■
C10	= +
C13	= /
C9	= *
C10	= I
C13	= >

knit up 88 (92–96) sts evenly around neck, incl sts from stitch holders.
Work 1 row K1, P1 rib.
Cont in rib, working 16 rows in stripes of 2 rows C1 and 2 rows C14 throughout.
Cast off loosely in rib, using C14.

Making Up

Using C9 and 'Stem Stitch', complete stem detail as indicated on Graphs. Cut 4cm lengths of C4 and C7 and thread through stitch on garter st ridge, randomly throughout Background C, and knot to secure. Join left shoulder and neckband seam. Join side and sleeve seams. Sew sleeves in position. Fold neckband in half onto wrong side and slip-stitch loosely in position.

NOTES TO GRAPHS:
For Front and Sleeves: Read right side rows from right to left and wrong side rows from left to right.

For Back: Read right side rows from left to right and wrong side rows from right to left.
Each square on Graphs represents one stitch or one bobble.

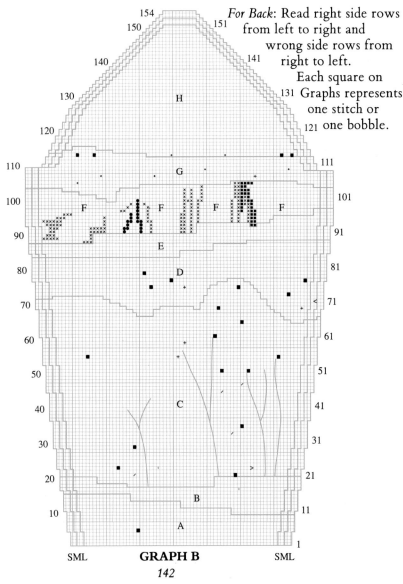

SML **GRAPH B** SML
142

For Bobbles: (see abbreviations at start of pattern)

For Embroidery: — = Stem Stitch, using C9. Heavy lines represent changes in Background as listed below.

A = Using C2, knit in garter st, noting bobbles.

B = Using C3, knit in garter st, noting bobbles.

C = These 28 rows form patt for Background C on Back, Front and Sleeves. For Back and Front, Background C begins on Row 18 of Graph A, with the 1st row of patt. For Sleeves, Background C begins on Row 18 of Graph B, with the 17th row of patt. Rep these 28 rows throughout area marked 'C', noting bobbles.
1st and 2nd Rows: Using C6, knit.
3rd Row: Using C4, purl.
4th Row: Using C7, purl.
5th and 6th Rows: Using C6, knit.
7th Row: Using C5, purl.
8th Row: Using C7, knit.
9th Row: Using C5, purl.
10th and 11th Rows: Using C6, purl.
12th Row: Using C4, knit.
13th Row: Using C6, purl.
14th Row: Using C4, purl.
15th Row: Using C6, purl.
16th Row: Using C5, knit.
17th and 18th Rows: Using C6, purl.
19th Row: Using C7, purl.
20th Row: Using C4, knit.
21st Row: Using C5, purl.
22nd and 23rd Rows: Using C6, knit.
24th Row: Using C4, knit.
25th Row: Using C6, purl.
26th Row: Using C6, knit.
27th Row: Using C7, purl.
28th Row: Using C5, knit.

D = Using C11, work in stocking st, noting bobbles.

E = Using C12, work in stocking st.

F = Using C8, work in stocking st, noting C9, C10 and C13 detail.

G = Using C1, work in stocking st, noting bobbles.

H = Using C14, work in stocking st, noting bobbles.

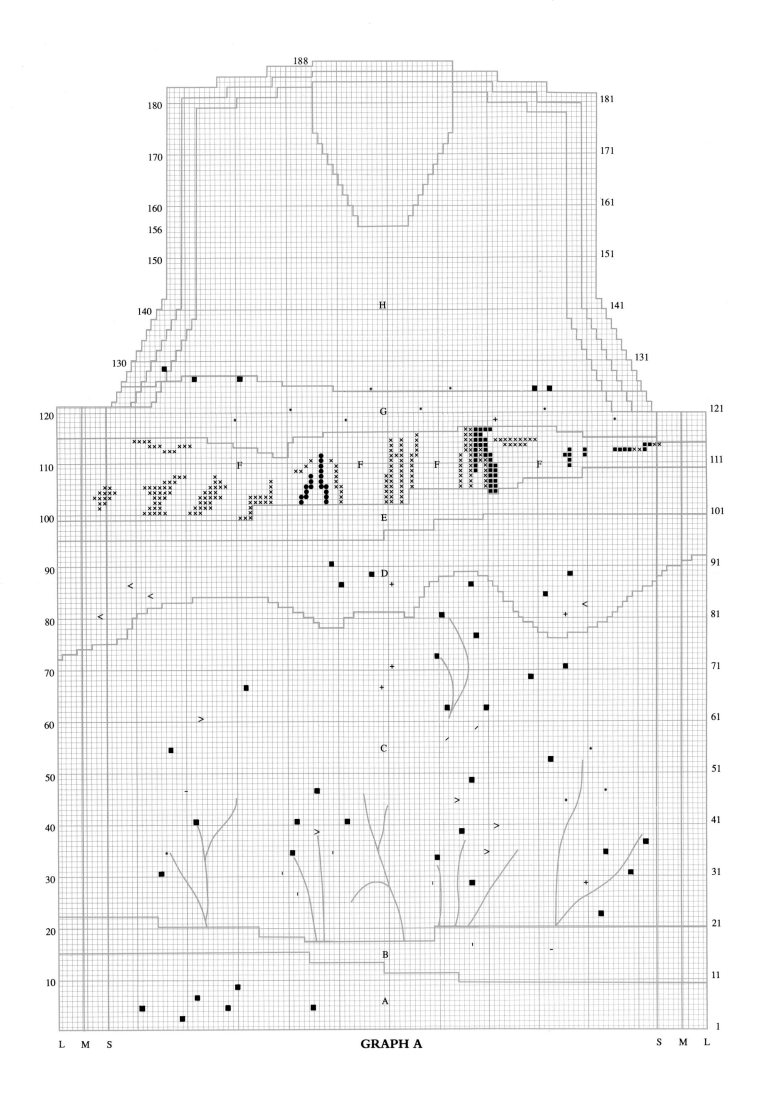

GRAPH A

City Light

DENISE GREEN

Interpreted by Maria Galinovic

The rather minimal painting became a colourful garment—depicting many city lights.

As I live in Albury, I had not had any previous contact with the work of Denise Green. But after seeing a print of *City Light*, I thought it would make an excellent pattern for a jumper.

Its vivid colours would appeal to the wearer and its geometric shape would make it relatively simple to knit.

I decided to reproduce the painting several times by doing a series of small patterns instead of one large pattern, which I thought could have been too overpowering.

Translating a completed work into a garment of your own often poses many difficulties. What the artist meant to be a square or a wide shape has to be altered to be wearable. And this often changes the mood of the picture.

But filling the body of the jumper with many city lights seemed to solve the problem of dimension. The pattern was still recognisably like the painting without having to worry about the impact of size. The rather minimal painting became a colourful garment—depicting many city lights rather than one.

Denise herself is known for her repeated use of simplified images—markers, buoys, arrows, pointing hands, letters, numerals and dotted lines—in paintings and drawings, which symbolise linkage, indication and direction.

Denise Green was born in Melbourne, grew up in Brisbane, and left Australia for Europe when she was seventeen. After studying at the Sorbonne in Paris, she moved to New York in 1970 where she has been living and working ever since.

Although Australian, Green's work seems to reflect her cosmopolitan and international education. *City Light* is a good example of such a lifestyle and it could reflect any city anywhere.

Measurements

	Small	Medium	Large
Actual Garment Measures:	110	122	135 cm
Length (*approx*):	75	76	77 cm
Sleeve Seam:	47	47	47 cm

Materials

CLECKHEATON MOHAIR 12 PLY (*50g balls*)

	Small	Medium	Large
Main Colour (MC) Bright Yellow	7	8	9 balls
Contrast 1 (C1) Red	1	1	1 ball
Contrast 2 (C2) Black	1	1	1 ball
Contrast 3 (C3) Orange	1	1	1 ball
Contrast 4 (C4) Cobalt Blue	1	1	1 ball
Contrast 5 (C5) Sky Blue	1	1	1 ball

One pair each 4.00mm (No 8) and 6.00mm (No 4) knitting needles; 2 stitch holders; 6 buttons (2 blue, 2 black, and 2 red); knitters needle (and plain yarn—if desired) for sewing seams.

Tension

16 sts and 19 rows to 10cm over stocking st, using 6.00mm needles.

Back

Using 4.00mm needles and MC, cast on 90 (100–110) sts.

KEY

MC = ⬜
C1 = ⬤
C2 = ▬
C3 = ▣
C4 = ◯
C5 = ✚

Work 20 rows K1, P1 rib.
Change to 6.00mm needles.**
Work in patt as shown on Graph A until
row 132 (134–136) has been completed.
Work 4 rows K1, P1 rib.

SHAPE SHOULDERS:
Keeping rib correct, cast off 12 (13–14) sts
at beg of next 4 rows, then 11 (13–15) sts
at beg of foll 2 rows.
Leave rem 20 (22–24) sts on a stitch
holder.

Front

Work as for Back to **.
Work in patt as shown on Graph A until
row 120 has been completed, reversing
Graph as indicated.

SHAPE NECK:
Next Row: Patt 40 (45–50), *turn*.
Keeping Graph A correct, dec one st at
neck edge in alt rows 5 (6–7) times, noting
to tie a coloured marker at end of 5th row
(126th row of Graph A) . . . 35 (39–43)
sts.
Work 1 row, thus completing Graph A.
Work 4 rows K1, P1 rib.

SHAPE SHOULDER:
Keeping rib correct, cast off 12 (13–14) sts
at beg of next row and foll alt row.
Work 1 row. Cast off rem 11 (13–15) sts.
With right side facing, slip next 10 sts
onto stitch holder and leave. Join yarn to
rem sts and keeping Graph A correct,
complete other side of neck to correspond
(omitting coloured marker and working
one row more before shaping shoulder).

Sleeves

Using 4.00mm needles and MC, cast on 33
(35–37) sts.
Work 20 rows K1, P1 rib.
Change to 6.00mm needles.
Work in patt as shown on Graph B until
row 76 is completed, AT SAME TIME inc
one st at each end of 3rd and foll 4th rows
14 (13–13) times in all, then in alt rows 7
(9–9) times . . . 75 (79–81) sts.

Neckband

FRONT PIECE:
Join shoulder seams. With right side
facing, using 4.00mm needles and MC, beg

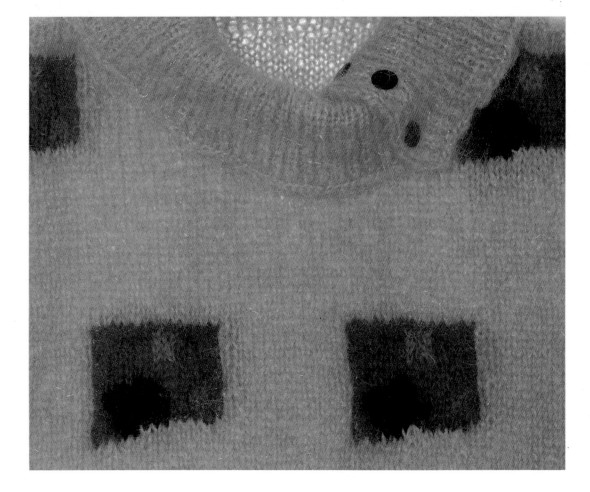

where coloured thread was tied on right side of Front neck and knit up 60 (62–64) sts evenly around neck to shoulder seam, then knit across first 9 sts from back neck stitch holder—noting to inc in each st. Work 25 rows K1, P1 rib on these 78 (80–82) sts.
Cast off loosely in rib.

Front Piece and knit across rem sts on Back neck stitch holder—noting to inc in each st, knit up 25 (27–29) sts evenly around Front neck edge to coloured thread, *turn*, then cast on 8 sts.
Work 7 rows K1, P1 rib on these 63 (69–75) sts.
8th Row: Rib 3, yfwd, K2tog, rib to last 5

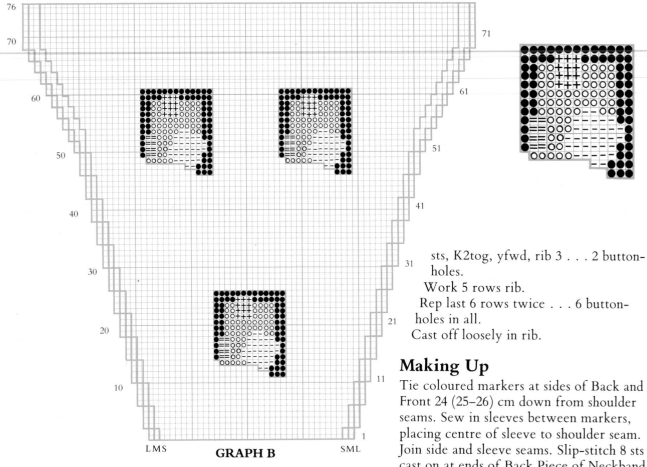

GRAPH B

sts, K2tog, yfwd, rib 3 . . . 2 button-holes.
Work 5 rows rib.
Rep last 6 rows twice . . . 6 button-holes in all.
Cast off loosely in rib.

Making Up

Tie coloured markers at sides of Back and Front 24 (25–26) cm down from shoulder seams. Sew in sleeves between markers, placing centre of sleeve to shoulder seam. Join side and sleeve seams. Slip-stitch 8 sts cast on at ends of Back Piece of Neckband to inside of Front Piece along where sts were picked up. Sew buttons to Front Piece to match buttonholes (sewing red buttons near cast off edge, blue near neck edge, and black in middle) at each end. Roll Neckband onto right side.

BACK PIECE:
Using 4.00mm needles and MC, cast on 8 sts, then with right side facing, beg at st next to where last st was knitted up for

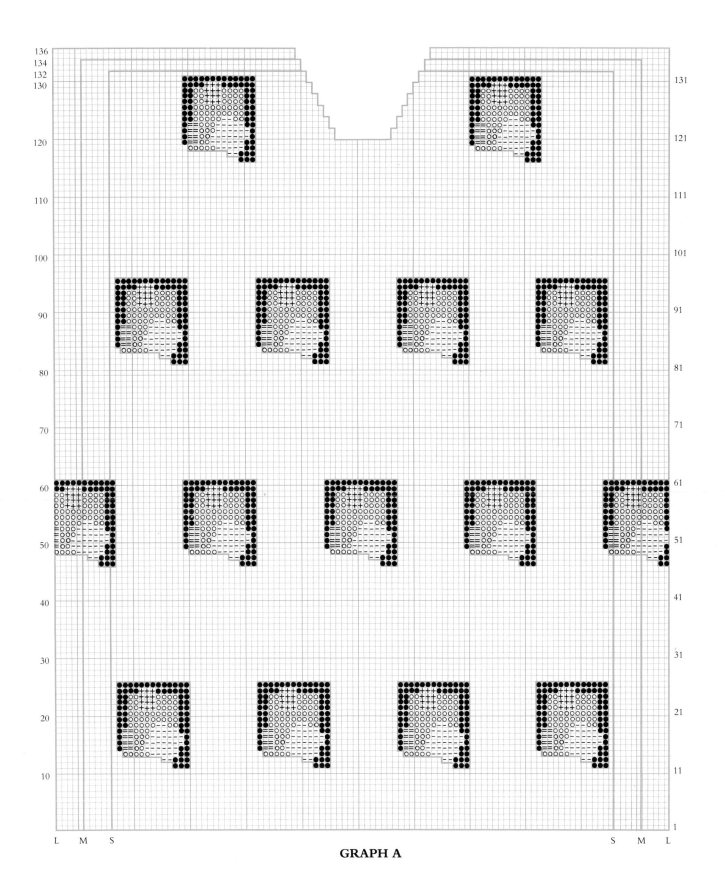

GRAPH A

The Jacaranda Tree

BRETT WHITELEY

Interpreted by Ruth Fitzpatrick

I wanted this garment to feel like a Brett Whiteley
painting—full of life!

To me, Brett Whiteley is one of Australia's best modern artists. I have always loved the boldness of his subjects, the beautiful colours he uses in his paintings and the way he captures Australian images.

The Jacaranda Tree is part of Whiteley's Lavender Bay series and I decided to interpret it into a garment because it represented something dear to the artist; it showed his use of colours in a modern way with all their starkness and clarity; and it was a wonderful representation of his special style. I love the blues he uses in this painting—they are such spiritual colours to me.

In the knitted garment, I was limited by the actual colours I could use in the yarn, which is why I used several blues rather than the darker blue actually used in Whiteley's painting. I also outlined the subjects to give them a more dramatic presence, as it is necessary to define images in knitwear very clearly. The shape was also important as I felt the painting had a modern feeling, so I wanted the shape to follow through and be avant-garde as well.

As the garment is my version of Brett Whiteley's painting, I wanted to catch the mood and colour of *The Jacaranda Tree* even though I have eliminated all the subtle colours and tones shown on the original painting. I wanted this garment to feel like a Brett Whiteley painting—full of life!

Natural Inspiration

Ruth Fitzpatrick lives in Uralla, a small town with a population of 3000 people, 20 minutes drive from Armidale, the university town situated on the New England Plateau in northern New South Wales. In a Victorian house, surrounded by a large garden, Ruth Fitzpatrick lives with her three young children, managing a large hand-knit industry and running a commercial gallery.

Uralla produces some very fine wool and each year the Wool Expo sponsors a competition with encouraging prize money in a variety of sectors. This year Ruth won the $1000 award for the most original evening wear in a knitted garment, as well as the Local Designer's Award. The design is very avant-garde, and the knitting expertise it demonstrates is remarkable.

Ruth began knitting at the age of 10, when she went to live with her great grandmother, then aged 96, who was a lace-maker and knitter. Ruth reminisces about the first garment she made: 'It was a jumper for myself made of scrap wool and I had numerous colours to play with. I called it my rainbow jumper. I loved that jumper. The kids at Pittown laughed at me when they saw it. Unfortunately that precious jumper was washed down the Hawkesbury River in the 1964 floods when my family lost everything.'

Ruth grew up as one of four children on a farm in the Windsor area outside Sydney. As a child she says she used to paint a lot and bury herself in knitting. At the age of 16 she started taking both her design skills and her knitting seriously when she won a scholarship to study Fine Art at East Sydney Technical College where she studied between 1968 and 1971.

Commuting for four hours each day by train between Windsor and Sydney, Ruth had ample time to knit. She found ready customers for her garments on the train itself and as she says, 'After four years there were many passengers on that train

wearing my garments.' Conversely in the sculpture course at East Sydney her knitting was never popular and was not recognised as an art form by the establishment. Ruth says, 'I used to knit up three-dimensional sculptures but the lecturers wouldn't accept it as art—it was knitting.'

When Ruth finished her studies at the technical college she enrolled at the Julian Ashton Art School at The Rocks in Sydney to gain more experience in life drawing, portraiture and painting. Like others, she had attended art school at a time when conceptual art was popular, and when as she says 'You could run a car tyre over a canvas and call it art.' But she felt she needed a more disciplined approach in order to achieve the technical skills necessary to express herself.

During college vacations she worked as an assistant animator at Air Programs International where the discipline and deadlines to be met proved valuable in her own business enterprises at a later stage.

She exhibited in small galleries in Darlinghurst and at times rented empty shops for a week and staged knitting exhibitions herself. As she wanted to travel but was impecunious, she joined an airline as an air hostess and for the next six years travelled both overseas and in Australia. She continued to knit, even in such incongruous places as Weipa and Groote Eylandt in the tropical north.

Ruth married in 1980 and in 1982 formed a business and started recruiting and training a team of knitters who today number about 200 and are scattered throughout Australia.

During the 1980s, Ruth exhibited in a prestigious range of exhibitions and galleries around Australia. She has shown her paintings, soft sculptures, quilts and knitwear since 1968, but in the last ten years she has leapt to the forefront in art knit circles. She was included in the *Salute*

to *Australia* exhibition at the Neiman Marcus store in Dallas, Texas, in 1987; the *Art Knits* exhibition at the Art Gallery of New South Wales in 1988; and was the only art knitter to represent Australia in the Australian Pavilion at Expo in Brisbane, 1989. She has exhibited at numerous Wool Corporation exhibitions as well as the Dorian Scott exhibitions held at David Jones and Georges in Melbourne.

Her garments are now worn by such luminaries as Elton John, Kiri Te Kanawa, Molly Meldrum and Pamela Stephens. Her knitwear makes regular appearances on the television production 'A Country Practice', which is filmed at Pittown, her former hometown.

Ruth receives a lot of her design inspiration from the country environment around her. Her cape for the Bicentennial *Art Knits* exhibition depicted the historic houses around Windsor and boating, water skiing and swimming activities on the Hawkesbury. The farms surrounding

Windsor and the airbase were also included in the circular cape, and wool dyes were applied to give a painterly feel to the piece.

At times Ruth's garments reflect her political allegiances. Her coat to celebrate the Bicentenary was designed as a 'Dreamtime Coat' and was a celebration of the survival of the Aborigines after 200 years of genocide.

Ruth prefers country living because she feels the lifestyle is more beneficial for her children. As a single, divorced mother who recently moved to New England she has been gratified by the extent of local support for her work and her enterprise. She feels the stimulus of an adjoining university town keeps her intellectually alive and in touch, while allowing her an informal way of life.

Ruth sees her immediate future as being in knitting, but one day she would like to have enough leisure time to take up painting again.

Measurements

Actual Garment Measures	Medium	Large
(at armholes, approx):	101	104 cm
Length (approx): (allow for dropping when worn)	90	90 cm
Sleeve Seam (approx):	41	42 cm

Materials

CLECKHEATON 12 PLY MACHINE WASH (*50g balls*)

	Medium	Large
Colour 1 (C1) Navy Blue	8	9 balls
Colour 2 (C2) Mid Blue	11	13 balls
Colour 3 (C3) Bright Blue	9	9 balls
Colour 4 (C4) Black	3	4 balls
Colour 5 (C5) White	2	2 balls
Colour 6 (C6) Rust	1	1 ball
Colour 7 (C7) Yellow	1	1 ball

AND CLECKHEATON MOHAIR MYSTIQUE 12 PLY (*50g balls*)

Colour 8 (C8) Purple Fleck	2	2 balls

AND CLECKHEATON SENSATION 12 PLY (*50g balls*)

Colour 9 (C9) Green Fleck	1	1 ball

NOTE: *Quantities are approximate as they vary between knitters.*

One pair each 4.50mm (No 7) and 5.50mm (No 5) knitting needles; 4.50mm circular needle, 80cm long; 2 stitch holders; knitters needle for sewing seams and embroidery; padding for bands; 2 large buttons.

Tension

17 sts and 23 rows to 10cm over stocking st using 5.50mm needles and Machine Wash.

Back

Using 5.50mm needles and C1, cast on 152 (160) sts.
Work in patt as shown on Graph A for *Back* (noting to reverse design as indicated on Graph), dec one st at each end of 3rd and alt rows 15 times in all, then in foll 4th rows 11 (16) times, then in foll 6th rows 6 (4) times . . . 88 (90) sts, row 111 (119) completed.
Cont in patt without shaping until row 194 has been completed, noting to omit buttonholes.

SHAPE SHOULDERS:

Keeping patt correct from Graph, cast off 14 (15) sts at beg of next 2 rows.
Leave rem 60 sts on a stitch holder.

Left Front

Using 5.50mm needles and C1, cast on 11 (15) sts.
Work in patt as shown on Graph A for *Left Front*, inc 2 sts at front edge in 2nd and every row 18 times in all AT THE SAME TIME dec one st at side edge in 3rd and alt rows 9 times in all . . . 38 (42) sts, row 19 completed.
Inc one st at front edge in every row 51 times AT THE SAME TIME dec one st at side edge in foll alt rows from previous dec 6 times, then in foll 4th rows 9 times . . . 74 (78) sts, row 70 completed.
Dec one st at side edge in next and foll 4th rows 2 (7) times in all then in foll 6th rows 6 (4) times AT SAME TIME inc one st at front edge in foll alt rows from previous inc 14 times, in foll 4th rows 7 times then in foll 5th row/s 1 (2) time/s . . . 88 (90) sts, row 13 (13) completed.

KEY

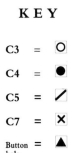

C3 = ◯

C4 = ●

C5 = ╱

C7 = ✕

Button hole = ▲

Cont in patt without shaping until row 194 has been completed, noting to omit buttonholes.
Cast off loosely.

Right Front

Work to correspond with Left Front until row 194 has been completed, reversing shaping and working as indicated for Right Front on Graph A and noting to work buttonholes as indicated by casting off 10 sts, on row 185.

SHAPE SHOULDERS:

Keeping patt correct from Graph, cast off 14 (15) sts at beg of next 2 rows.
Leave rem 60 sts on stitch holder.

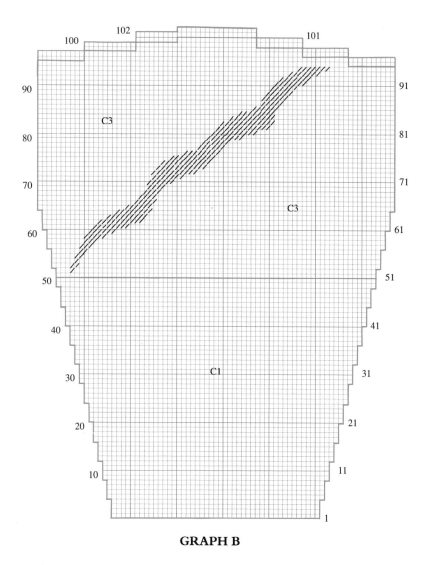

GRAPH B

Sleeves

Using 5.50mm needles and C1, cast on 45 sts.
Working in K2, P2 rib, work as shown on Graph B until row 50 has been completed, inc one st at each end of 5th and foll 4th rows 12 times in all ... . 69 sts.
Change to C2 and work in patt as shown from row 51 onwards, inc one st at each end of foll 4th rows from previous inc 4 times . . . 77 sts.
Cont in patt without shaping until row 94 (96) has been completed.
Using C2 only for rem, SHAPE TOP:
Cast off 10 sts at beg of next 6 rows.
Cast off rem 17 sts.

Polo Collar

Join shoulder by slip stitching right front over and onto left front at top of work, then joining front and back shoulders together.
With right side facing, using 4.50 circular needle and C1, knit up 120 sts from stitch holders.
Work in rounds of K2, P2 rib as shown on Graph A from round 197 onwards, dec one st at each end of front neck and one st each end of back neck in 2nd and alt rounds 8 times in all . . . 88 sts.
Cont in rib without shaping until round 229 has been completed.
Cast off *loosely* in rib.

Bands

Sew in sleeves, placing centre of sleeve to shoulder. Join side and sleeve seams.
Using 4.50mm needles and C3, cast on 20 sts.
Work in stocking st until work measures length required to fit around left armhole, along right front edge, across lower edge of back and along left front edge (to top of C1 section), noting to continue design of bird's tail to match right front. Slip stitch band to body. Fill band with padding, slip stitching other side to body. Slip stitch open ends.
Work band for right armhole in same manner.

Making Up

Sew on buttons. Using satin st, embroider right front as illustrated.

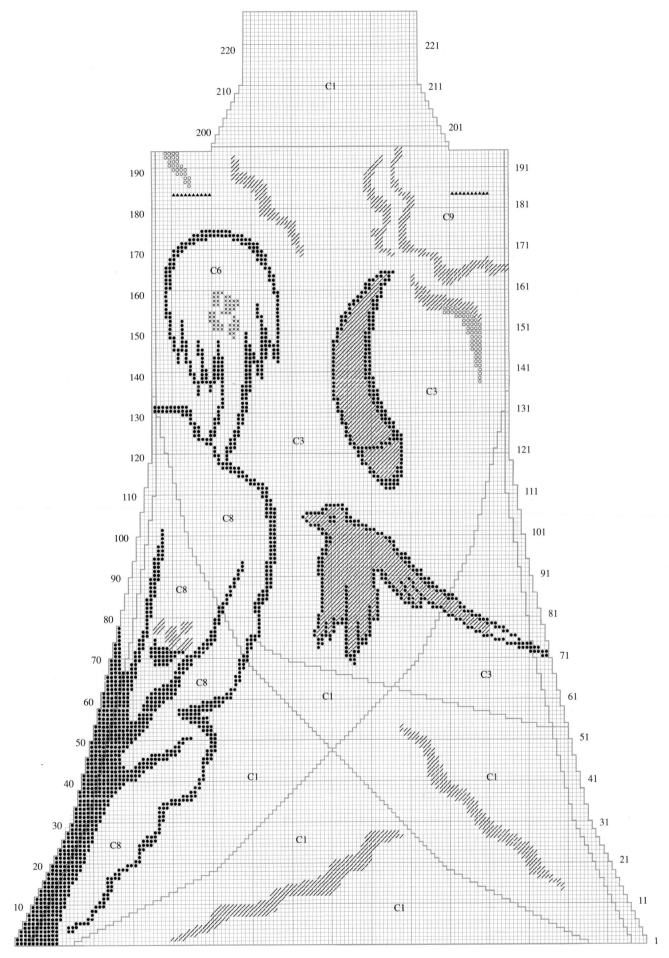

GRAPH A

The Parrot House

HAROLD SEPTIMUS POWER

Interpreted by Ruth Fitzpatrick

With its brilliant colours, strong brush strokes, the sulphur-crested cockatoo, macaws and other parrots and all the flowers crowded around the birds, the painting is a delight.

When asked to produce my interpretation of Harold Septimus Power's *The Parrot House* I felt daunted and wondered if such a busy, colourful and detailed painting could possibly be made up into an art knit garment, with its accompanying limitations.

I decided to accept the challenge and began the graphing, which I found exciting, especially trying to devise just how the garment could be knitted as it required so many colour changes.

With its brilliant colours, strong brush strokes, the sulphur-crested cockatoo, macaws and other parrots and all the flowers crowded around the birds, the painting is a delight. It has so much colour and energy.

With my painting background and a graphic approach to my own art knits, this painting was a wonderful challenge—a chance to show that art knits can be like 'paintings in wool'.

Harold Septimus Power originally came from New Zealand, arriving in Australia in 1898. He studied at the Academie Julian in Paris. He settled in England at Bushey, an artists' colony near London.

In 1915 he was appointed an official war artist and he spent his time on the battlefields where the Australians fought, in particular those of the Middle East where, like George Lambert, he served with the Australian Light Horse Brigade. His romanticised paintings of noble horse teams

at the front gave Australian war paintings of the First World War their most heroic image.

Septimus loved painting animals and birds, in fact he was a member of the Society of Animal Painters in London.

The Parrot House celebrates the beauty of the birds in the parrot family. It also reminds us that we should be protecting these and other exotic creatures from extinction by large-scale illegal trapping for the pet trade.

KEY

MC	=	☐
'Bobble'	=	■
C2	=	◁
C3	=	▷
C4	=	‖
C5	=	>
C6	=	◆
C7	=	△
C8	=	│
C9	=	•
C10	=	●
C11	=	◤
C12	=	✕
C13	=	◇
C14	=	☐
C15	=	╲
C16	=	✱
C17	=	═
C18	=	▲
C19	=	∧
C20	=	○
C21	=	∨

Measurements

	Small	Medium	Large
Actual Garment Measures (approx):	109	113	118 cm
Length (approx):	83	85	87 cm
Sleeve Seam (approx):	41	41	41 cm

Materials

CLECKHEATON MACHINE WASH 8 PLY *(50g balls)*

Main Colour (MC) Nutmeg	8	8	9 balls
Contrast 1 (C1) Salmon	4	4	4 balls
Contrast 2 (C2) Dark Green	3	3	3 balls
Contrast 3 (C3) Mid Pink	2	2	2 balls
Contrast 4 (C4) Emerald	1	1	1 ball
Contrast 5 (C5) Rust	1	1	1 ball
Contrast 6 (C6) Red	1	1	1 ball
Contrast 7 (C7) Bright Pink	1	1	1 ball
Contrast 8 (C8) Yellow	1	1	1 ball
Contrast 9 (C9) Turquoise	1	1	1 ball
Contrast 10 (C10) Black	1	1	1 ball
Contrast 11 (C11) Navy	1	1	1 ball
Contrast 12 (C12) White	1	1	1 ball

AND CLECKHEATON MOHAIR CLASSIQUE 12 PLY *(50g balls)*

Contrast 13 (C13) Royal Blue	1	1	1 ball
Contrast 14 (C14) White	1	1	1 ball
Contrast 15 (C15) Red	1	1	1 ball
Contrast 16 (C16) Yellow	1	1	1 ball
Contrast 17 (C17) Navy	1	1	1 ball

AND CLECKHEATON MOHAIR 12 PLY *(50g balls)*

Contrast 18 (C18) Mid Blue	1	1	1 ball
Contrast 19 (C19) Tan	1	1	1 ball

AND CLECKHEATON MERINO 8 PLY *(50g balls)*

Contrast 20 (C20) Light Green	1	1	1 ball
Contrast 21 (C21) Violet	1	1	1 ball

One pair each 3.25mm (No 10) and 4.00mm (No 8) knitting needles; 1 stitch holder; 10 large buttons; knitters needle for sewing seams.

Tension

22 sts and 30 rows to 10cm over stocking st, using 4.00mm needles and MC.

ABBREVIATION

'Bobble'=Join desired colour to loop between last st worked and next st (tie with a slip knot, leaving a 6cm end), (K1, P1, K1) in next st, turn, P3, turn, K3, turn, P3, turn, K3, pass 2nd and 3rd st over first st. Break off yarn, knot ends and thread through work to secure.

Back

Using 3.25mm needles and C1, cast on 121 (125–131) sts.
Work 12 rows K1, P1 rib, inc one st in centre of last row . . . 122 (126–132) sts.
Work in patt as shown on Graph A, beg with row 11 (7–1), until row 176 (172–166) has been completed.

SHAPE RAGLAN ARMHOLES:

Keeping patt correct from Graph A, dec one st at each end of next and alt rows until 54 sts rem.
Work 1 row, thus completing Graph.
Leave these sts on stitch holder.

Left Front

Using 3.25mm needles and C1, cast on 71 (73–77) sts.
Work 11 rows K1, P1 rib.
12th Row: Rib and slip first 11 sts onto pin and leave for Left Front Band, rib to end, inc 1 (1–0) st/s in centre of row . . . 61 (63–66) sts.
Change to 4.00mm needles.
Work in patt as shown on Graph A as indicated for Left Front, beg with row 11 (7–1), until row 176 (172–166) has been completed.

SHAPE RAGLAN ARMHOLE:

Keeping patt correct from Graph A, dec one st at beg of next and alt rows until 42 sts rem, thus completing row 213.

SHAPE NECK:

Next Row: Cast off 8 sts, patt to end . . . 34 sts.

Dec one st at armhole edge in next and alt rows 3 times in all, AT SAME TIME dec one st at neck edge in every row 5 times . . . 26 sts.

Dec one st at each end of alt rows until 2 sts rem.

Work 1 row, thus completing Graph.

Next Row: K2tog. Fasten off.

Right Front

Using 3.25mm needles and C1, cast on 71 (73–77) sts.

Work 4 rows K1, P1 rib.

5th Row: Rib 4, cast off next 3 sts, rib to end.

6th Row: Rib to last 4 sts, cast on 3 sts, rib 4 . . . buttonholes.

Work a further 5 rows rib.

12th Row: Rib to last 11 sts, inc 1 (1–0) st/s in centre of row, slip last 11 sts onto a pin and leave for Right Front Band . . . 61 (63–66) sts. Complete to correspond with Left Front, reversing all shaping and working as indicated on Graph A for Right Front.

Left Sleeve

Using 3.25mm needles and C1, cast on 51 (55–59) sts.

Work 33 rows K1, P1 rib.

34th Row: Rib 4 (6–8), * inc in next st, rib 1, rep from * to last 1 (3–5) st/s, rib 1 (3–5) . . . 74 (78–82) sts.

Change to 4.00mm needles.

Work in patt as shown on Graph B, inc one st at each end of 7th and foll 6th rows until there are 104 (108–112) sts, then in alt rows until there are 108 (112–116) sts.

Work 1 row.

SHAPE RAGLAN:

Keeping patt correct from Graph B, dec one st at each end of every row until 74 (78–86) sts rem, then in alt rows until 24 sts rem.

Work 1 row. Cast off loosely.

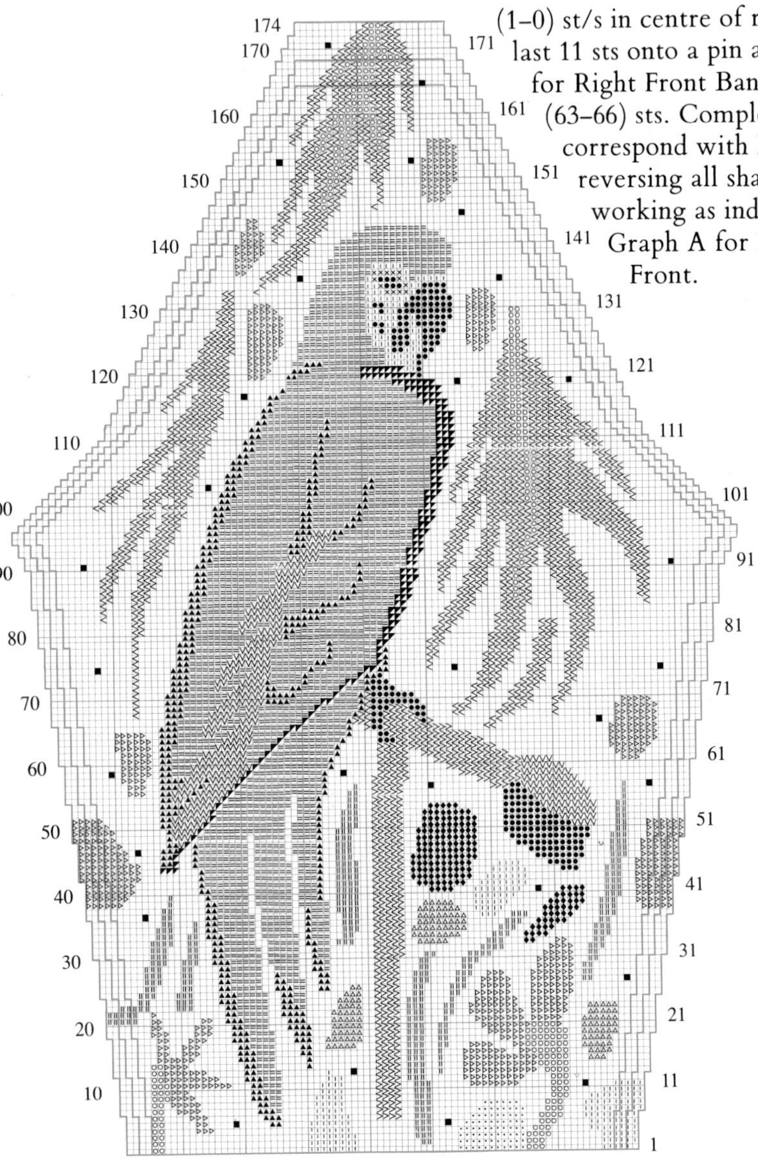

GRAPH B

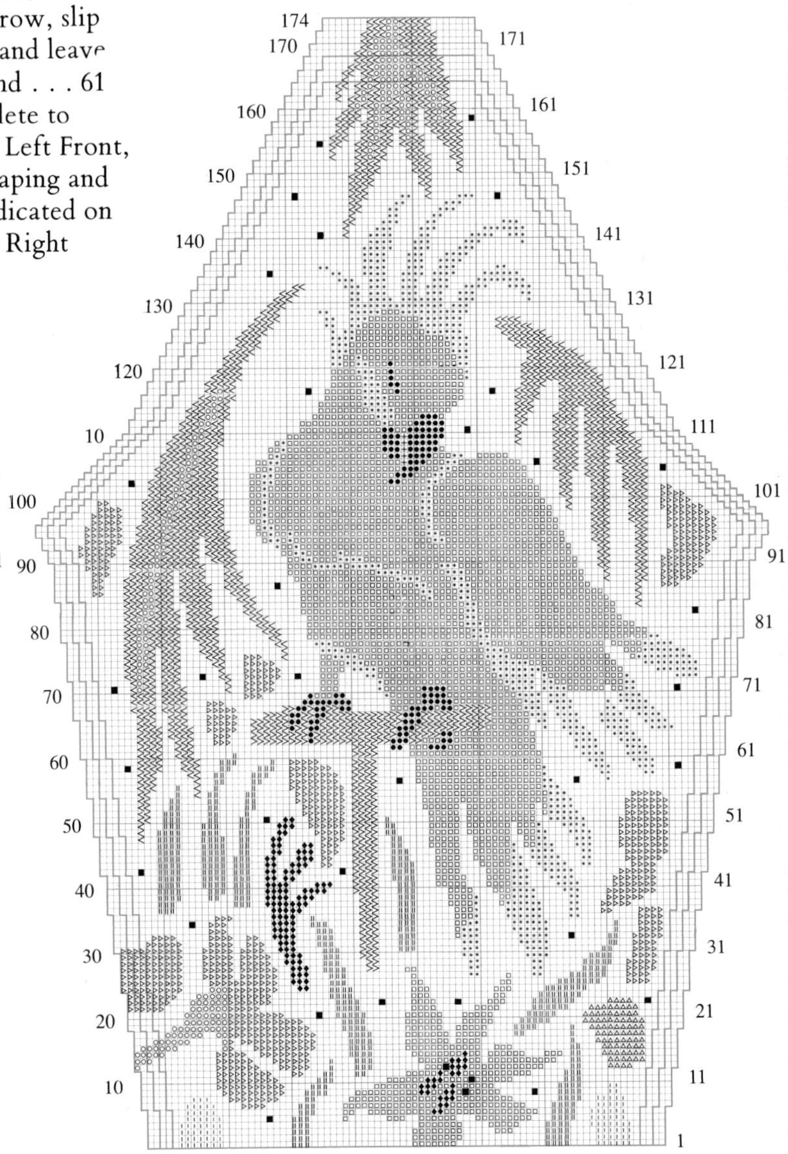

GRAPH C

Right Sleeve

Work as for Left Sleeve, working patt as shown on Graph C.

Left Front Band

Slip 11 sts left on pin on Left Front onto 3.25mm needle so that right side will be facing for first row.
Work 190 rows K1, P1 rib, working in C1 for first 24 (28–34) rows, C7 for next 23 rows, then in MC for rem 143 (139–133) rows, thus working last row on wrong side.
Break off yarn. Leave sts on pin.

Right Front Band

Slip 11 sts left on pin on Right Front onto 3.25mm needle so that wrong side will be facing for first row.
Work 192 rows K1, P1 rib, working a buttonhole (as before) in foll 23rd and 24th rows from previous button-hole 8 times and working in C1 for first 25 (29–35) rows, C7 for next 22 rows, then in MC for rem 145 (141–135) rows, thus working last row on right side. Do not break off yarn. Leave sts on needle.

Neckband

Join raglan seams, noting that tops of sleeve form part of neckline. With right side facing, using 3.25mm needle holding Right Front Band sts and attached MC ball, knit up 40 sts evenly along Right Front neck edge, 22 sts evenly across Right Sleeve, knit across Back stitch holder, noting to dec one st in centre, knit up 22 sts evenly across Left Sleeve, knit up 40 sts evenly along Left Front neck edge, then rib across Left Front Band sts . . . 199 sts.
Work 17 rows K1, P1 rib, beg with a 2nd row and working a buttonhole (as before) in foll 12th and 13th rows . . . 10 buttonholes in all.
18th Row: Cast off first 11 sts in rib, rib to last 11 sts, cast off last 11 sts in rib . . . 177 sts.
Rejoin MC and cont on these sts, working a further 17 rows rib.
Cast off loosely in rib.

Making Up

Join side and sleeve seams. Sew rem of front bands in position. Sew buttons in place. Fold neckband in half to wrong side and slip-stitch loosely in position, catching sides in place.

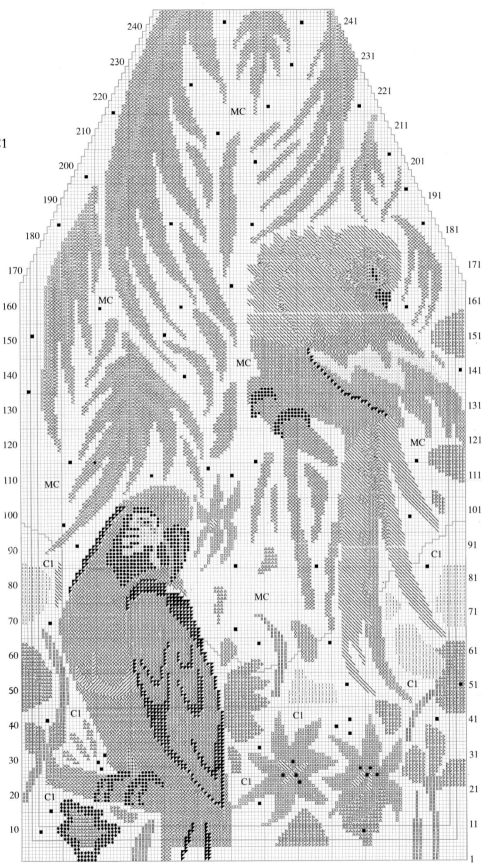

GRAPH A

When the World was Young

SEGLINDE BATLYE

Interpreted by Robyn McAleer

When the World was Young seems to state its 'Australianness' very clearly in a more sophisticated manner than a painting depicting gum trees and native fauna.

Linde and I met about ten years ago while students at Claremont Technical College (Western Australia), where a random assortment of students shared three years of learning and personal growth. There was a considerable range of ages among the students, which at first I thought could be a great disadvantage. What mattered to all of us though was developing skills, and the group dynamics worked for, rather than against us. Those years have left a lasting impression on me and mark my growing appreciation of Linde's work.

I have always loved Linde's compositional skills and seeming frivolity of element placement, which of course belies the very serious artist she is. *When the World was Young* is a good example of her approach to painting.

Linde's output and the variety of her paintings is quite overwhelming and making a decision on which painting to choose was very difficult. As usual I made a subjective choice. *When the World was Young* seems to state its 'Australianness' very clearly in a more sophisticated manner than a painting depicting gum trees and native fauna, which I was not interested in interpreting; others can do it with much more dexterity. The reds in the painting appeal to me greatly, as red is my favourite colour, and the circles and curves appeal to my romantic sense far more than angles ever could.

My interest as a designer was to take some of the colours and elements and to rearrange them into some kind of pattern that spoke of the painting, but took on a different life as the knitted design.

Looking to the Future

Now in mid-career and in mid-life Robyn McAleer has decided to sit back awhile and carefully consider her future creative efforts. For the past five years Robyn has worked non-stop.

Robyn says: 'I feel I should be specialising and I also need to learn how to market myself more successfully.' It is a quandary that often arises among those with multiple artistic talents, and limited marketing experience.

Robyn has an array of skills that makes a choice of specialisation quite difficult. She is a textile designer, painter, silk-screen printer, knitter and costume maker, and is attracted to all those areas.

Born in Melbourne, Robyn comes from an artistic background. Her grandfather, mother and father are all competent painters and her uncle is a sculptor. Her parents have worked together in creative film-making.

Robyn learnt to knit from her grandmother and as a child in Melbourne during winter, she and her mother and a girlfriend used to sit around the fire knitting football scarves and jumpers. In her teenage years Robyn made her own clothes and used to haunt the wool departments in the chain stores in search of knitting materials.

For seven years after she left school, Robyn worked in a variety of secretarial jobs. Commuting to work on trains she would knit, read and converse without missing a stitch. For a short period she worked in a chalet at Mt Buller and here learnt to knit Norwegian-style jumpers on a friend's knitting machine.

After marrying in 1970, Robyn and her husband Roger, who had a career in the public service, moved to Canberra. Here, without any formal training, Robyn worked as an interior decorator. Moving to

business. She became pregnant, but her son, who was born with spina bifida, died after six days. The death acted as a catalyst in Robyn's life.

Robyn explains:

I didn't know how to mourn. My friends lost patience with me and told me to keep a stiff upper lip. I started having migraines. I had a spiritual experience which helped the healing process and started me on a religious search. With unresolved grief, a five-year-old, a business to run and a husband studying full-time, I decided to either compound the problems or solve them by enrolling full-time in a Fine Arts degree at Claremont Technical College. I loved the course and the experience changed me as a person. Two years after finishing the degree I enrolled at Curtin University and gained my Bachelor of Craft in textiles in 1985. I found the course easy but it didn't occur to me that I had a natural ability for the work.

Sydney a year later, Robyn continued working in the same field and a daughter, Diana, was born in 1972.

When Roger decided to forgo his career in 1976 and return to university to study architecture, they settled in Perth. The climate was enticing and the cost of living more manageable for a one-income family.

To earn an income while Roger studied, Robyn began a gourmet delicatessen

While at university Robyn designed and printed fabric and found that she had a ready market for it. Post university Robyn launched into her own business, printing, designing and manu-facturing clothing, rainwear, boxes and a number of hand knits every season. Robyn's knitwear has always been ancillary to her textile production.

Inspiration for Robyn's designs comes she says: 'From just walking down the street, looking and laughing at things. I know my designs work because people get a laugh

out of them. In my work I try to make a statement about who and what I am and how I see the world. I tend to abstract if I can. Australiana doesn't interest me—it's too widely done.'

Between 1986 and 1990 Robyn exhibited in a number of prestigious exhibitions both in Australia and overseas. She was included in the *Commonwealth Exhibit of Textiles* at Edinburgh as well as the Nieman Marcus *Australasian Exhibition* at Dallas, Texas in 1986. She was part of the craft Expo in Melbourne in 1987 and was an exhibitor in the *Art knits* exhibition at the Art Gallery of New South Wales in 1988.

In 1988, Robyn collaborated with the Aboriginal painter and writer, Sally Morgan, to produce a small collection of clothing and stage a joint exhibition. Robyn says: 'Sally's work is very graphic, linear and stylised. Her work, with its brilliant colour, appeals to me very much. It was a great challenge to work with her.'

More recently Robyn designed theatrical costumes for the West Australian Ballet Company during the 1989 Festival of Perth. She would enjoy more involvement with design of this genre, but the scope is limited in Western Australia. Isolation from the eastern states restricts opportunities to participate in a wider field of theatrical design.

Isolation also has to be built in as a cost factor in Robyn's work. Her rainwear is designed by her in Perth, but laminated in Melbourne before returning to Perth for cutting and sewing. Robyn explains: 'In Perth I have to manufacture at such a cost. If I were big enough I could live in Sydney or Melbourne and have the cloth processed in South Korea or Taiwan.'

These are the sorts of problems and directions Robyn is now sitting back contemplating. Like other knitters she may consider production offshore for the general market.

Currently Robyn is taking classes in life drawing and planning a studio in her back garden. It seems like just the place to sort out a future direction.

Measurements

	Small	Medium	Large
Actual Garment			
Measures (*approx*):	102	112	122 cm
Length (*approx*):	50	51	52 cm
Sleeve Seam ¾			
length (approx):	34	34	34 cm

Materials

CLECKHEATON MACHINE WASH 8 PLY (*50g balls*)

	Small	Medium	Large
Main Colour			
(MC) Black	6	7	8 balls
Contrast 1			
(C1) Purple	2	2	2 balls
Contrast 2			
(C2) Mid Blue	1	1	1 ball
Contrast 3			
(C3) Light Blue	1	1	1 ball
Contrast 4			
(C4) Red	1	1	1 ball
Contrast 5			
(C5) Yellow	1	1	1 ball
Contrast 6			
(C6) Mustard	1	1	1 ball
Contrast 7			
(C7) Pink	1	1	1 ball

AND CLECKHEATON NEW CAPRICE 8 PLY (*50g balls*)

	Small	Medium	Large
Contrast 8			
(C8) Hot Pink	1	1	1 ball

AND CLECKHEATON MOHAIR 12 PLY (*50g balls*)

	Small	Medium	Large
Contrast 9			
(C9) Purple	2	2	2 balls

AND CLECKHEATON MERINO 8 PLY (*50g balls*)

	Small	Medium	Large
Contrast 10			
(C10) Dark Purple	1	1	1 ball

One pair each 3.75mm (No 9) and 4.50mm (No 7) knitting needles; knitters needle for sewing seams; 5 buttons.

Tension

21 sts and 28 rows to 10cm over stocking st, using 4.50mm needles and MC.

Back

Using 3.75mm needles and C9, cast on 110 (120–130) sts.
Work 20 rows K1, P1 rib in stripes of 2 rows C9 and 2 rows C1.
Change to 4.50mm needles.
Work in patt as shown on Graph A until row 120 (122–124) has been completed.

SHAPE SHOULDERS:
Keeping patt correct from Graph, cast off 13 (15–16) sts at beg of next 4 rows, then 13 (14–17) sts at beg of foll 2 row.
Cast off rem 32 sts loosely.

Left Front

Using 3.75mm needles and C9, cast on 65 (70–75) sts.

Work 19 rows K1, P1 rib in stripes as for Back band.
20th Row: Using C1, rib and slip next 10 sts onto a pin and leave for Left Front Band, rib to end . . . 55 (60–65) sts.
Change to 4.50mm needles.
Work in patt as shown on Graph B until row 40 has been completed.

SHAPE FRONT SLOPE:
Keeping patt correct from Graph, dec one st at end of next and foll 4th rows until 47 (52–57) sts rem, then in foll 6th rows until 39 (44–49) sts rem.
Work 3 (5–7) rows patt, thus completing row 120 (122–124) of Graph.

SHAPE SHOULDER:
Cast off 13 (15–16) sts at beg of next row

KEY

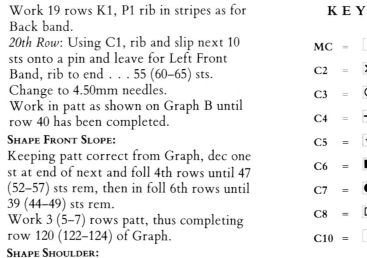

MC	=	□
C2	=	✕
C3	=	○
C4	=	✛
C5	=	✳
C6	=	■
C7	=	●
C8	=	▫
C10	=	❘

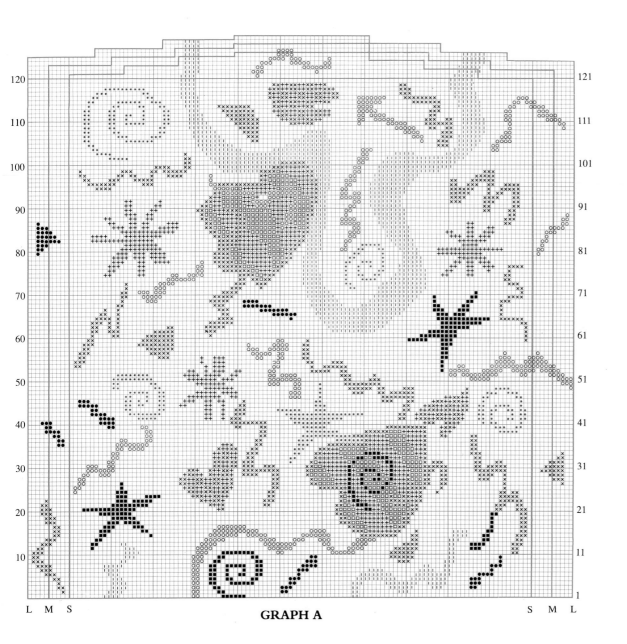

GRAPH A

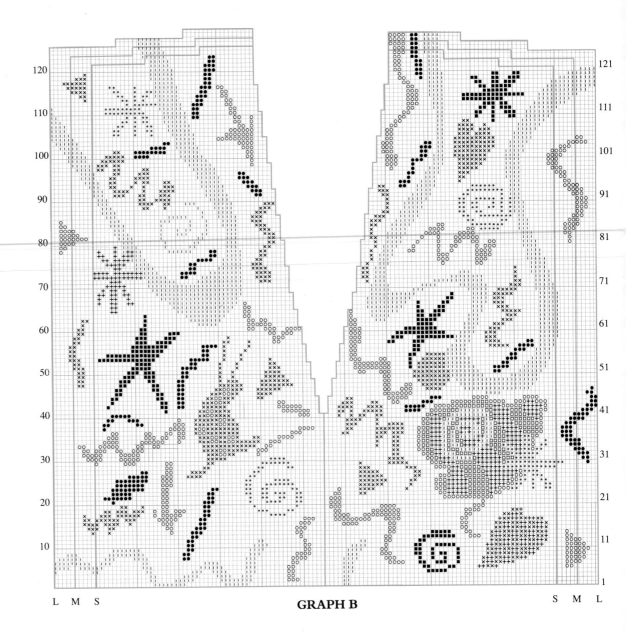

GRAPH B

and foll alt row:
Work 1 row. Cast off rem 13 (14–17) sts.

Right Front

Using 3.75mm needles and C9, cast on 65
(70–75) sts.
Working in K1, P1 rib in stripes as for
Back band, work 4 rows.
5th Row: Rib 4, cast off 2 sts, rib to end.
6th Row: Rib to last 4 sts, cast on 2 sts, rib
4 . . . buttonhole.
Work a further 13 rows rib.
20th Row: Rib to last 10 sts, slip last 10 sts
onto a pin and leave for Right Front
Band . . . 55 (60–65) sts.
Complete to correspond with Left Front,
reversing all shaping and working as
indicated on Graph B for Right Front.

Left Sleeve

Using 3.75mm needles and C9, cast on 48
(50–52) sts.
Work 16 rows K1, P1 rib in stripes as for
Back band, inc 6 (8–10) sts evenly across
last row . . . 54 (58–62) sts.
Change to 4.50mm needles.
Working in patt as shown on Graph C,
inc one st at each end of 3rd and alt rows
until there are 66 (70–74) sts, then in foll
4th rows until there are 98 (102–106) sts.
Work 3 rows patt, thus completing
Graph.
Cast off very loosely.

Right Sleeve

Work as for Left Sleeve, working patt as
shown on Graph D.

Right Front Band

Join shoulder seams. Slip 10 sts left on pin on Right Front onto 3.75mm needle so that wrong side will be facing for first row.

Using C1, rib 1 row.

Working in K1, P1 rib in stripes of 2 rows C9 and 2 rows C1 throughout, ** *Next Row*: Rib 4, cast off 2 sts, rib 4. *Next Row*: Rib 4, cast on 2 sts, rib 4. Work 14 rows rib. **

Rep from ** to ** 3 times . . . 5 buttonholes in all.

Cont in rib stripes until work is length required to fit (slightly stretched) along Right Front and across half of back neck, ending with 2 rows C9.

Cast off in rib, using C9.

Left Front Band

Slip 10 sts left on pin on Left Front onto 3.75mm needle so that right side will be facing for first row.

Complete to correspond with Right Front Band, omitting buttonholes and ending with 2 rows C1.

Cast off in rib, using C1.

Tails

Using 4.50mm needles and C3, and leaving a 6cm end, cast on 11 sts.

Cast off firmly, knitways.

Fasten off, leaving a 6cm end.

Stitch to garment along C2 and C3 'squiggles' as desired.

Bobbles

Using C3 and leaving a 6cm end, place a slip knot on 4.50mm needle.

Work K1, P1, K1, P1 into slip knot . . . 4 sts.

Work 4 rows stocking st.

Pass 2nd, 3rd and 4th sts over first st.

Fasten off, leaving a 6cm end. Turn bobble to purl side and knot ends. Attach to C3 areas as desired.

Making Up

Tie a coloured marker 23 (24–25) cm down from beg of shoulder shaping on side edges of Back and Fronts to mark armholes. Sew in sleeves between markers, placing centre of sleeve to shoulder seam. Join side and sleeve seams. Sew front bands in place, joining at centre back neck. Sew buttons in place.

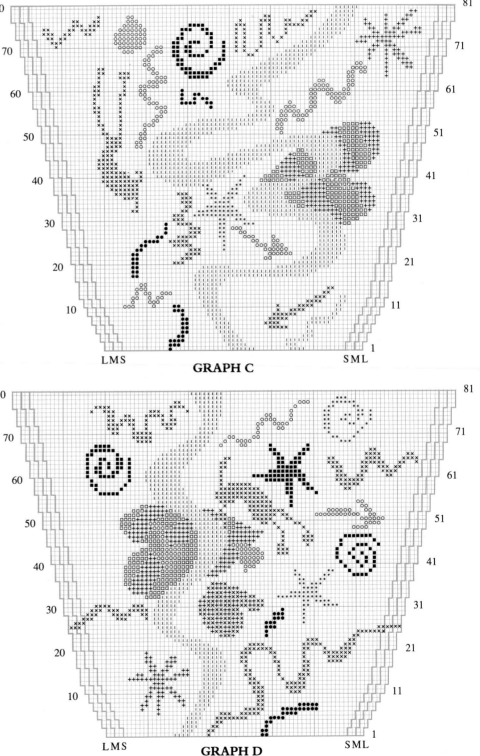

GRAPH C

GRAPH D

Lunchtime

VIDA LAHEY

*A small vase of pansies, providing splashes of colour and contrasting spots of black,
stands beside a shining jug and a glass, all bathed in warm midday sunlight—a
scene of simplicity and quietude.*

The Cretonne Curtain

Interpreted by Libby Jones

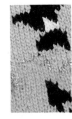

For many years now, my abiding passion for the fashions of the 1920s, 1930s and 1940s has grown to a point that I sometimes find myself imbuing my designs—both personal and professional—with more than just a touch of the old world. What fascinates me is not just the cut of clothes worn in this era, but the era itself. The innocence, the gentility and the carefree attitude to life towards the beginning of the century has a lure to it; for me there is always a temptation to visit the past, especially when the past seems so rosy.

To me, the works of Vida Lahey encapsulate the very essence of these times. I had not heard of her until I visited the Queensland Art Gallery's *Songs of Colour—the Art of Vida Lahey* retrospective exhibition in 1989. There, I found an artist whose gentle works illustrated an old-time Australia that I, unfortunately, believe has almost disappeared. I immediately admired her obvious flair with colour and light, used carefully, but not insipidly, on simple domestic scenes, flower studies, landscapes and portraits, and I felt there was much about the character and style of her work with which I could identify. When presented with the idea of taking the work of an artist to interpret into knitwear, Vida Lahey was my first and only choice.

Born in Queensland in 1882, Vida Lahey was an artist whose talent came to the fore very easily in life; she held her first exhibition at the age of twenty. She subsequently spent many years travelling, studying and establishing herself as a respected artist. In 1912 she became art mistress at Brisbane Girls High School (later known as Somerville House), which incidentally was the high school I attended. She painted and lectured extensively throughout Australia and the world for the next 50 years, working consistently through two world wars and many social changes, until her death in 1968. She has left Queensland with a legacy of paintings that not only underscore her own development as a painter, but are a valuable glimpse of life in earlier days.

For me, the choice of painting from such an artist was, from the first, difficult. What I wanted to achieve was a design that captured the sensibilities of the 1930s, a mellow and calm memory of morning teas, garden parties and sunny days. I knew with such a design I would be ameliorating times that were in fact troubled, but my intention above all was to combine a fairly modern design with my own vision of the 1930s, rather than aim for a reproduction of the period itself. As many of the works of Vida

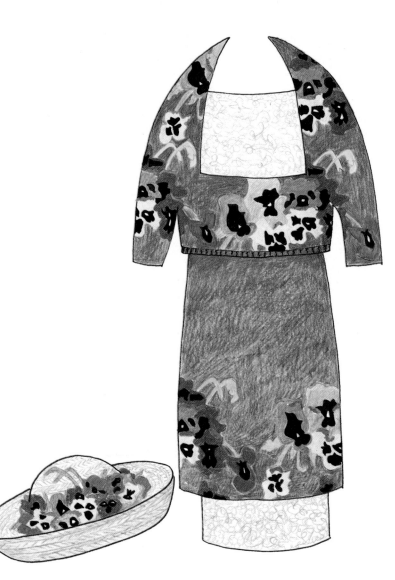

Lunchtime

Measurements

Top   One Size (Small–Medium)

Actual Garment
Measures (*approx,
at armholes*):   107 cm
Length (*approx*):   50 cm
Sleeve Seam
(*approx*):   36 cm

Skirt

Length (*approx,
excluding waistband*):   78 cm

Materials

CLECKHEATON 8 PLY MACHINE WASH (*50g balls*)

	Top	Skirt	Leg Warmers
Main Colour (MC) Brown	7	14	3 balls
Contrast 1 (C1) Black	2	1	sm. qn. ball/s

Contrast 2 (C2) White	1	1	″	″	ball
Contrast 3 (C3) Yellow	1	1	″	″	ball
Contrast 4 (C4) Pale Pink	1	1	″	″	ball
Contrast 5 (C5) Pink	1	1	″	″	ball
Contrast 6 (C6) Red	1	1	″	″	ball
Contrast 7 (C7) Lilac	1	1	″	″	ball
Contrast 8 (C8) Blue	1	1	″	″	ball

AND CLECKHEATON MERINO 8 PLY (*50g balls*)

Contrast 9 (C9) Green	1	1	″	″	ball

AND GOLD METALLIC THREAD (C10)

(worked double)	1	1	″	″	ball

Small quantities of all colours used for
Hat Trimming.

NOTE: *Quantities are approximate as they vary
between knitters.*

One pair each 4.00mm (No 8) and 3.25mm
(No 10) knitting needles; a stitch holder *for
top*; 1 pkt yarn bobs; lace *for insert of Top
and for underskirt of Skirt*; knitting-in elastic
for Skirt; length of round elastic *for Skirt*;
hat *for trimming*; crochet hook *for trimming*;
knitter's needle for sewing seams.

Tension

22 sts and 30 rows to 10cm over stocking
st using 4.00mm needles and Machine
Wash.

NOTE: *Gold Metallic thread is worked double at all
times.*

Back

Using 3.25mm needles and MC, cast on
101 sts.
Work 9 rows stocking st.
Next Row: Knit. (ridge for hemline)
Change to 4.00mm needles.
1st Row: K1, * P1, K1, rep from * to end.
1st row forms moss st patt.
Work a further 9 rows moss st, dec once
in centre of last row . . . 100 sts.
Work in patt as shown on Graph A, inc
one st at each end of 6th and foll 5th rows
until there are 120 sts (row 51 completed).
Tie a coloured marker at each end of last

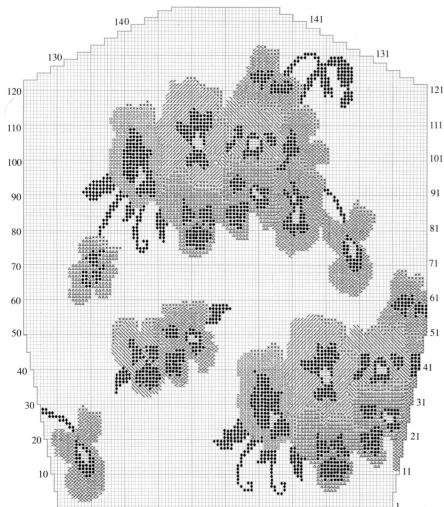

GRAPH A

row to mark armholes.
Cont straight in patt as shown on Graph until row 122 has been completed.

SHAPE SHOULDERS:
Keeping patt correct from Graph, cast off 4 sts at beg of next 22 rows.
Cast off rem 32 sts loosely.

Front

Work as for Back (working from Graph B) until row 50 of Graph has been completed . . . 118 sts.

SHAPE NECK:
Next Row: Inc in first st, patt 26, turn.
Tie a coloured marker at beg of last row to mark armhole.
Cont on these 28 sts.
Cont straight in patt as shown on Graph until row 78 has been completed.
Keeping patt correct, inc one st at end (neck edge) of next and foll 4th rows until there are 39 sts. (row 119 completed)
Work 3 rows straight in patt as shown on Graph.

SHAPE SHOULDER:
Keeping patt correct from Graph, cast off 4 sts at beg of next and alt rows 10 times in all, AT SAME TIME inc one st at neck edge in foll 4th rows from previous inc 5 times . . . 4 sts.
Work 1 row.
Cast off.
Slip next 64 sts on to stitch holder and leave.
With right side facing, join yarn to rem sts and work to correspond with side just completed, reversing shaping and working from Graph for right side of neck.

Left Sleeve

Using 3.25 mm needles and MC, cast on 47 sts.
Work 10 rows moss st as for Back, inc once in centre of last row . . . 48 sts.
Change to 4.00mm needles.
Work in patt as shown on Graph C, inc one st at each end of 2nd and foll 3rd rows until there are 114 sts.
Work 2 rows patt (row 100 completed).
Cast off loosely.

Right Sleeve

Work as for Left Sleeve, noting to work from Graph D instead of Graph C.

Neckband

Join shoulder seams. With right side facing, slip sts from front stitch holder on to a 3.25mm needle.
Using MC, 1st Row: K31, K2 tog, K31.
Work 11 rows moss st.
Next Row: Moss 10, cast off next 43 sts, moss 10.
Cont in moss st on last 10 sts until work is length required to fit (slightly stretched) up right side of neck and across half back neck.
Cast off.
With wrong side facing, join MC to rem 10 sts and work other side to correspond.
Join ends of neckband at centre back neck.

Making Up

Sew neckband in position. Join sleeve and side seams to coloured markers. Sew in sleeves. Fold lower edge on to wrong side at ridge and slip stitch in position. Sew lace insert in position on front.

KEY

MC	=	□
C1	=	●
C2	=	—
C3	=	△
C4	=	╱
C5	=	╲
C6	=	<
C7	=	○
C8	=	>
C9	=	◆
C10	=	✕

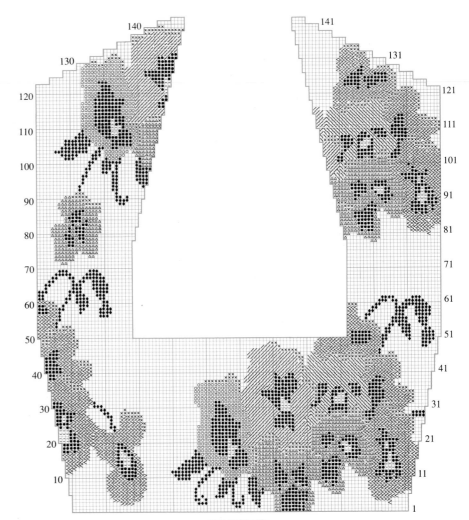

GRAPH B

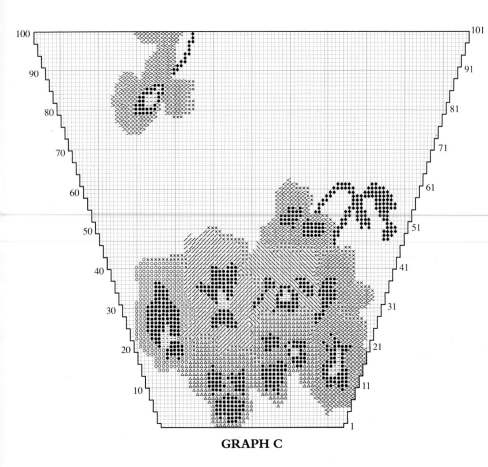

GRAPH C

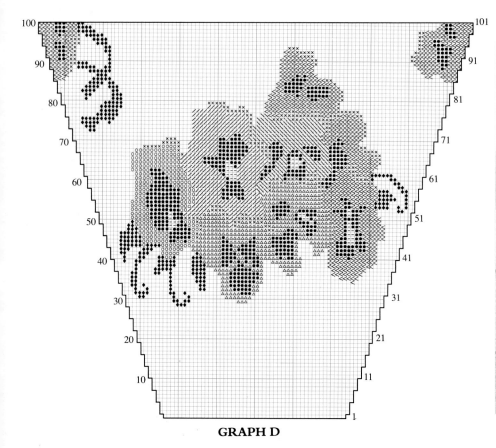

GRAPH D

Skirt
Back and Front (alike)
Using 3.25mm needles and MC, cast on
111 sts.
Work 10 rows stocking st.
Next Row: K1, * y fwd, K2 tog, rep from *
to end. (eyelet row)
Work 9 rows stocking st, beg with a purl
row and dec once in centre of last
row . . . 110 sts.
Change to 4.00mm needles.
Work in patt as shown on Graph E until
row 180 has been completed.
Keeping patt correct from Graph, dec one
st at each end of next and foll 4th rows
until 88 sts rem (row 221 completed).
Work 3 rows straight.
Change to 3.25mm needles, MC and
knitting-in elastic tog.
Work 20 rows K1, P1 rib.
Cast off in rib.

Making Up
Join side seams. Fold lower edge on to
wrong side at eyelet row and slip stitch in
position. Thread round elastic through
rows of rib at waist and draw up to
desired measurement. Make underskirt so
that 12cm will be showing at lower edge
when underneath skirt.

Leg Warmers

Using 3.25mm needles, MC and knitting-in elastic tog, cast on 64 sts.
Work 20 rows K1, P1 rib.
Change to 4.00mm needles and yarn only.
Work in patt as shown on Graph F, inc one st at each end of first and foll 10th rows until there are 80 sts (row 71 completed).
Cont straight as shown on Graph until row 84 has been completed.
Change to 3.25mm needles, MC and knitting-in elastic tog.
Work 26 rows K1, P1 rib.
Cast off loosely in rib.

Making Up

Join side seams.

Hat Trimming

Using 3.25mm needles and stocking st, make 3 pansies (see Graph G) in each colour except green, black, white, brown and metallic thread. Oversew top edges with doubled metallic thread. Attach pansies randomly over crown of hat. Vines (make 4) – Crochet a simple chain stitch either side of a pipe cleaner. Turn over top and catch stalk with remaining thread. Bind into S shapes and tuck end under pansy. Attach firmly.

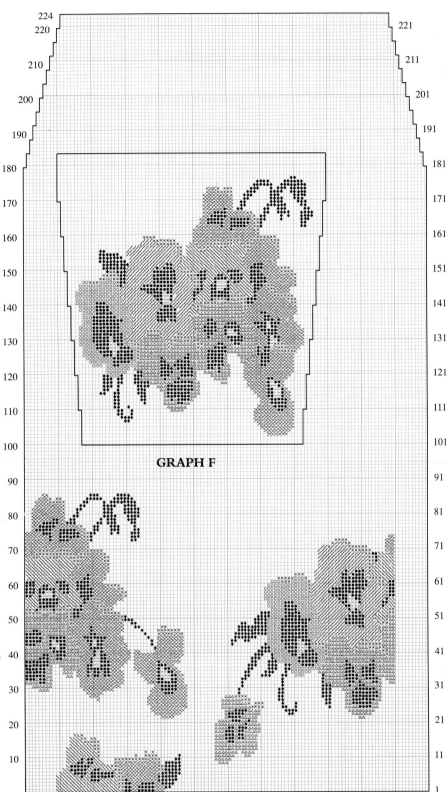

GRAPH F

GRAPH G

GRAPH E

KEY

MC	=	●
C1	=	I
C2	=	△
C3	=	II
C4	=	▲
C5	=	◮
C6	=	O
C7	=	✚
C8	=	✕
C9	=	◇
C10	=	◥

Cretonne Curtain

Measurements

Jumper	Small	Medium	Large
Actual Garment			
(approx, at armholes):	111	116	121 cm
Length (approx):	66	67	68 cm
Sleeve Seam			
(approx):	39	39	39 cm

Shorts	One Size only	
Fits Hips (approx)	80–95	cm
Length (approx,		
including waistband):	55	cm

Materials

CLECKHEATON 8 PLY MACHINE WASH (*50g balls*)
Main Colour
(MC) Black

	Small	Medium	Large
Jumper	5	5	6 balls
Shorts		10	balls
Contrast 1			
(C1) White			
Jumper	3	3	4 balls
Shorts		4	balls
Contrast 2			
(C2) Pink			
Jumper only	7	7	8 balls
Contrast 3			
(C3) Red			
Jumper only	3	3	4 balls
Contrast 4			
(C4) Grey			
Jumper only	3	3	3 balls
Contrast 5			
(C5) Pale Pink			
Jumper	1	1	1 ball
Shorts		1	ball
Contrast 6			
(C6) Lilac			
Jumper	1	1	1 ball
Shorts		1	ball
Contrast 7			
(C7) Light Grey			
Jumper only	1	1	1 ball
Contrast 8			
(C8) fuchsia			
Jumper	1	1	1 ball
Shorts		1	ball
Contrast 9			
(C9) Tan			
Jumper only	1	1	1 ball

AND CLECKHEATON MERINO 8 PLY (*50g balls*)
Contrast 10
(C10) Green

	Small	Medium	Large
Jumper only	1	1	1 ball

NOTE: *Quantities are approximate as they vary between knitters.*

One pair each 3.25mm (No 10) and 4.00mm (No 8) knitting needles; 2 stitch holders *for Jumper:* 2 small and 2 large beads for bird eyes *for Jumper;* shoulder pads *for Jumper* (optional); length of flat elastic *for Shorts;* length of braid *for Shorts* (optional); knitters needle for sewing seams and embroidery.

Tension

22 sts and 30 rows to 10cm over stocking st using 4.00mm needles.

Jumper
Back

Using 3.25mm needles and MC, cast on 104 (110–116) sts.
Work 20 rows K1, P1 rib, inc one st at each end of last row . . . 106 (112–118) sts.
Change to 4.00mm needles.
Work in patt as shown on Graph A, inc one st at each end of 6th and foll 5th rows 6 times in all, then in foll 10th rows 3 times . . . 124 (130–136) sts.
Cont without shaping until row 102 has been completed.
Tie a marker at each end of last row to mark armholes. **
Cont without shaping until row 178 (180–182) has been completed.

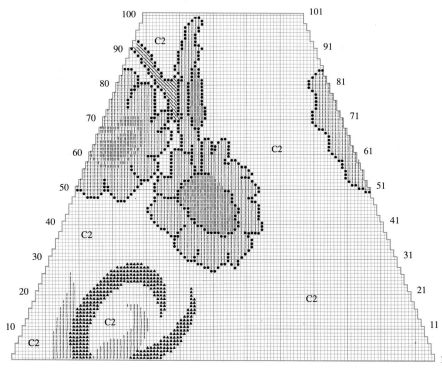

GRAPH B

GRAPH A

SHAPE SHOULDERS:
Keeping colours correct as placed in last row, cast off 13 (14–15) sts at beg of next 4 rows, then 14 (15–16) sts at beg of foll 2 rows.
Leave rem 44 sts on a stitch holder.

Front

Work as for Back to **.
Cont without shaping until row 164 has been completed.

SHAPE NECK:
Next Row: Patt 45 (48–51), turn.
Cont on these 45 (48–51) sts.
Keeping patt correct, dec one st at neck edge in alt rows 5 times . . . 40 (43–46) sts.
Work 5 rows patt.

SHAPE SHOULDER:
Keeping colours correct as placed in last row, cast off 13 (14–15) sts at beg of next row and foll alt row, then 14 (15–16) sts at beg of foll alt row.
Slip next 34 sts onto stitch holder and leave. With right side facing, join yarn to rem sts and work to correspond with other side, reversing shaping.

Sleeves

Using 4.00mm needles and C2, cast on 126 sts.
Work in patt as shown on Graph B, dec one st at each end of 3rd and 6th rows, then in foll 2nd and 3rd rows alternately until 48 sts rem.

Work 2 rows patt, thus completing row 100.
Change to 3.25mm needles and C2.
Work 18 rows K1, P1 rib.
Cast off loosely in rib.

Neckband

Join right shoulder seam. With right side facing, using 3.25mm needles and MC, knit up 104 (108–112) sts evenly around neck, incl sts from stitch holders.
Work 21 rows K1, P1 rib.
Cast off loosely in rib.

Making Up

Join left shoulder and neckband seam. Sew beads on bird for eyes, on back and front as illustrated. Using stem st embroider detail on back and front as illustrated. Join sleeve and side seams to markers. Sew in sleeves. Fold neckband in half on to wrong side and slip stitch loosely

---

Shorts
Right Side

Using 4.00mm needles and MC, cast on 160 sts.
Work 6 rows stocking st.
Work in patt as shown on Graph C, until row 30 has been completed.
Keeping patt correct from graph, dec one st at each end of next and foll 10th rows 6 times in all . . . 148 sts.
Work 8 rows patt.

SHAPE CROTCH:
Keeping patt correct from graph.
Next Row: Cast off 16 sts, patt to end.
Next Row: Cast off 11 sts, patt to end.
Next Row: Cast off 4 sts, patt to end.
Next Row: Cast off 2 sts, patt to end.
Next Row: Cast off 2 sts, patt to end.
Cont in patt from graph from row 95 onwards, noting casting off and dec, until row 166 has been completed . . . 76 sts.
NOTE: *When turning, bring yarn to front of work, slip next st on to right-hand needle, yarn back, slip st back on to left-hand needle, then turn and proceed as instructed. This avoids holes in work.*

Working rem in MC. *Next Row*: K25, turn.
Next Row: Purl to end.
Next Row: Knit across all sts to end.
Next Row: P35, turn.

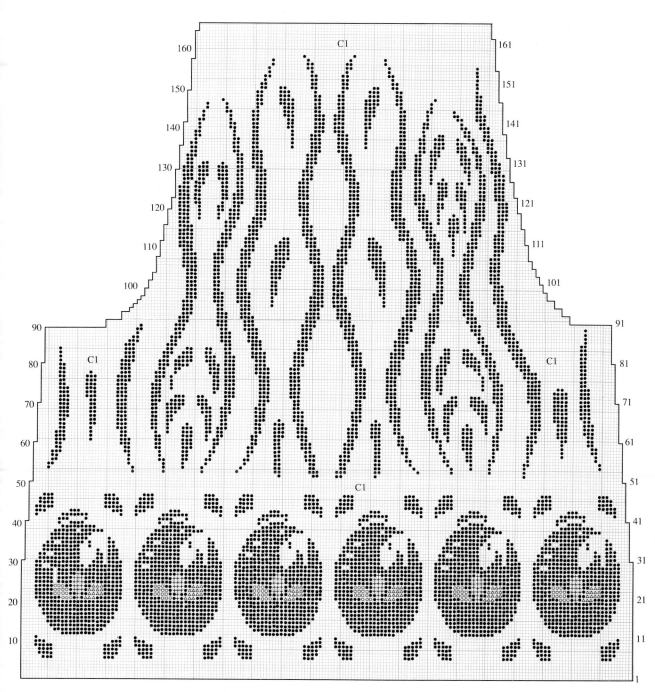

GRAPH C

Next Row: Knit to end.
Next Row: Purl across all sts to end . . . 76 sts.
Change to 3.25mm needles and MC.
Work 20 rows K1, P1 rib.
Cast off loosely in rib.

Left Side

Work to correspond with Right Side, reversing patt (as indicated on Graph C) and shaping.

Making Up

Join fronts and back together from waistband to crotch. Join front and back inside leg seams. Fold ribbed waistband in half on to wrong side and slip stitch loosely in position leaving 3cm unsewn for elastic insertion. Thread elastic through waistband and draw up to desired measurement. Sew braid around hem, if desired.

A View of the Artist's House and Garden in Mills Plains, Van Diemen's Land

JOHN GLOVER

Interpreted by Moreen Clark

John Glover's painting was a surprising mixture of the old and the new—a lovely English garden amidst the Tasmanian wilderness and flourishing under blue skies with a familiar backdrop of gumtree-covered hills.

John Glover's painting of his house and garden at Mills Plains near Launceston, has always been one of my favourites since I saw it for the first time in the Art Gallery of South Australia when I was a young high school student.

Weekends in Adelaide in those days were fairly quiet, particularly on a Sunday, so the art gallery and museum next door were places of interest where a lazy afternoon could be spent looking at original paintings and sculptures. Art was my favourite subject at school so I became a frequent visitor to the gallery studying the techniques of the various artists, and becoming familiar with Australian scenery as it was depicted by the early European artists.

John Glover's painting was a surprising mixture of the old and the new—a lovely English garden amidst the Tasmanian wilderness and flourishing under blue skies with a familiar backdrop of gumtree-covered hills. It seemed to me an odd mixture at the time, but nevertheless a very beautiful idea. I could imagine the rose perfume in that garden in the morning, with the dew heavy on the roses, as a powerful presence in the valley.

As I lived in the driest state in Australia with a rainfall of ten inches every year, the first thing that occurred to me when looking at the massive, planned garden was how, in 1835, did they water it? But of course there was convict labour in those days and the rainfall in that part of Tasmania is both consistent and high. The

tree ferns in the painting are completely unsheltered and look rather out of place because I am used to seeing them in a rainforest. These practical considerations added another dimension to the charm of the painting.

Memories of these early impressions made the choice of interpreting John Glover in knitting, an easy one. A shawl captures the sense of that period and is a garment a woman may well have worn as she strolled through the garden. Vests were worn by gentlemen of the time—but not quite in the manner I have chosen to knit. In that sense I chose to bring the painting into the twentieth century.

The technical details of the interpretation, the drawing of the graphs and the writing of the patterns were the hardest part of the exercise for me, because I usually work in a free-style manner or on impulse.

I've used a wide range of wools and fibres because I wanted the visual impact to mirror the original painting but in brighter, clearer colours; age and varnish have darkened the colours originally used.

Contrary to the painting, whenever I have visited Launceston the sky has either been very blue with a few clouds, or grey and wintry, so I've made the upper sky quite blue and introduced that colour lower down in some of the flowers and leaves.

The afternoon sun that backlights the whole area of the painting haloes the distant trees with a golden light throwing shadows forward. The sun also highlights the flowering broom, hollyhocks and roses, giving some brilliant colours while shading others, so I've juxtaposed many different shades of pink, red and yellow to this effect. Anyone attempting this embroidery will be able to experiment as I have done to gain different and exciting effects. I hope they will feel free to try out their own ideas.

The shades of green in the embroidery have caused me the most angst. Because they are so varied in the painting and any wool range is limited, I've used combinations of browns and greens, blues and greens, blues and yellows, and yellows and greens to gain the impression of the Australian greens in the original.

painting was birds. Tasmania is full of blackbirds and plovers. They love water, and the pond in Glover's painting would have encouraged a lot of birdlife. Perhaps Glover didn't think them important enough. For a man who painstakingly painted each fallen petal, it seems odd not to have a flight of birds in the background somewhere.

As an artistic setting for his house and studio, Glover's flowering garden seems slightly impractical in some ways, but still a marvellous achievement in successfully transplanting a beautiful, scented, English garden into a wild Australian setting.

Having the full range of Cleckheaton colours to choose from has made this possible, and in some instances multi-coloured threads have been placed alongside single colours to get the changes of sunlight and shadow in the foreground, on the distant slopes, in the trees and on the background slopes.

Where I have used one or two stitches only of colour, I have Swiss darned rather than knitted the wool in, therefore avoiding a lot of joins on the back of the garment. I have glass-beaded in places to accentuate the colour, texture and sparkle of leaves and flowers as they catch the light.

The one thing I found missing in the

Glover waited for it to grow and at the age of 63, he painted it. In 1835 he exhibited the painting at the *London Exhibition* for the whole art world to see. This was Glover's record of what he knew would be his final resting place. It was to be an answer to all his critics as he proclaimed that 'here was his new house and studio, his new garden and his new country'—Tasmania, Australia.

I feel honoured to have the permission of the Art Gallery of South Australia to interpret John Glover's work.

Creative Dimensions

Moreen Clark, the 'Grandma Moses' of Australian art knits, lives near the Murray River in Mannum, South Australia. Moreen has been a school-teacher for more than 30 years, has nine children and numerous grandchildren. She began knitting as a child and like many women of her generation has always sewed and knitted for her children. But it was with the birth of her first granddaughter about eight years ago that Moreen began to explore new creative dimensions.

As Moreen says:

I never really had the time with my own children to develop aspects of embroidery and knitting which interested me. With my first grandchild, I wanted to create something memorable, more exuberant and colourful than my former efforts.

I've always loved the landscape around me and its colours. The river, the Flinders Ranges, the desert, the birds and the wildflowers, the sheep grazing and their beautiful fleece moved me to interpret them in my knitting and embroidery. Living here amongst it all, it seems natural that the childrens' garments should reflect this.

A springtime trip to the Flinders Ranges with her husband, Don, some years ago was such a visual delight that the images of cockatoos, eagles, galahs, wildflowers and changing light over the ranges made her realise that she had found the vocabulary for which she had been searching.

Recently Moreen visited one of her daughters who was living at Mount Elvira

Station, near Lake Barlee in Western Australia. She describes the landscape: 'It is such a beautiful place, full of blue hills, salt lakes, granite outcrops, orange and cream and purple breakaways, salmon gums, saltbush and bluebush, wild goats and kangaroos'. She was so taken by the richness of it all that she knitted and embroidered a full coat, capturing the essence of the place.

The garment, which is called *Over the Bluebush and Breakaways the Cockatoos are Flying*, is covered in West Australian wildflowers, which grow on the property along the bushtracks and near the billabongs where the wild horses drink. It is a poem about Australia.

Moreen uses both natural fleeces and commercial wools for her knitted pieces. The natural fleece lends itself to a more earthy, chunky look, and the commercial yarn to a more sophisticated garment.

Moreen says: 'I usually hand pick my own fleeces and have them spun for me. I have in the past dyed my own wool with vegetable dyes, but because it is so time consuming I now use chemical dyes. However, I'm growing gums in my garden so that I can use the bark for further wool dyeing when I have the time'.

Because of Moreen's duties as a full-time schoolteacher at the local high school, and her occasional forays with Don to remote country areas, her time for knitting is limited. But four or five nights a week and most weekends she either knits or embroiders.

Although Moreen has had little formal art training except for part-time instruction, she has an innate colour and design sense. Her work has a naive, primitive feel, reminiscent of Grandma Moses and a vitality and freshness, which is very appealing.

She either has knitted for her, or knits herself, the basic garment in suitable background colours. Then, usually without reference to a sketch of any kind, she begins encrusting the surface with a multi-coloured landscape. Recently she has added beading, which further enriches the work. A major piece may take Moreen a couple of

months or more, so her output is not large.

Because she chooses to knit and embroider for her large family, commercial orders are sandwiched in between. When I first visited Moreen in her secluded stone farmhouse set among fruit trees, drying on the clothes line were two tiny, black, knitted and embroidered children's dresses. These were garments belonging to Maya and Angelique her small granddaughters who live with her. Strewn around the verandah were other such potential heirlooms, drying in the sun.

Over the centuries needlework has been mostly a woman's province, and the skills have been handed down from mother to daughter. Moreen's mother used to spend the evenings knitting and sewing and Moreen's daughter, Jo and future daughter-in-law Kaylene, are also following in her footsteps. Jo knits and fashions the beautiful handmade buttons that adorn her mother's jumpers. Kaylene has just knitted and embroidered her first major piece. The Clark household has an ambience that encourages garments to be created in a uniquely Australian idiom.

Giving expression to their talents in their own idiosyncratic vernacular, they are aspiring through traditionally female creative avenues to achieve a valid place in the milieu of Australian art.

Moreen's work was shown in a major exhibition for the first time at the Art Gallery of New South Wales in 1988, in *Art Knits*, curated by Jane de Teliga. Her work was also selected to be shown at the Victoria and Albert Museum in London in the 1989 *Contemporary Art of Dress* exhibition. The Powerhouse Museum in Sydney has commissioned a tea cosy, which will be added to their collection this year.

In Moreen's words: 'If no one bought my coats I would still make them because that is how I express myself and my love for this country'.

Shawl

Measurements

Width (*across top*)	244 cm
Length (*from point to centre of long edge, excluding fringe*)	90 cm

Materials

CLECKHEATON 8 PLY MACHINE WASH (*50g balls*)

Bright Blue	2 balls
Mid Blue	2 balls
Pale Blue	2 balls
Aqua	2 balls

1 ball each of all other colours and yarns used in Vest (see page 198), AND 4 balls of desired colour for fringe (*Note*: fringe may be worked in colours to match knitting but you may require an extra ball of some colours).

One long 4.00mm (No 8) circular knitting needle; 7.00mm (No 2) crochet hook; tapestry needle for embroidery; knitters needle for sewing seams; hanks of compatible crewel or tapestry yarns in a selection of contrasting colours as listed for Vest; a selection small glass beads to enhance flowers and foliage.

NOTE: *Foreground colours are worked in random stripes in various yarns and colours as indicated on Graph. Before commencing garment, wind off lengths of various yarns and colours into balls (using mixtures as indicated on Graph as a guide), joining together with knots and leaving ends 15cm long. This will enable yarns in each section to be knitted in at random.*

CODE

Light green	=	L GR
Dark green	=	D GR
Dark brown	=	D BR
Goldy brown	=	G B
Black	=	BL
Ochre brown	=	O
Rust	=	R
Brown	=	BR

KEY

Gold/Green	=	✗
Gold/Brown	=	O

Tension

22 sts and 30 rows to 10cm over stocking st, using 4.00mm needles.

Shawl

Using Dull Brown and a 4.00mm circular needle, cast on 3 sts.
Using browns, red, greens and dark purples, work in stocking st, inc one st at each end of 3rd and every row until there are 295 sts.
Work in patt as shown on Graph, inc one st at each end of every row until row 110 has been completed . . . 515 sts.
Using Bright Blue, work 11 rows stocking st, inc one st at each end of every row . . . 537 sts.
Next Row: (wrong side – foldline) knit.
Using Bright Blue work 10 rows stocking st, dec one st at each end of every row . . . 517 sts.
Cast off loosely.

Making Up

Using 'knitting stitch' embroider Gold green and Gold brown as indicated on Graph. Using Diagram and photographs as a guide, embroider flowers and foliage in foreground using suitable and varied embroidery sts. Attach matching beads, concentrating on leaves and grass. Fold top edge onto wrong side at foldline and stitch in position. Using hook and desired colour (or colours to match garment) attach fringe to shaped edges and along cast on edge, having 2 strands of yarn 44cm long for each piece of fringing.

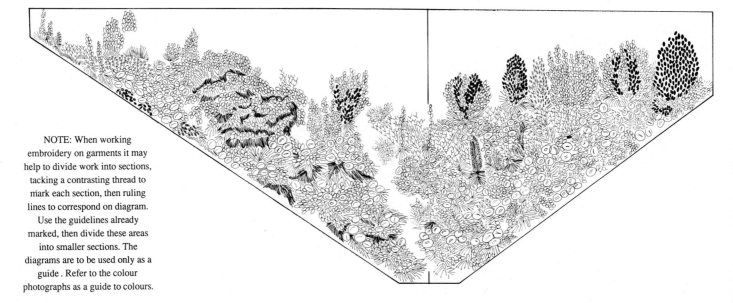

NOTE: When working embroidery on garments it may help to divide work into sections, tacking a contrasting thread to mark each section, then ruling lines to correspond on diagram. Use the guidelines already marked, then divide these areas into smaller sections. The diagrams are to be used only as a guide. Refer to the colour photographs as a guide to colours.

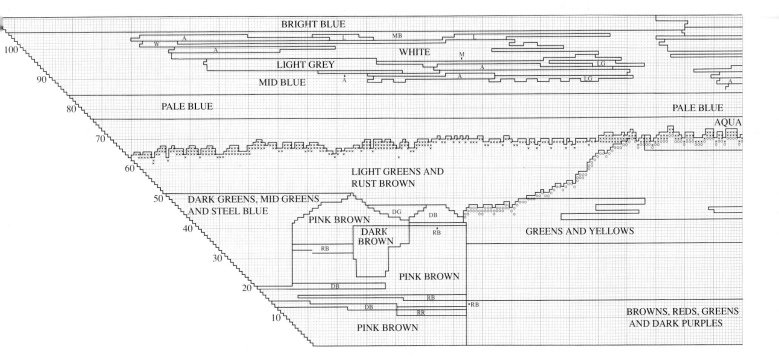

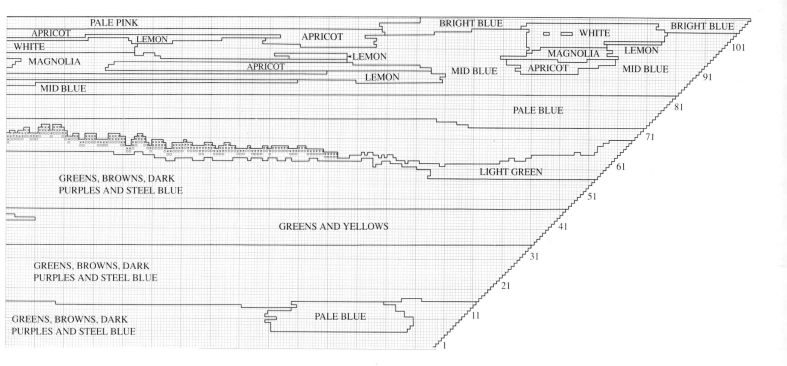

Vest

Measurements (one size only)

Actual Measurement (*approx*):	112 cm
Length (*approx*):	54 cm

Materials

CLECKHEATON 8 PLY MACHINE WASH (*50g balls*)

Mid Blue	2 balls
Dark Blue	2 balls
Pale Blue	2 balls
Black	1 ball
Dark Navy	1 ball
Dark Grey	1 ball
Taupe	1 ball
Light Grey	1 ball
Cream	1 ball
White	1 ball
Magnolia	1 ball
Bright Yellow	1 ball
Apricot	1 ball
Coral Pink	1 ball
Bright Pink	1 ball
Pale Apricot	1 ball
Pale Lavender	1 ball
Lemon	1 ball
Pale Pink	1 ball
Lilac	1 ball
Aqua	1 ball
Bright Blue	1 ball
Dark Green	1 ball
Goldy Brown	1 ball
Rust Brown	1 ball
Scarlet	1 ball
Wine Red	1 ball
Bright Red	1 ball

AND CLECKHEATON HIGHLAND 8 PLY (*50g balls*)

Steel Grey	}	1 ball
Green	with flecks of	1 ball
Purple	red, blue and	1 ball
Red Brown	aqua	1 ball

AND EMBERS 8 PLY BY CLECKHEATON (*50g balls*)

Mid Pink	1 ball
Musk	1 ball

AND COUNTRY 8 PLY BY CLECKHEATON (*50g balls*)

Rose Pink	1 ball
Dark Red	1 ball

AND WOOLRICH 8 PLY BY CLECKHEATON (*50g balls*)

Dark Green	1 ball

AND CLECKHEATON NATURAL 8 PLY (*50g balls*)

Dull Yellow	1 ball
Khaki	1 ball
Denim Blue	1 ball
Dull Brown	1 ball
Dark Brown	1 ball
Light Green	1 ball

AND CHELSEA 8 PLY BY CLECKHEATON (*50g balls*)

Blue Green	1 ball
Purple Heather	1 ball
Pink	2 balls
Brown	2 balls

NOTE: *Foreground colours are worked in random stripes in various yarns and colours as indicated on Graph. Before commencing garment, wind off lengths of various yarns and colours into balls (using mixtures as indicated on Graph as a guide), joining together with knots and leaving ends 15cm long. This will enable yarns in each section to be knitted entirely throughout using colours at random and/or in stripes to underarm (noting to keep shed and house in correct position and colours), using photographs as a guide to blending shades throughout. Try to use predominately darker shades of black, browns, greens, reds and purples nearer to cast-on edge, varying to predominately lighter shades of browns, greens and purples nearer to armhole. Keep Graph correct above underarm. It should be noted that no two garments will be alike and that your garment may vary from photograph.*

Three 4.00mm (No 8) circular knitting needles (80cm long); one pair 4.00mm (No. 8) knitting needles; stitch holder; tapestry needle for embroidery; knitters needle for sewing seams; selection of crewel or tapestry yarns in a range of suitable colours.
Greens (not bright emerald),
blue, grey, goldy greens, pale greens (not apple green), apricots, pinks, reds, purple, lavender, yellow, creamy browns, rusts, goldy browns, ochre browns and grey browns) for foliage and foreground embroidery; selection of small coloured glass beads to enhance flowers and foliage.

Tension

22 sts and 30 rows to 10cm over stocking st, using 4.00mm needles.

Vest (worked in one piece to armholes)

Using 4.00mm circular needle and Dull Brown, cast on 222 sts.
Working in stocking st from Graph throughout or using colours in random stripes throughout, work 2 rows.
Cast on 2 sts at beg of next 8 rows, then inc one st at each end of next and alt rows 4 times . . . 246 sts.
Work 63 rows patt.

DIVIDE FOR RIGHT FRONT AND SHAPE FRONT SLOPE:

Next Row: Patt 58, turn.
Cont on these 58 sts for Right Front.
Keeping Graph correct, noting that sts represented by symbols are to be embroidered on afterwards in knitting st, dec one st at end of alt rows 5 times, AT SAME TIME dec one st at beg of 2nd and foll 4th rows 18 times . . . 35 sts.
Using Bright Blue, work 9 rows stocking st. Cast off.

DIVIDE FOR BACK:

With right side facing, join yarn to rem sts, cast off next 10 sts, patt 110, turn.
Cont on these 110 sts for Back.
Keeping Graph correct, dec one st at end of alt rows 5 times . . . 100 sts.
Work 69 rows patt, noting that sts represented by symbols are to be embroidered on afterwards in knitting st.

SHAPE SHOULDERS:

Using Bright Blue, cast off 35 sts at beg of next 2 rows.
Leave rem 30 sts on stitch holder.

LEFT FRONT:

With right side facing, join yarn to rem sts, cast off next 10 sts and patt to end.
Cont on these 58 sts for Left Front.

SHAPE ARMHOLE AND FRONT SLOPE:

Keeping Graph correct, noting that sts represented by symbols are to be embroidered on afterwards using knitting st, dec one st at beg of alt rows 5 times, AT SAME TIME dec one st at end of 2nd and

foll 4th rows 18 times . . . 35 sts.
Using Bright Blue, work 9 rows stocking st.
Cast off.

Bands

Join shoulder seams. With right side facing, using three 4.00mm circular needles and Pink Brown CHELSEA 8 ply, knit up required number of sts evenly around entire outside edge, beg at centre of lower edge taking care not to stretch fabric and working in approx 3 out of every 4 sts.
Purl 10 rounds.
Cast off very loosely.
Work same band around armholes.

Making Up

Allow band to roll onto wrong side and fill by threading 4 strands of thick yarn along inside of roll. Slip stitch band neatly in position on wrong side, using small, even sts.
Using knitting st, embroider colours from Graph represented by symbols on garment above armholes. Using Diagram and photographs as a guide, embroider flowers, foliage and outline of shed and house in foreground in a variety of embroidery sts. Using knitting st and colours as desired, refering to photographs as a guide, fill in foreground around flowers and foliage to blend with and enhance rest of embroidery.
Attach matching beads, concentrating on centres of flowers, leaves and around edges of trees.

KEY

Bright yellow	=	☐
Apricot	=	●
Aqua	=	╱
Goldy green	=	▲
Pale pink	=	=
Lemon	=	‖
Light grey	=	✕
Khaki	=	✛
Pale blue	=	╲
White	=	■
Magnolia	=	○

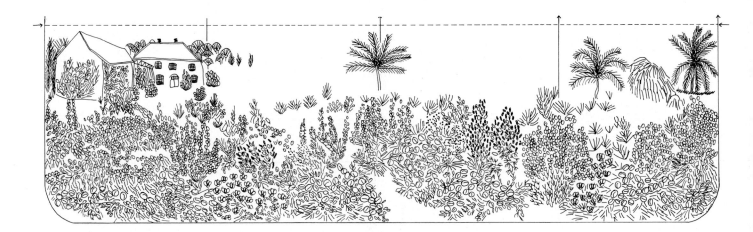

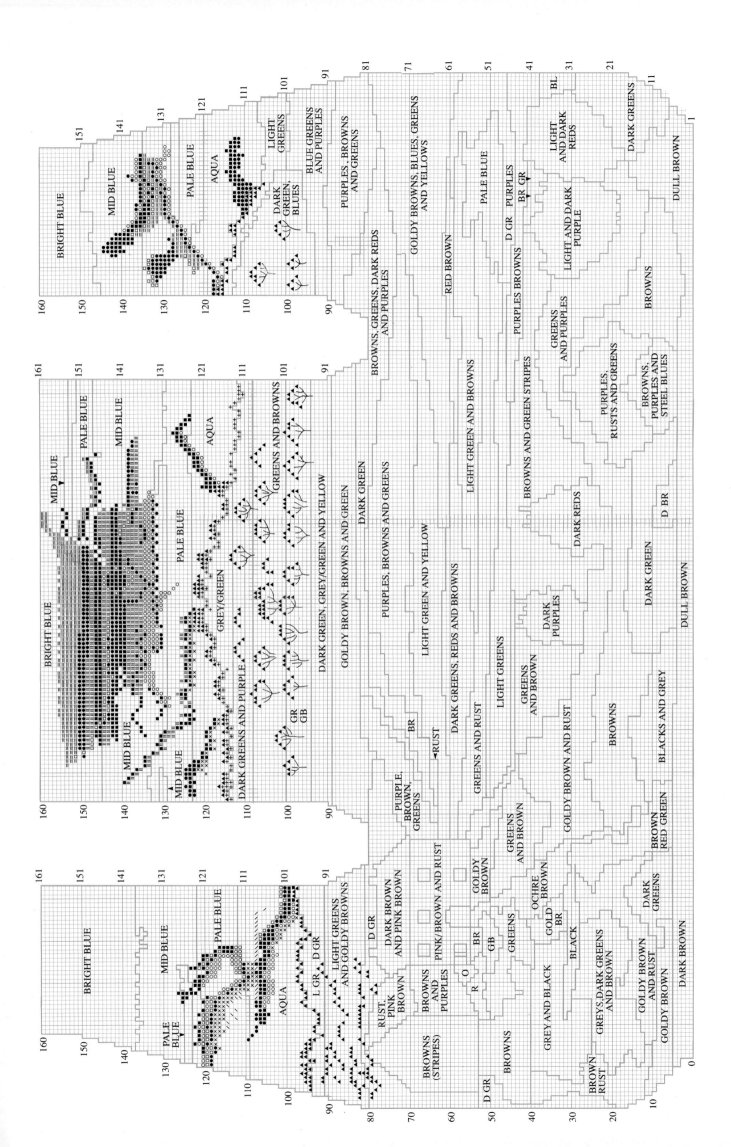

Unidentified
Found Object

CHRISTOPHER BURY

Interpreted by Michael Glover

The painting is like a static movie in an abstract vision. I see the innocent looking out to sea—and the ship sails on. The wealth of pictorial imagery is seen through the abstraction of colour, line, texture and shape.

Christopher Bury's painting *Unidentified Found Object* hangs in my living room and is a constant source of wonder and pleasure to me. I feel I have completely internalised it. I never tire of studying it.

I love the sea and it has always been a source of inspiration to me in my work. I grew up in a family who shared this affinity and my father traded in boats and made and mended his own fishing nets all his life. One of my brothers is a professional fisherman. Storm and tempest is an aspect of the sea that has never frightened me. I relate closely to this feeling of turbulence in Christopher's painting and feel at home in it.

For me the painting is like a static movie in an abstract vision. I see the innocent looking out to sea—and the ship sails on. The wealth of pictorial imagery is seen through the abstraction of colour, line, texture and shape. The imagery stirs up the emotions and I always find this a romantic notion.

In a vision, I see the shoreline as a refuge of warmth from the great force of the sea's stormy nature. Yet a sensitivity also prevails, especially through the use of colour. Primary colours have been worked in such a way as to produce over-tones. These are distinct in the nature of the painting, which combines both masculine and feminine elements. Within the painting, the forceful nature of the strong, primary colours contrasts with the softer feminine lilacs and greens. Together

they give a panoramic picture that hints at the fantastic marine world lying hidden beneath the surface.

The bottom right-hand corner of the painting reveals a rather obscure figure, which I have taken as a major component in my interpretation. Revealing itself in the shape of a shawl, this shape is repeated time and again throughout the painting. The painting presents a wild and turbulent scene yet, for me, it has a capacity to calm just through the sound of the sea alone.

I see the figure safe ashore wrapped in the warmth of a knitted garment. But its very safety places even greater emphasis on the spirit of the sea predominant in the painting. We are told many myths of what lies beneath the surface of the sea. I have approached the interpretation of this painting from what lies hidden within myself—my subconscious. From here I have wound my own myths around the painting. In the sea we are literally and figuratively out of our depth. It houses the primal mystery from which we evolved. It can never be known.

In choosing the shawl to work through my interpretation of the painting, I have chosen symbolically to allude to the shapes inherent in sails and rigging. Historically the shawl has been a garment worn by women in fishing communities since the invention of weaving. When I visited the island of Aran, the home of traditional patterned knitting, and saw the women there wrapped in the warmth of their shawls, I realised fully the practicality of the shape. Crossing over the breasts and knotted around the back, the garment keeps both the chest and the kidneys warm, but leaves the arms free for movement.

After some trial and error, I feel I have captured the true colours essential to the spirit of the painting. The bias neckline, the bib front and the tassels extend the concept of a shawl as such into the realms of a fashionable garment. I feel that women will both enjoy wearing and making the piece.

An Elusive Quality

Defining the essential Michael Glover is rather like trying to hold a cloud or a wisp of fog in your hands. The problem seems to be one of content—Michael is 90 per cent spirit and 10 per cent corporeal substance. Words like 'leprechaun' and 'sprite' spring to mind when describing him as they capture some of his elusive qualities.

Michael shares a small terrace house in Carlton with his black poodle, Poppy, his piano, his small collection of paintings and his large assortment of yarns. Looped across the ceiling of his living room is one of the fishing nets his father made and mended when Michael was a child. Above a side table hangs Christopher Bury's painting of the wild and stormy sea, *Unidentified Found* *Object*, which Michael has chosen to interpret. Michael has a deep affinity with the sea, which is the main creative force in his life:

It doesn't matter how wild the sea is, it can calm me down. Even when faced with 30-foot waves off the south-west coast of Tasmania in my father's small fishing boat, I saw the sea as a grey heaven. I spent four years surfing in huge waves off the west coast of Tasmania and I loved it. But I had to choose between doing that full time or using the sea creatively in an artistic sense. I chose the latter, but I return to the seashore constantly and swim in all weather. Lying on the beach listening to the waves always puts my mind at rest.

Currently Michael is preparing for a major exhibition based on the sea, which combines painting, knitting, music and performance. Seven knitted pieces are to be exhibited, three of which, a gown, a pillow and a shawl have already been completed. The exhibition explores the Celtic myth of the Selkie, the story of a boy lost at sea and believed drowned but who turns instead into a sea creature half seal and half man. Michael indentifies closely with the myth of the Selkie.

Michael's paintings and knitting interrelate with performance. In his 1988 exhibition at the Crafts Council Gallery in Melbourne, he knitted a tree, inhabited the trunk and with arms waving like branches gave a performance with musical accompaniment. His creative knitting is breathtaking in its audacity and originality.

Michael is of Celtic origin and is part of a large Anglo–Irish family who live in Tasmania. He grew up in Hobart near the water and remembers that his father always had a boat at anchor, ready to go fishing. Whatever spare time Michael had as a child was divided between the sea and pastoral properties owned by close relatives in the north-east of the state. His other passion, horseriding, was fostered during these years.

Michael was about eight when he learnt to knit:

My aunt taught me how to put yarn on a needle, but I taught myself how to knit. It was a necessity. I needed a pair of mittens to keep my hands warm when I was practising the piano on winter mornings. I'd watched my father making and mending his fishing nets since I was born and I think I knew intuitively how to go about knitting.

Michael absorbed other useful lessons from his parents, both of whom painted and were also creative in a practical way. They built their own house and sheds on the property and by 'making do' and improvising they became thoughful role models for Michael and his siblings.

Michael's father would convert worn-out canvas trousers, with a dinner plate as a pattern and a small hand-worked sewing machine into fishing hats for himself. Michael's mother always knitted.

Michael was educated at St Virgil's College, but transferred to Rosney College to study for his HSC. Here he took art, music and ancient history, which allowed him to explore his love of myth. He says of his schooling: 'The Brothers really understood me and I was encouraged to develop my own loves and interests.'

After graduating, Michael enrolled at the Conservatorium of Music and four years later attained a Bachelor of Arts in Music and Dance. During the course Michael took part in an opera. This awakened in him the potential for expression not only in performance but in the creation of textiles: 'I've always loved dressing up and the fantasy which comes with it. But dancing and moving inside a created garment taught me a lot more about how fabric drapes on the body. Knitted garments can be draped and shaped so expressively.'

In the latter period of his time at the Conservatorium, Michael was part of an avant-garde quartet and was strongly influenced by working with a visiting English puppeteer whose huge puppets with long tails wore exquisite fabrics. He was inspired then to pursue the creation of imaginative textiles, realising how important they were to any concept.

Michael also took a part-time course in fashion at Hobart technical college. In conjunction with his Conservatorium studies, he sketched, painted and knitted in his free time for two years. At the end of the four years, rich with ideas, Michael was ready to launch into the commercial fashion world of Melbourne.

In 1981 Michael gained a sponsorship from fashion designer, Ross Weymouth and spent a year learning the finer points of the craft through observation and practice: 'I watched everything they did as I used to watch my Dad making the fishing nets.' During the evening he attended a course at the technical college in cutting and construction of garments. Frustrated by the conventionality of the high fashion garments usually worn at the Melbourne Cup, Michael designed and wore his own knitted creation, causing quite a stir.

When Michael's apprenticeship with Ross Weymouth terminated he spent the next few years exploring techniques and creating some extraordinary one-off art knits. One knitted garment Michael undertook had 1000 stitches around the hemline and took three months to complete. Not interested in commercial production lines, Michael designed, made and sold individual pieces to suitable boutiques and individual clients.

In 1987, with a grant from the Crafts Council to study yarn innovation, Michael went to London. He visited Italy and in Florence at the 'Pitti Filati' fashion show met a British knitwear designer, Elishka Turina, with whom he shared a workroom back in London, absorbing much about yarn innovation.

Commissioned by another important Irish knitwear designer, Brinion Heaton, he designed original models that were sold in limited editions of six to wealthy American and Japanese clients. Brinion Heaton worked from Bath in England during the week and employed more than 2000 knitters throughout the British Isles. During the weekend she would return to Ireland, and Michael took the opportunity to do the same. He travelled to Donegal in Galway and visited the countryside from which his paternal grandparents, the Knights, had set forth for Australia in their own boat in 1857. Michael says of the experience: 'I felt I'd come home. I loved the countryside, the environment and the extraordinary creativity of the people.'

In 1987 Michael returned to Melbourne and re-experienced an overwhelming sense of the beauty of Australia, the colour of its skies and the quality of its light. As he says: 'There is such a wealth of resources here for the artist that I knew in spite of the many tempting offers to remain abroad that Australia was central to my vision in art.'

Within three months of his return Michael was preparing for a major exhibition at the Crafts Gallery in Melbourne for which he created several large and spectacular pieces.

Preferring to create individual garments, Michael designed one-off art knits for a special clientele and in 1988 also joined RMIT as a part-time teacher in textiles. He encourages hand knitting and is a wonderful role model in the garments he both knits

and wears. In an area where few teachers in textiles seriously promote the artistic and unique possibilities of hand knitting, the next generation of creative hand knitters in Victoria may owe their vision to Michael Glover's efforts. Michael does not deny the value of machine knitting, particularly from a commercial point of view. Pragmatically he realises that most students will be forced to earn their living using this technique. ·

Michael knits constantly. A range of one-off hats, using a variety of handspun and commercial yarns, have found a ready market. The short, black, curly hair from his poodle, Poppy, is soon to be spun into yarn for one of Michael's hats. Michael loves the sociable nature of knitting and even takes his current creation with him to the movies. He says that he can 'feel' the colours in the dark and has no trouble changing over from one to the other. 'Like a knitter drowsed, whose fingers play in skilled unmindfulness', Michael personifies Thomas Hardy's vision of the knitter.

In the future, Michael would like to explore further the knowledge of yarn innovation he acquired in Europe and the United Kingdom. He would like to develop and be instrumental in marketing a much wider range of yarns in Australia, but would need a future grant to do so as he lacks the resources himself. As he points out: 'This year's grants of any size have once again gone to painters and sculptors. Textiles are the poor relation and not considered seriously worthy of substantial funding. But I'll keep applying.'

Perhaps in view of Michael Glover's high fashion profile the decision-makers may be convinced that Michael's vision is worthy of support in future grants. Michael was featured prominently in the Bicentennial edition of *Fashion Australia* and was included in the *Art Knits* exhibition curated by Jane de Teliga in 1988. Michael helped curate and was a contributor to *Men Knitting*, an exhibition held at the Argyle Centre in Sydney in 1988. His name is synonymous with art knits in Australia.

Measurements (one size only)

Width (*across top – approx*)	270 cm
Length (*from point to centre of long edge, excluding edging – approx*):	118 cm

Materials

CLECKHEATON – THE BOUTIQUE COLLECTION:
RIVERINA 5 PLY (*50g balls*)

Main Colour (MC) Royal Blue	12 balls
Contrast 1 (C1) Navy Blue	5 balls
Contrast 2 (C2) Light Green	1 ball
Contrast 3 (C3) Mauve	1 ball

AND CLECKHEATON WOOLRICH 8 PLY (*50g balls*)

Contrast 4 (C4) Dark Green	5 balls
Contrast 5 (C5) Yellow	1 ball

AND CLECKHEATON 8 PLY MACHINE WASH (*50g balls*)

Contrast 6 (C6) Light Blue with coloured flecks	1 ball

AND CLECKHEATON 5 PLY MACHINE WASH (*50g balls*)

Contrast 7 (C7) Red	1 ball
Contrast 8 (C8) Bright Pink	1 ball

One 4.00mm (No 8) circular knitting needle (80cm long); 4.00mm (No 8) crochet hook; 2 of a set of 4.00mm knitting needles; knitters needle for sewing seams.

Tension

23 sts and 31 rows to 10cm over stocking st, using 4.00mm needles and MC.

NOTE: *This garment has been designed at a looser tension than normally recommended for 5 ply and uses a mixture of 5 and 8 plys for texture.*

Left Side

Using 4.00mm needles and MC, cast on 3 sts.

Work 16 rows stocking st, inc one st at end (left edge) of 7th and foll alt rows . . . 8 sts.

17th Row: Work first 4 sts of 25th row of Graph A, using MC, knit to last st, inc in last st . . . 9 sts.

** Keeping Graph correct as *placed* in last row, cont until the 32nd row has been completed, AT SAME TIME inc one st at end of alt rows.

Using MC, work 2 rows stocking st, inc one st at end of first row.

Next Row: Using C1, knit to last st, inc in last st.

Next Row: Using C1, knit.

Next Row: Using C1, purl to last st, inc in last st.

Next Row: Using C1, knit. **

31st Row: Work first 6 sts of 21st row of Graph A, using MC, knit to last st, inc in last st . . . 16 sts.

Rep from ** to ** . . . 24 sts.

49th Row: Work 17th row of Graph A across next 16 sts, using MC, knit to last st, inc in last st . . . 25 sts.

Rep from ** to ** . . . 35 sts.

71st Row: Work 13th row of Graph A across next 16 sts, using MC, knit to last st, inc in last st . . . 36 sts.

Rep from ** to ** . . . 48 sts.

97th Row: Work 9th row of Graph A across next 16 sts, using MC, knit to last st, inc in last st . . . 49 sts.

Rep from ** to ** . . . 63 sts.

127th Row: Work 5th row of Graph A across next 16 sts, using MC, knit to last st, inc in last st . . . 64 sts.

128th Row: Using MC, purl to last 16 sts, work 2nd row of Graph A across last 16 sts.

*** Keeping graph correct as *placed* in last row, cont until the 32nd row has been completed, AT SAME TIME inc one st at left edge in every row.

Using MC, work 2 rows stocking st, inc one st at left edge in every row.

Next Row: Using C1, knit to last st inc in last st.

Next Row: Using C1, inc in first st, knit to end.

Next Row: Using C1, purl to last st, inc in last st.

Next Row: Using C1, inc in first st, knit to end. ***

161st Row: Work 1st row of Graph A across next 16 sts, using MC, knit to last st, inc in last st . . . 97 sts.

Rep from *** to *** . . . 134 sts.

Using MC, work 2 rows stocking st, inc one st at left edge in both rows . . . 136 sts.

201st Row: Work 1st row of Graph B across next 16 sts, using MC, knit to last st, inc in last st . . . 137 sts.

Keeping graph correct as *placed* in last row, cont until the 32nd row has been completed, AT SAME TIME inc one st at left edge in every row . . . 168 sts.

**** *Next Row*: Using C1, knit to last st, inc in last st.

Next Row: Using C1, inc in first st, knit to end.

Next Row: Using C1, purl to last st, inc in last st.

Next Row: Using C1, inc in first st, knit to end.

Using MC, work 2 rows stocking st, inc one st at left edge in both rows. ****

239th Row: Work 1st row of Graph B across next 16 sts, using MC, knit to last st, inc in last st . . . 175 sts.

Keeping graph correct as *placed* in last row, cont until the 28th row has been completed, AT SAME TIME inc one st at left edge in every row . . . 202 sts.

Rep from **** to **** . . . 208 sts.

273rd Row: Work 1st row of Graph B across next 16 sts, using MC, knit to last st, inc in last st . . . 209 sts.

Keeping graph correct as *placed* in last row, cont until the 24th row has been completed, AT SAME TIME inc one st at left edge in every row . . . 232 sts.

Rep from **** to **** . . . 238 sts.

303rd Row: Work 1st row of Graph B across next 16 sts, using MC, knit to last st, inc in last st . . . 239 sts.

Keeping graph correct as *placed* in last row, cont until the 20th row has been completed, AT SAME TIME inc one st at left edge in every row . . . 258 sts.

Rep from **** to ****, using C3 in place of C1 . . . 264 sts.

329th Row: Work 1st row of Graph B across next 16 sts, using MC, knit to last st, inc in last st . . . 265 sts.

Keeping graph correct as *placed* in last

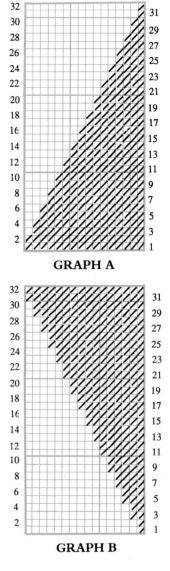

GRAPH A

GRAPH B

MC = ☐

⟋ = C8 for 17th row,
C5 for 31st row,
C6 for 49th row,
C7 for 71st row,
C4 for 97th row,
C2 for 127th row,
C3 for 161st row,
C3 for 201st row,
C2 for 239th row,
C4 for 273rd row,
C7 for 303rd row,
C6 for 329th row,
C5 for 351st row,
and C8 for 369th row.

*Keep nominated contrast colour correct until graph has been completed in each section.

row, cont until the 16th row has been completed, AT SAME TIME inc one st at left edge in every row . . . 280 sts.
Rep from **** to **** . . . 286 sts.
351st Row: Work 1st row of Graph B across next 16 sts, using MC, knit to last st, inc in last st . . . 287 sts.
Keeping graph correct as *placed* in last row, cont until the 12th row has been

completed, AT SAME TIME inc one st at left edge in every row . . . 298 sts.
Rep from **** to **** . . . 304 sts.
369th Row: Work 1st row of Graph B across next 16 sts, K48MC, K4C5, K3MC, K4C6, K3MC, K4C7, K3MC, K4C4, K3MC, K4C2, K3MC, K4C3, using MC, knit to last st, inc in last st . . . 305 sts.
Keeping graph and 4 sts in C3, C2, C4, C7, C6, and C5 correct as *placed* in last row, cont in stocking st until the 8th row of Graph B has been completed . . . 312 sts.
377th Row: Using C4, inc in first st, knit to last 2 sts, K2tog.
378th Row: Using C4, K2tog, knit to last st, inc in last st.
379th Row: Using C4, inc in first st, purl to last 2 sts, P2tog.
380th Row: As 378th row.
Using C1, work 2 rows stocking st, inc one st at right edge and dec one st at left edge in each row . . . 312 sts.
383rd Row: Using C2, work as for 377th row.
384th Row: Using C2, work as for 378th row.
385th Row: Using C2, work as for 379th row . . . 312 sts.
386th Row: Using C2, K2tog, knit to last 2 sts, K2tog.
Using C1, work 2 rows stocking st, dec one st at each end of both rows . . . 306 sts.
389th Row: Using C3, work as for 386th row.
390th Row: Using C3, work as for 386th row.
391st Row: Using C3, P2tog, purl to last 2 sts, P2tog.
392nd Row: As 390th row.
Using C1, work 2 rows stocking st, dec one st at each end of both rows . . . 294 sts.
Cast off loosely in C1.

Right Side

Using 4.00mm needles and MC, cast on 3 sts.
Work 16 rows stocking st, inc one st at beg (right edge) of 7th and foll alt rows . . . 8 sts.
17th Row: Using MC, inc in first st, work first 4 sts of 25th row of Graph A, using MC, knit to end . . . 9 sts.
Work as for Left Side until 71st row has

been completed, noting that the patt (triangles) placement remains at beg of rows and to inc at right edge of rows instead of left edge (as placed in 17th row) using MC in first st before commencing graphs (where applicable).
Rep from ** to **, using C3 in place of C1.
Cont as for Left side, reversing inc as placed in 17th row, until 161st row has been completed.
Rep from *** to *** of Left Side, noting to use C2 in place of C1.
199th Row: Using MC, inc in first st, knit to last 15 sts, work 1st row of Graph C across last 15 sts . . . 135 sts.
200th Row: Work 2nd row of Graph C across first 15 sts, using MC, purl to last st, inc in last st . . . 136 sts.
Keeping placement of Graph C correct until it has been completed then working rem in patt (as before), cont until the 368th row has been completed . . . 304 sts.
369th Row: Using MC, inc in first st, work 1st row of Graph B across next 16 sts, using MC, knit to end . . . 305 sts.
Keeping graph correct as placed in last row, cont until the 8th row of Graph B has been completed . . . 312 sts.
Complete as for Left Side from 377th row to end but noting to dec at right edge in every row and to omit shaping at straight edge, thus there will be 306 sts upon completion of 382nd row, 303 sts upon completion of 385th row, 300 sts upon completion of 388th row and 294 sts upon completion of last row.

Crochet Edging

Using 4.00mm hook and C4, make 6ch.
1st Row: Miss 2ch, 1dc in each of next 4ch.
2nd Row: 1ch, 1dc in each of next 4dc, 1dc in top of turning ch.
3rd Row: 1ch, 1dc in each of next 5dc.
4th Row: 1ch, 1dc in each of next 4dc, 1dc in top of turning ch, make 24ch, turn.
5th Row: Miss 3ch, 4tr in each of next 20ch, 1tr in each st to end.
6th Row: 1ch, 1dc in each of next 5tr, turn.
Using C1, rep rows 3 to 6 inclusive once.
Last 8 rows form patt for edging.
Cont in patt until work is long enough to fit along shaped edge of Left Side of Shawl between first and 2nd last purl ridges, ending with a 5th row. Fasten off.
Work same edging for Right Side of Shawl.

Making Up

Join pieces together along straight edges leaving seam open at lower point to top of first C8 triangle and sewing Right Side under shaping at top of Left Side – thus leaving shaping free to form a flap. Attach crochet edging to sides as illustrated.

Tubes

Using double pointed 4.00mm needles and C3, cast on 4 sts.
Knit one row. DO NOT TURN.
Slide sts to other end of needle, bring yarn firmly around back of work to beg and knit one row.
Cont throughout in this manner (knitting all rows and thus forming a tube automatically), until Tube measures 37cm from beg.
Cast off.
Make another Tube in same manner and attach one each of these Tubes around top corners of Shawl between end of edging and edge of cast off row, forming a loop with excess tubing at top of Shawl.
Make 3 more Tubes 23cm long, one in C6, one in C7 and one in C8.
Attach these Tubes in same order through C1 ridge at 323rd row of Right Side piece of Shawl so they form loops through work, having C7 in centre of Right Side and other Tubes 13 sts apart at either side.
Make another Tube 23cm long in C5 and attach to centre of Shawl in seam just below C2 ridge to form a loop.
Make another Tube 24cm long in C8 and attach in a loop to point of flap at top of Shawl so it forms a mock tassle. Catch point of flap down onto C2 ridge on Right Side of Shawl at top.
Make 3 Tubes 80cm long, one in C5, one in C6 and one in C7.
Attach each Tube to first row of C1 ridge under corresponding block of colour at top of Left Side of Shawl. Plait Tubes so that plait lies in centre third of length. When plait is completed, secure it by winding a length of C7 around where plait ends. Join ends together and attach to shaped edge above fringe.
Make 3 more Tubes 67cm long, one in C4, one in C2 and one in C3.
Attach Tubes under rem blocks so that colours correspond and complete as before.
Make 3 large Tassles using all colours and attach to each corner.

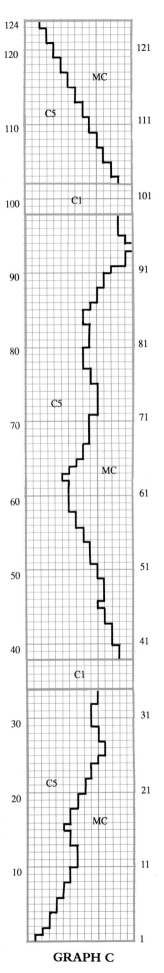

GRAPH C

Parakeets in my Garden

SALI HERMAN

Interpreted by Meryl Lloyd

The depth of the background in blacks and purples brings a feeling of mystery to the painting, a quality I am trying to achieve in the garment.

Parakeets in my Garden (1967) by Sali Herman has provided the inspiration for this early evening dress in mohair. In this semi-abstract painting with no definite lines, the relationship between vegetation and the parakeets is harmonised. I have chosen mohair as the yarn to execute this design; the fuzzy quality of mohair will help achieve this effect.

The depth of the background in blacks and purples brings a feeling of mystery to the painting, a quality I am trying to achieve in the garment, along with an ease and comfort of wearing. To achieve this depth, I picked up stitches where the green areas were and knitted three-dimensional shapes out from the surface; this also added to the movement of the garment.

The parakeets have a special place in this painting as they are united both with the painting and each other. In order to achieve this in my garment, I knitted the parakeets in a raised fancy stitch and made a feature of them on one shoulder.

I find this painting most appealing because the sense of foliage and nature are enveloped in mystery and depth. The palm leaves convey strength and the parakeets gentleness as they nestle in ones and twos, sitting contented and happy with the environment. I hope I have achieved those qualities in my mohair design.

Classic Lines

The best advertisement for a Meryl Lloyd knitted creation is Meryl Lloyd herself. Slim, attractive, blonde, blue-eyed and soft-voiced, her elegant garments seem a natural adjunct to her appearance. In a pair of tight fitting, two-toned, ski-type pants and a matching jumper she is an eye-catching display of her knitting skills.

Meryl Lloyd lives in an outer Melbourne garden suburb where she, and a newly recruited young apprentice, machine knit each day a range of garments for boutiques. They have just spent three months intensive work creating and delivering Meryl's new winter range. Hanging on a rack are a few beautiful dresses of classical design and fluid line in a range of colours. Other multi-coloured ensembles in subtle shades hang beside them. Her designs suggest the wearer's body under the soft fall of wool; the approach is very sophisticated. The attention to detail is meticulous, the finishing off exquisite, and the designs are very wearable. Meryl's garments have a timeless quality about them and you feel that an investment in one would be an astute move. They are heirlooms and the price is relative.

Meryl directs my attention to two identical ensembles, one knitted in a range of European wools, the other in Japanese processed wool. Unhappy with the latter product she explains its shortcomings to the untrained eye: 'The quality of the Japanese wool is excellent but they've dyed their wool without regard to the tonal range. Unlike the European approach, the way the Japanese eye has seen the colours is not from a feeling point of view. The blending and muting of shades in the European range is far superior and produces a more subtle finished garment.' Like all knitters she's very aware of the quality of the materials with which she has to work.

Meryl began knitting when she was very young, learning the skill from her mother. When she was five, she knitted a jumper for her small teddy bear, which he still wears as he sits on a shelf in her living room. Knitting continued as a creative recreation during her teen years and her teacher training course at Armadale, Melbourne. As part of her training at RMIT she also undertook her art training for four years.

Finishing her studies in 1971, Meryl taught as a home economics teacher for the next 12 years. During these years Meryl both painted and knitted. Of her painting she says:

In retrospect when I looked at my paintings prior to 1983, I realised that somewhere in them I had unwittingly painted a tunnel ending in darkness. It was only when I was looking at a painting I'd finished in 1984 after separation and divorce, that I actually recognised the tunnel element in my paintings and that the tunnel in the just completed piece had light at the end of it. For the latter part of my ten-year marriage I'd been subconsciously aware of problems in my marriage and expressed them in my art, but I wasn't conscious of this insight until the dilemma had worked itself through.

Fine seascapes on her walls are the distilled essence of further emotional trauma and resolution within Meryl's life. Meryl explains their history:

I became ill just before my second marriage and tried to postpone the wedding but it was as if I'd lost all my power to do so. Three days after the wedding my immune system began breaking down and within eight weeks I was taking high levels of cortisone and I wasn't getting any better. I moved up to New South Wales, leaving my husband, and lived in isolation for eighteen months slowly regaining my health. During this period and some later time at Mornington Peninsula I painted my way through again. The sea was a healing factor.

Meryl continues: 'After this time my life turned around. I think I was allergic to marriage. Unless you're married to a man of like sensibility it seems the more creative a woman is, the more difficult it can be for her. For me, in both marriages, that was the dividing line and the crippling factor. I could not be a whole person within those confines.'

During her first marriage Meryl says she knitted frenetically because her chosen career was not allowing her to express herself enough creatively. The principal at the school where she was teaching during the 1970s forbade knitting at all staff meetings. He felt she would be a bad example encouraging other female teachers to knit also. She was often the butt of sexist jokes from other male staff members for her knitting. She says: 'They never saw it as creative and original work but as something suburban and mundane. Weaving they considered "art" and was acceptable, but knitting had no status at all and was debunked.'

Meryl knitted a lot of abstract patterns during these years and explored both texture and colour. As with almost all other art knitters, colour is the siren song leading her on to create. In 1976 Meryl won two first prizes at *The Sheep Show* in Melbourne for garments knitted from very

Colour 10
(C10) Pale Pink   1   1   1 ball
Colour 11
(C11) Palest Blue   1   1   1 ball

AND CLECKHEATON MOHAIR MYSTIQUE 12 PLY
(50g balls)
Colour 12
(C12) Black with
coloured flecks   2   2   3 balls
Colour 13
(C13) Purple with
coloured flecks   2   2   3 balls
Colour 14
(C14) Jade with
coloured flecks   2   2   3 balls

AND CLECKHEATON MOHAIR 12 PLY
(50g balls)
Colour 15
(C15) Bright Red   1   1   1 ball

AND CLECKHEATON ANGORA SUPREME 8 PLY
(50g balls)
Colour 16
(C16) Yellow   1   1   1 ball

NOTE: *Quantities are approximate as they vary between knitters.*

One pair each 4.00mm (No 8) and 5.50mm (No 5) knitting needles; 4.00mm circular knitting needle . . . 80cm long; 2 stitch

GRAPH A

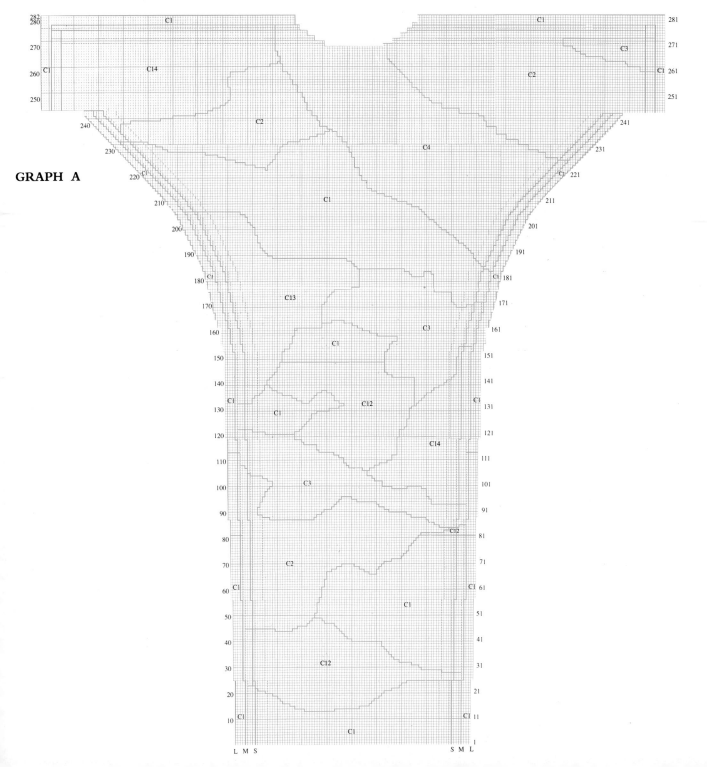

holders; knitters needle for sewing seams and embroidery; shoulder pads (optional).

Tension

17 sts and 23 rows to 10cm over stocking st, using 5.50mm needles and Mohair Classique.

SPECIAL ABBREVIATION — 'Moss St' = *1st Row*: K1, *P1, K1, rep from * to end. Rep 1st Row.

Back

Using 4.00mm needles and C1, cast on 79 (87–95) sts.
Work 6 rows Moss St.
Change to 5.50mm needles. **
Noting to keep 5 Moss Sts correct at each end in C1 until row 81 has been completed, in C12 until row 113 has been completed then in C1 for rem, work in patt as shown on Graph A (noting inc at each end) until row 152 has been completed . . . 87 (95–103) sts.

SHAPE FOR SLEEVES:
Cont in patt as shown on Graph (noting inc at each end) until row 244 has been completed (thus completing Moss St sections at sides as well) . . . 201 (209–217) sts.
Cast on 17 sts in C1 at beg of next row, then 17 sts in C14 at beg of foll row . . . 235 (243–251) sts, row 246 completed.

NOTE: *A circular needle might be easier to use at this point. Cont in patt without shaping until row 270 has been completed.*

SHAPE NECK:
Next Row: Patt 106 (110–114), turn.
Cont on these 106 (110–114) sts.
Keeping patt correct from Graph (noting to cont in Moss St and C1 from row 272 (274–278) onwards as indicated), cast off 4 sts at beg of next row, 3 sts at beg of foll alt rows twice, *Sizes Medium and Large only* — then 2 sts at beg of foll alt row, *Size Large only* — then 2 sts at beg of foll alt row.
Work 2 rows patt.

ALL SIZES — 96 (981–100) sts.
Cast off rem sts.
Slip next 23 sts on to a stitch holder and leave.
With right side facing, join yarn to rem sts and work to correspond with side just completed, reversing shaping, and working in patt as shown on Graph.

Front

Work as for Back to **.
Noting to keep 5 Moss Sts correct at each

end in C1 until row 114 has been completed, in C12 until row 166 has been completed then in C12 for rem on left side of front and C1 for rem on right side of front (see Graph B), work in patt as shown on Graph B (noting inc at each end of same rows as Back) until row 152 has been completed . . . 87 (95–103) sts.

SHAPE FOR SLEEVES:
Cont in patt as shown on Graph (noting inc at each end of same rows as Back) until row 244 has been completed . . . 201 (209–217) sts.
Cast on 17 sts in C2 at beg of next row, then 17 sts in C1 at beg of foll row . . . 235 (243–251) sts, row 246 completed.

NOTE: *A circular needle might be easier to use at this point. Cont in patt without shaping until row 250 has been completed.*

SHAPE NECK:
Next Row: Patt 112 (116–120), turn.
Cont on these 112 (116–120) sts.
Keeping patt correct from Graph, cast off 5 sts at beg of next row, 3 sts at beg of foll alt row, 2 sts at beg of foll alt rows twice, then dec one st at neck edge in next and alt rows 4 (6–8) times in all . . . 96 (98–100) sts.
Work 6 (4–4) rows patt.
Work 5 rows Moss St in C1.
Cast off rem sts.
Slip next 11 sts on to stitch holder and leave.
With right side facing, join yarn to rem sts and work to correspond with side just completed, reversing shaping, and working in patt as shown on Graph.

Neckband

Join top sleeve and shoulder seams. With right side facing, using 4.00mm circular needle and C4, knit up 107 (115–131) sts evenly around neck, incl sts from stitch holders.
Work 4 rounds K1, P1, rib.
Knit 11 rounds.
Cast off loosely.

Leaves

Small Leaf (knit up one across right shoulder from front to back and one at top of left sleeve). With right side facing, using 4.00mm needles and C3, knit up 25 sts.
Work in Moss St and keeping patt correct, inc one st at each end of 4th row, then dec one st at each end of 8th, 10th, 12th, 14th, 16th, 17th, 18th, 19th and 20th rows . . . 9sts. Cast off loosely.

Medium Leaf (knit up one in C4 section at top of right front). With right side facing, using 4.00mm needles and C3, knit up 29 sts.

Work in Moss St and keeping patt correct, inc one st at each end of 2nd, 4th, 6th and 8th rows.

Dec one st at each end of next and every row until 3 sts rem.

Next Row: Sl 1, K2 tog, psso. Fasten off.

Large Leaf (knit up 2 across C8 and C14 sections at top of left front, as illustrated). With right side facing, using 4.00mm needles and C3 knit up 33 sts.

inc one st at each end of 2nd, 4th and 6th rows.

Dec one st at each end of 8th and every row until 9sts rem.

Cast off loosely.

Making up

Join side lower and sleeve seams, leaving side seams open for last 68cm for splits. Fold neckband and last 4 sts of sleeves onto right side and catch in position. Using C7, make 2 pom-pons and attach to left shoulder, as illustrated.

GRAPH B

KEY

C1 = ●
C2 = +
C3 = △
C4 = ▲
C5 = ◇
C6 = ╱
C7 = |
C8 = ○
C9 = ✖
C10 = ◆
C11 = ╲
C12 = ✕
C13 = ＞
C14 = ■
C15 = ✱
C16 = □

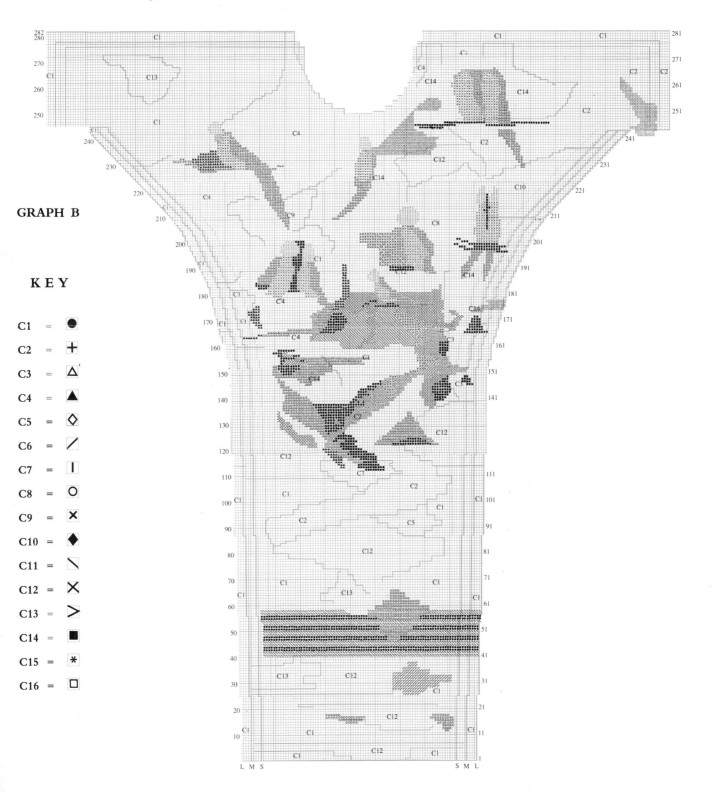

The Bridge in Curve

GRACE COSSINGTON SMITH

Interpreted by Meryl Lloyd

Grace Cossington Smith has attempted to capture the political and social atmosphere of Sydney in the 1930s in a subtle and clever way.

What impressed me most about *The Bridge in Curve*, 1930, was the subtleness of colour, and the way in which colour has been used to convey movement and mood. As colour is of paramount importance to me as a designer, I felt this painting could be interpreted into a knitted design, hopefully without losing too much of what Cossington Smith has captured so successfully. I find the painting appealing because it conveys the excitement that must have been felt by the people who lived in Sydney at this time. Grace Cossington Smith has attempted to capture the political and social atmosphere of Sydney in the 1930s in a subtle and clever way.

Grace Cossington Smith is one of my favourite female artists. I admire her independence and devotion to creativity in a time when women had little choice in their careers. Marriage was considered the best option and women had to live their lives through their 'successful husbands'.

The Bridge in Curve has great power and movement. The rural landscape has been married with the urban landscape extremely successfully, and the unfinished bridge dominates the skyline with the more masculine qualities of harshness and insensitivity. The masculinity of the bridge is conveyed not only by its domination of the landscape, but by its mechanical structure and harshness, which brings a brutality to the painting. Cossington Smith has anchored the bridge into the earth and nestled the rural Sydney around it.

I have taken those aspects, which I feel to be the artist's intention, and separated

them into simple design forms, hopefully without losing sight of their deeper meaning. I have simplified the bridge shape, still keeping the sense of its strength and shape against the blue sky and repeated it to convey a feeling of additional power over the landscape.

The second image I have depicted is rural Sydney with barns, sheep and trees—implying a rustic harmony with nature—while also showing the power poles beginning to exert their influence. The colours I have used are earthy and solid.

The third image is mechanisation, and I have shown the factories with power poles, while still keeping the tree to remind us of rural landscape.

I have repeated each of these designs horizontally across the garment and then vertically, separating each design horizontally with a block of moss stitch. I chose moss stitch because it has an earthy quality as well as being simple to execute. It is also in keeping with the simplicity and strength I feel the painting conveys.

KEY

MC	=	□
C1	=	·
C2	=	▲
C3	=	\
C4	=	<
C5	=	/
C6	=	●
C7	=	◇
C8	=	~
C9	=	—
C10	=	◆
C11	=	*
C12	=	O
C13	=	>
C14	=	□
C15	=	I
C16	=	=
C17	=	×
C10	=	+
C19	=	■
C20	=	II

Measurements

	Small	Medium	Large
Actual Garment Measures (*approx*):	110	120	130 cm
Length (*approx*):	53	54	55 cm
Sleeve Fits:	43	43	43 cm

Materials

CLECKHEATON COUNTRY 8 PLY (*50g balls*)

	Small	Medium	Large
Main Colour (MC) Cobalt	5	5	6 balls
Contrast 1 (C1) Mid Blue	4	4	5 balls
Contrast 2 (C2) Pale Blue	4	4	5 balls
Contrast 3 (C3) Bottle Green	2	2	3 balls
Contrast 4 (C4) Jade	1	1	1 ball
Contrast 5 (C5) Pale Grey	1	1	1 ball
Contrast 6 (C6) Dark Grey	1	2	2 ball/s
Contrast 7 (C7) Black	1	2	2 ball/s
Contrast 8 (C8) Gold	1	1	1 ball
Contrast 9 (C9) White	1	1	1 ball
Contrast 10 (C10) Maroon	1	1	1 ball
Contrast 11 (C11) Navy	1	1	1 ball
Contrast 12 (C12) Pale Pink	1	1	1 ball
Contrast 13 (C13) Soft Pink	1	1	1 ball
Contrast 14 (C14) Orange	1	1	1 ball

AND CLECKHEATON CHELSEA 8 PLY (*50g balls*)

	Small	Medium	Large
Contrast 15 (C15) Beige Fleck	2	2	3 balls
Contrast 16 (C16) Muted Jade	2	2	3 balls
Contrast 17 (C17) Grey Mauve	1	1	1 ball
Contrast 18 (C18) Muted Plum	1	1	1 ball
Contrast 19 (C19) Muted Purple	1	1	1 ball
Contrast 20 (C20) White	1	1	1 ball

NOTE: *Quantities are approximate as they vary between knitters.*

One pair each 3.25mm (No 10) and 4.00mm (No 8) knitting needles; a stitch holder, knitters needle for sewing seams and embroidery; 6 buttons.

Tension

21 sts and 38 rows to 10cm over moss st using 4.00mm needles and Country 8 ply.

SPECIAL ABBREVIATION: '*Moss St*'= 1st Row: * K1, P1, rep from * to end. 2nd Row: *P1, K1, rep from * to end. Rep last 2 rows.*

Back

Using 3.25mm needles and MC, cast on 82 (92–102) sts.
Work 15 rows K1, P1 rib.
16th Row: Rib 2 (6–12), * inc in next st, rib 1, rep from * to last 0 (6–10) sts, rib 0 (6–10)   122 (132–142) sts.

Change to 4.00mm needles.
Work in patt as shown on Graph as indicated for Back, until row 138 has been completed.
Working rem in C2 Moss St, work 16 (20–24) rows.

SHAPE NECK:
Next Row: Moss 45 (49–53), turn.
Cont on these 45 (49–53) sts.
Dec one st at neck edge in next row.

SHAPE SHOULDER:
Keeping moss st correct, cast off 14 (15–17) sts at beg of next row and foll alt row, AT SAME TIME dec one st at neck edge in next 2 rows . . . 14 (16–16) sts.
Work 1 row. Cast off rem sts.
With right side facing, slip next 32 (34–36) sts on to stitch holder and leave.
Join C2 to rem sts and work to correspond with side just completed, reversing shaping.

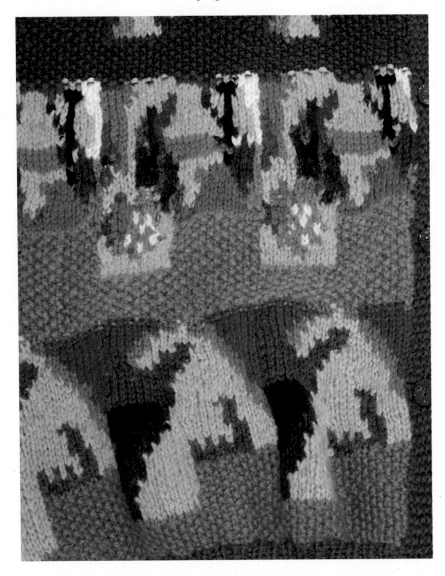

Left Front
Using 3.25mm needles and MC, cast on 40 (44–50) sts.
Work 15 rows K1, P1 rib.
16th Row: Rib 10 (0–4), * inc in next st, rib 0 (1–1), rep from * to last 9 (0–4) sts, rib 9 (0–4) . . . 61 (66–71) sts.
Change to 4.00mm needles.
Work in patt as shown on Graph as indicated for Left Front, until row 138 has been completed.
Working rem in C2 Moss St, work 11 rows.

SHAPE NECK:
Next Row: Keeping patt correct, cast off 10 (10–11) sts at beg of next row . . . 51 (56–60) sts.
Dec one st at neck edge in every row until 45 (49–57) sts rem, *Sizes Medium and Large only* – then in alt row/s until (48–52) sts rem.
All Sizes – Work 0 (1–1) row/s Moss St.

SHAPE SHOULDER:
Keeping moss st correct, cast off 14 (15–17) sts at beg of next row and foll alt row, AT SAME TIME dec one st at neck edge in every (alt-alt) rows from previous dec 3 (2–2) times . . . 14 (16–16) sts.
Work 1 row. Cast off rem sts.

Right Front
Work to correspond with Left Front, reversing shaping and working as indicated on Graph for Right Front.

Sleeve Centre Panel (make 2 alike)
Using 4.00mm needles and mid blue, cast on 22 sts.
Work in patt as shown on Graph as indicated for Sleeve Panel until row 138 has been completed.
Work 4 rows in C2 Moss St.
Cast off loosely.

Sleeve Right Side Pieces (make 1 each in MC and C1.)
Using 4.00mm needles, cast on 16 (18–20) sts.
Work in Moss St, inc one st at beg of 5th and foll 4th rows until there are 44 (46–48) sts, then in foll 6th rows until there are 48 (50–52) sts.
Work 1 row Moss St.

SHAPE TOP:
Keeping moss st correct, cast off 16 (17–17) sts at beg of next row and foll alt

row, then rem 16 (16–18) sts at beg of foll alt row.

Sleeve Left Side Pieces (make 1 each in C1 and MC.)

Using 4.00mm needles, cast on 16 (18–20) sts.
Work in Moss St, inc one st at end of 5th and foll 4th rows until there are 44 (46–48) sts, then in foll 6th rows until there are 48 (50–52) sts.
Work 2 rows Moss St.

SHAPE TOP:

Keeping moss st correct, cast off 16 (17–17) sts at beg of next row and foll alt row, then rem 16 (16–18) sts at beg of foll alt row.

Cuffs

Join a right side piece and left side piece either side of sleeve centre panel.
With right side facing, using 3.25mm needles and MC, knit up 40 (40–44) sts evenly around sleeve edge.
Work 15 rows K1, P1 rib.
Cast off loosely in rib.

Neckband

Join shoulders. With right side facing, using 3.25mm needles and MC, knit up 86 (96–108) sts evenly around neck, incl cast off sts and sts on stitch holder.
Work 9 rows K1, P1 rib.
Cast off loosely in patt.

Right Front Band

With right side facing, using 3.25mm needles and MC, knit up 112 sts evenly along right front and end of neckband.
Work 5 rows Moss St.
Next Row: Moss 5, * cast off 3 sts, moss 17, rep from * 4 times, cast off 3 sts, moss 4.
Next Row: Moss 4, * cast on 3 sts, moss 17, rep from * 4 times, cast on 3 sts, moss 5 . . . 6 buttonholes.
Work 4 rows Moss St.
Cast off loosely.

Left Front Band

Work as for Right Front Band, omitting buttonholes.

Making Up

Tie a marker at side edges of Back and Fronts 27 (28–29) cm down from shoulder. Sew in sleeves between marker. Join side and sleeve seams. Sew buttons in place.

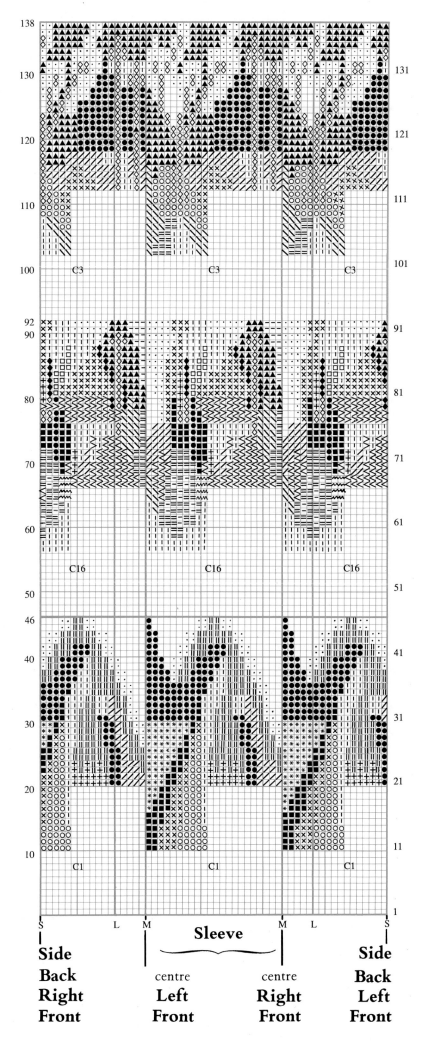

Mount Nameless, Morning

The inspiration for much of my own work (the imagery, colours, application of ideas, particularly for performance work) has stemmed from my contact with the desert—the 'inland', the 'red centre'—and the bush in all its manifestations.

Mount Nameless,
Afternoon

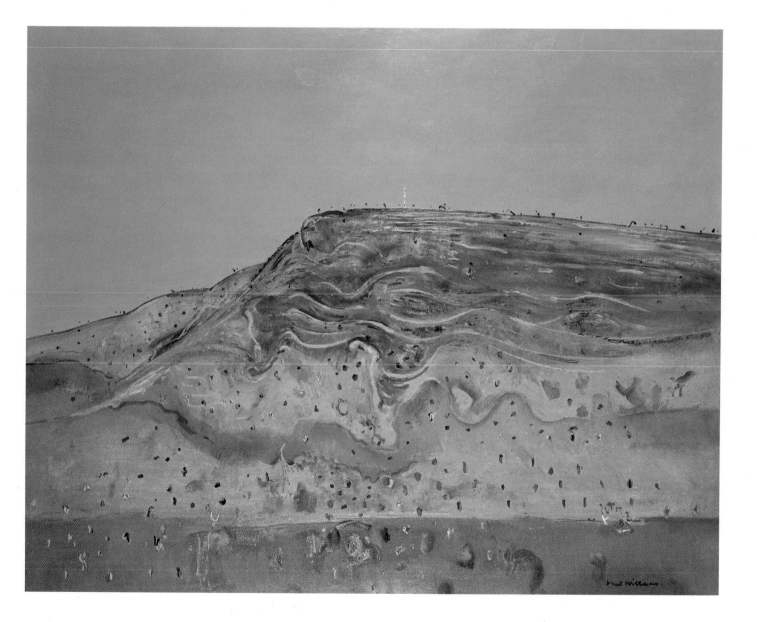

FRED WILLIAMS

Interpreted by Jenni Dudley

Why Fred Williams? Thinking about reasons for this choice I remembered a conversation in Bruce Chatwin's *The Songlines* between the author and a barrister called Hughie, who suggests that Australia is the most abstract country on earth:

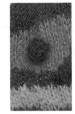

'It's a weird country,' I said.
'It is.'
'. . . this country's old. Old rock! . . . Old, weary and wise. Absorbent too! No matter what you pour on to it, it all gets sucked away . . .'
'I love it here,' he said thoughtfully. 'The abstraction, you understand me?'
'I think so.'
'Suitable for marsupials, but never meant for man. The land, I mean. Makes people do the most peculiar things . . .'

Fred William's *Red Landscape* was the cover illustration for *The Songlines*, an appropriate choice as it reflects both the artist and the writer trying to comprehend our paradoxical existence in this land.

The inspiration for much of my own work (the imagery, colours, application of ideas, particularly for performance work) has stemmed from my contact with the desert—the 'inland', the 'red centre'—and the bush in all its manifestations. I had to choose Fred Williams.

Lateral Parameters

Jenni Dudley lives in a beachside suburb of Adelaide where she is about to restore a big, old octagonal house. Currently she is marketing a range of children's modular play furniture called Whopper Blocks, which she has designed and manufactured. Bright, colourful and flexible, the units are open-ended in structure. Rather like some of Jenni's community arts projects, the parameters have been very loosely set, encouraging participants to create using the given framework, but not to be limited by it. Jenni is a lateral thinker and adept at transferring basic concepts across a number of areas.

Jenni's artistic talents are as flexible and adaptable as her concepts. Her many artistic skills include knitting as a means of expression. Taught to knit by her mother and her Geordie grandmother when she was eight years old, her repertoire included scarves and face-washers. When she was twelve, she attempted to knit a 4-ply Fair Isle jumper of her own design. It was meant for her about-to-be-born baby brother, but she never finished it. Recently, sorting through cupboards in the family home, she unearthed it, and included it as part of her profile in the *Art Knits* exhibition.

Although encouraged as a teenager to attend art classes, make her own clothes, paint murals on bedroom walls and knit, Jenni's parents were not keen on her choice of art as a vocation. Instead, with a Commonwealth Scholarship to pay her fees and $48 a month living allowance, she attended Flinders University, enrolling in Social Sciences and graduating in 1969 with an Honours Arts degree in History and Fine Arts.

Post-university, and not quite sure what she wanted to do, Jenni spent some months working in a crayfish canning factory, followed by an Easter stint as a sales assistant in a Darrell Lea chocolate shop. Jenni then began teaching high school in Adelaide and studying sculpture part-time at the South Australian School of Art. The following year, she moved to Sydney and began teaching at Chiron College, a progressive free-discipline school, with very small classes, and without the traditional authoritarian structures. The experience was difficult, rewarding and insightful. She was also enjoying her part-time ceramics course at East Sydney Technical College. Praising her mentors in sculpture and ceramics, she says: 'They all gave me theoretical and practical disciplines which have been invaluable.'

At the end of 1972, Jenni resigned from teaching, having decided to travel overseas and become apprenticed to a potter in Europe. She planned a two-week stopover in Indonesia, intending to take a short course in batik making, which would be useful for teaching. Two years and several visa extensions later, she was still in Yogyakarta, and about to have her first exhibition of batik paintings. Intrigued by

the craft and the culture, she had studied with Bagong Kussudiardja, a painter and batik-maker, who was also famous as a dancer, choreographer and director of Indonesia's foremost contemporary dance company. At that time, Yogyakarta was a hotbed of contemporary cultural activity, with artists and theatre people forging new expressions from social change, and the impact of Western thought and art practice on traditional artistic approaches and forms in Indonesia.

Jenni was fascinated by this process and by the Indonesian aesthetic sense: 'I saw the value of textiles in everyday life, and the fact that they were part of the fine art tradition in Indonesia. Textiles and carving were the innate forms of pictorial expression there, not easel painting, which

had been introduced from the West.' She continued:

It was the first time I'd seen people working in textiles in a highly professional way and I was surprised to

*see so many men working in the medium.
Though I was interested in the traditional
woven textiles in a theoretical sense, I didn't
want to work in that way. It was batik as a
direct medium of folk and contemporary
expression that impressed me. It was very
highly valued and very alive. It was an eye-
opener because the parallels in Australia were
embroidery and knitting—and maybe screen
printing at the commercial level—and at that
time they were really dull. They had no status
at all, whereas batik, made at the domestic,
commercial and artistic levels, had the status of
Fine Art. I consciously used batik as a painting
medium, exploring it in this way, but also
aware of its own particular 'language'.*

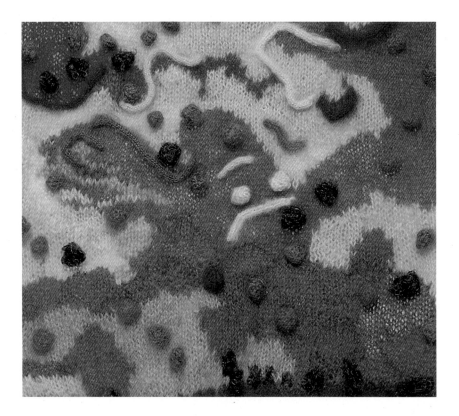

The Indonesian experience introduced
Jenni to new dimensions and possibilities in
art practice. Consequently when she
returned to Australia and began teaching a
textile course for TAFE in Adelaide in
1975, she was able to promulgate these
ideas.

As she needed suitable working space for
her rather messy craft, Jenni set up studio
production with an artistically like-minded
group. For the next three years, Jenni
designed and made one-off batiked
garments for exhibitions, private clients
and markets. She also gave workshops and
gradually began working on community
arts projects.

A Workshop Development grant from
the Crafts Board of the Australia Council
in 1978 enabled her to relocate her studio
(twice), and reassess her work practice.
This eventually led to the production of
small ranges of limited edition, unusual
garments (using all kinds of textile
techniques), and a growing interest in
costume design.

When Jenni married Rodney
Weathersbee in 1979, they moved to the
Adelaide Hills where they built a house in
the Japanese style, and established a garden,
which took over Jenni's art practice for
some time! She continued to work with
mutually supportive groups, such as the
Designer's Collective, through which she
could present her work in lively ways in
unconventional settings such as wineries,
shop-windows and garden nurseries, as well
as galleries and other commercial venues.
Working in a community context, the
Designer's Collective collaborated with the
South Australian Museum on a travelling
exhibition, *Fur and Feathers*, with associated
design workshops.

Rodney died early in 1982, and as
portable therapy, Jenni began knitting
again. Her garments were well received
and with borrowed capital of $2000 she
went into production. Her label, 'Bold
Strokes' dates from this time. Beginning
with a neighbour and friend as knitters, she
soon found herself employing more knitters
and having to raise the overdraft
considerably. She has the highest praise for
the core of knitters she employed: 'They
would often make suggestions on how best
to technically knit the garment. They were

highly skilled professional craft workers, and very loyal. Their names were on each garment they knitted. I was delighted to be giving such women regular and reasonably paid employment.'

Jo Renfrey, who knitted Jenni's piece for *The Art of Knitting*, made her first jumper at the age of seven. She continued to knit for her large and conservative family, and welcomed the chance to knit Jenni's intricate patterns and interwoven colours. Knitting provided Jo with relaxation from the stress of her demanding position as Senior Speech Pathologist with the Education Department of South Australia.

From 1984–1988, Jenni marketed her garments reasonably successfully. But the costs of yarn had spiralled, the margin of profit had narrowed and several of her designs were pirated, appearing on the market vastly reduced in price and quality.

She decided to change direction. Since then, she has sold the house in the Hills and finished commercial production in hand knits.

Jenni's work was included in the 1988 Bicentennial *Art Knits* exhibition at the Art Gallery of New South Wales. Her curriculum vitae is studded with exhibitions at prestigious galleries and commercial venues. She has taught in tertiary art institutions, given many workshops on design, textile crafts and costume, and worked on a variety of community arts projects, most recently 18 embroidered banners for a public library.

Now, living by the sea, Jenni is contemplating the future. She will continue to knit individual and exhibition pieces, and she is hopeful that her play furniture will find an expanding market. With so many skills at her fingertips who knows what will be next?

Measurements

	Small	Medium	Large
Actual Garment Measures (at underarm):	103	115	127 cm
Length (*approx*):	73	73	73 cm
Sleeve Fits (with cuff turned back—approx):	37	37	37 cm

Materials

CLECKHEATON MOHAIR 12 PLY (*50g balls*)

Main Colour			
(MC) Pale Pink	2	2	3 balls
Contrast 1 (C1) Lilac	1	2	2 ball/s
Contrast 2 (C2) Red	1	1	1 ball
Contrast 3 (C3) Ochre/Mustard	2	2	3 balls
Contrast 4 (C4) Dark Red	1	1	1 ball
Contrast 5 (C5) Grey	2	2	2 balls
Contrast 6 (C6) Bright Pink	1	1	1 ball
Contrast 7 (C7) Sky Blue	2	2	2 balls

AND CLECKHEATON MOHAIR CLASSIQUE 12 PLY (*50g balls*)

Contrast 8 (C8) Dark Lilac	1	1	1 ball
Contrast 9 (C9) Pale Blue	1	2	2 ball/s
Contrast 10 (C10) Pale Yellow	1	2	2 ball/s

AND CLECKHEATON NOSTALGIA (*50g balls*)

Contrast 11 (C11) Boucle-Grey/ Black blend	1	1	1 ball

One pair each 4.50mm (No 7), 5.50mm (No 5), and 2 of a set of 3.25mm (No 10) double pointed knitting needles; 2 stitch holders; knitters needle (and plain yarn—if desired) for sewing seams.

Tension

16.5 sts and 23 rows to 10cm over stocking st, using 5.50mm needles.

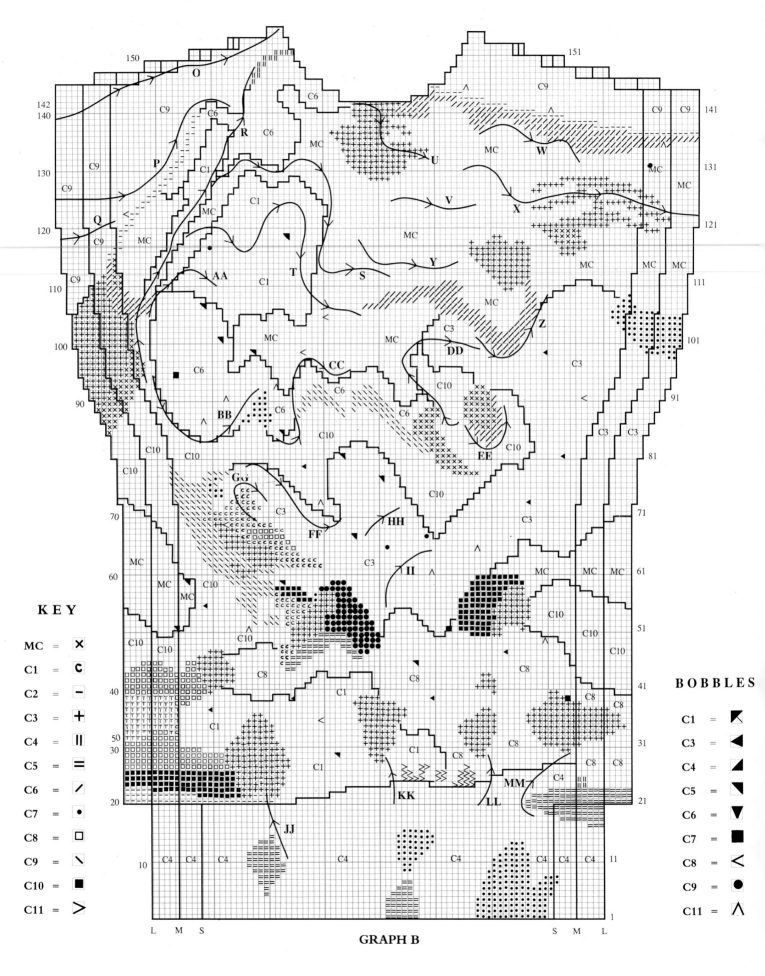

KEY

MC	=	✖
C1	=	c
C2	=	−
C3	=	✚
C4	=	‖
C5	=	=
C6	=	╱
C7	=	•
C8	=	☐
C9	=	╲
C10	=	■
C11	=	❯

BOBBLES

C1	=	◤
C3	=	◀
C4	=	◢
C5	=	◥
C6	=	▼
C7	=	■
C8	=	❮
C9	=	●
C11	=	⋀

GRAPH B

Abbreviation

'Bobble' = Join appropriate colour to loop between last st worked and next st (tie with a slip knot, leaving 6cm at end), (K1, P1, K1, P1, K1) in next st, *turn*, P5, *turn*, K5, *turn*, P5, *turn*, K5, pass 4th, 3rd, 2nd, and first sts on right hand needle over last st worked. Break off yarn, knot ends and thread through work to secure.

Back

Using 4.50mm needles and C4, cast on 63 (71–81) sts.
** Work in patt as shown on Graph A in K1, P1 rib until row 20 has been completed, inc 8 (10–10) sts evenly across last row and noting to change colours on wrong side of work, using a separate ball of yarn for each section—DO NOT carry colours not in use across back of work . . . 71 (81–91) sts.
Change to 5.50mm needles.
Cont in patt from Graph A until row 72 has been completed.

SHAPE TOP:

Keeping Graph A correct, inc one st at each end of next row, then at each end of foll 8th row, then at each end of foll 4th row, then at each end of alt rows 5 times . . . 87 (97–107) sts.
Tie a coloured marker at each end of last row to mark beg of armholes.
Inc one st at each end of foll 5th row, then at each end of foll 6th row, then at each end of foll 7th row, and finally at each end of foll 8th row . . . 95 (105–115) sts. **
Cont in patt from Graph A until row 144 has been completed.

SHAPE SHOULDERS:

Keeping Graph A correct, cast off 5 (6–7) sts at beg of next 2 rows, 7 (8–9) sts at beg of foll 2 rows, then 6 (7–8) sts at beg of foll 2 rows . . . 59 (63–67) sts.

SHAPE BACK NECK:

Next Row: Cast off 5 (6–7) sts, patt 13 (14–15)—counting st left on right hand needle from cast off as first of these sts, *turn*.
Keeping Graph A correct, cast off 4 sts at beg of next row.
Next Row: Cast off 5 (6–7) sts, patt 2—

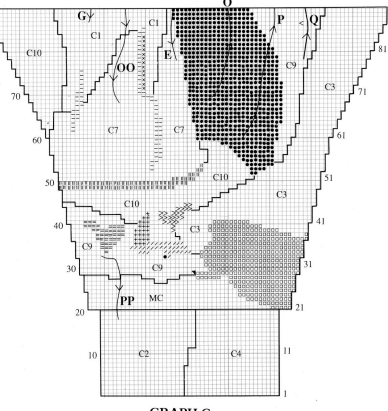

GRAPH C

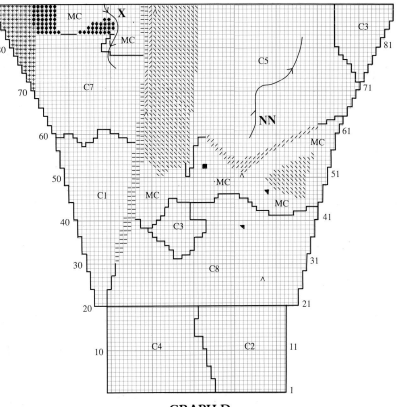

GRAPH D

counting st left on right hand needle from cast off as first of these 2 sts, K2tog.
Work 1 row on these 3 sts. Cast off.
With right side facing, slip next 23 sts onto a stitch holder and leave. Join yarn to rem 18 (20–22) sts, patt to end.
Keeping Graph A correct, cast off 5 (6–7) sts at beg of next row, then 4 sts at beg of foll row.
Next Row: Cast off 5 (6–7) sts, patt 2—counting st left on right hand needle from cast off as first of these 2 sts, P2tog.
Work 1 row on these 3 sts.
Cast off.

Front

Using 4.50mm needles, cast on 33 (37–42) sts using C4, 6 sts using C5, 10 sts using C4, 13 sts using C7 and 1 (5–10) st/s using C4.
Cont on these 63 (71–81) sts and work as for Back from ** to **, noting to work from Graph B instead of Graph A.
Cont in patt from Graph B until row 142 has been completed.

SHAPE NECK:
Next Row: Patt 41 (46–51), *turn*.
Keeping Graph B correct, cast off 3 sts at beg of next row . . . 38 (43–48) sts.

SHAPE SHOULDER AND REMAINDER OF NECK:
Keeping Graph B correct, cast off 5 (6–7) sts at beg of next row, 3 sts at beg of foll row and 7 (8–9) sts at beg of foll row.
Next Row: P2tog, patt to end.
Next Row: Cast off 6 (7–8) sts, patt to last 2 sts, K2tog.
Work 1 row.
Next Row: Cast off 5 (6–7) sts, patt to last 2 sts, K2tog.
Rep last 2 rows once.
Work 1 row on rem 3 sts.
Cast off.
With right side facing, slip next 13 sts onto stitch holder and leave. Join yarn to rem 41 (46–51) sts, patt to end.
Work 1 row.
Keeping Graph B correct, cast off 3 sts at beg of next row, 5 (6–7) sts at beg of foll row, 3 sts at beg of foll row and 7 (8–9) sts at beg of foll row.
Next Row: K2tog, patt to end.
Next Row: Cast off 6 (7–8) sts, patt to last 2 sts, P2tog.
Work 1 row.
Next Row: Cast off 5 (6–7) sts, patt to last 2 sts, P2tog.
Rep last 2 rows once.
Work 1 row on rem 3 sts. Cast off.

Left Sleeve (One size fits all)

Using 4.50mm needles, cast on 26 sts in C4 and 17 sts in C2. Cont on these 43 sts and work in patt as shown on Graph C in K1, P1 rib until row 20 has been completed, inc 6 sts evenly across last row (3 in C4 and 3 in C2) . . . 49 sts.
Change to 5.50mm needles.
Cont in patt from Graph C until row 90 has been completed, AT SAME TIME inc one st at each end of 5th and foll 4th rows 10 times in all, then at each end of alt rows 13 times . . . 95 sts. Cast off loosely.

Right Sleeve (One size fits all)

Using 4.50mm needles, cast on 20 sts in C2 and 23 sts in C4.
Complete as for Left Sleeve, working from Graph D instead of Graph C.

Neckband

Join right shoulder seam. With right side facing, using 4.50mm needles and C7, knit up 100 sts evenly around neck edge, incl sts from stitch holders.
Work 27 rows in K1, P1 rib.
Cast off loosely in rib.

To Make Up

Join left shoulder seam. Sew in Sleeves evenly between coloured markers, placing centre of Sleeve to shoulder seam. Join side and Sleeve seams, reversing seam on Sleeve in first 10 rows. Fold cuffs in half onto right side. Fold Neckband in half onto wrong side and slip-stitch loosely in position.
Make Tubes as follows and attach to garment as indicated on Graphs, noting that arrows point to end of Tubes to indicate which way they should be sewn on and that some Tubes will extend across from Front and Back to Sleeves:-

Tube A
Using double pointed 3.25mm needles and C10, cast on 4 sts. Knit one row. DO NOT TURN.
Slide sts to other end of needle, bring yarn around back of work to beginning and knit one row.
Continue throughout in this manner (knitting all rows and thus forming Tube

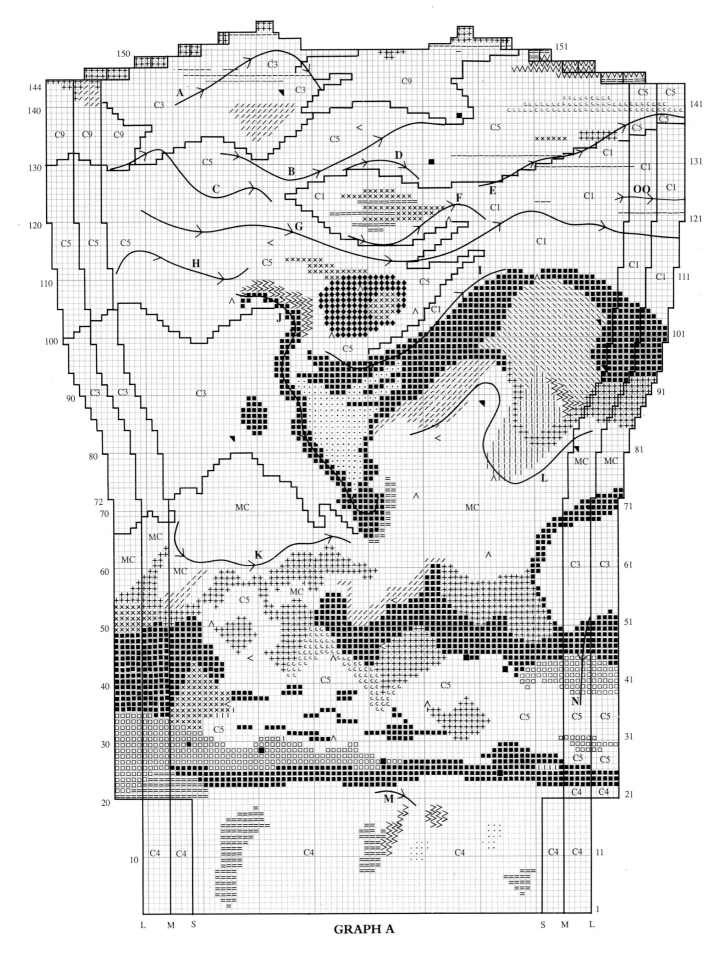

GRAPH A

automatically), until Tube measures 20cm from beg. Cast off firmly.
Work all Tubes in this manner using colours as specified.

Tube B
Work for 16.5cm in C10, 7cm in C4 and 7cm in C10.

Tube C
Work for 14cm in C10, 4cm in C4 and 5.5cm in C10.

Tube D
Work for 9cm in C10.

Tube E
Work for 8cm in C6, and 16 (19–22) cm in C10, noting that when attaching to garment sew extra at end over side seam and on to Right Sleeve.

Tube F
Work for 17cm in C10.

Tube G
Work for 62 (65–68) cm in C10, noting that when attaching to garment sew extra at end over side seam and on to Right Sleeve.

Tube H
Work for 8.5cm in C10, 3cm in C3 and 6.5cm in C10.

Tube I
Work for 21.5cm in C3.

Tube J
Work for 28.5cm in C10.

Tube K
Work for 23.5cm in C6.

Tube L
Work for 20cm in C3 and 12cm in C6.

Tube M
Work for 6.5cm in C5.

Tube N
Work for 6.5cm in C11. (Sew this Tube over side seam for first size, parallel to where indicated for other sizes).

Tube O
Work for 21 (26–31) cm in C9 and 9.5cm in C3, noting that when attaching to garment, begin where indicated on Right Sleeve and sew extra at end over side seam and on to Front.

Tube P
Work for 19.5 (24.5–29.5) cm in C1, 8cm in C6 and 5cm in C2, noting that when attaching to garment, begin where indicated on Right Sleeve and sew extra at end over side seam and on to Front.

Tube Q
Work for 6 (11–16) cm in C3, noting that when attaching to garment, begin where indicated on Right Sleeve and sew extra at end over side seam and on to Front.

Tube R
Work for 20cm in C3 and 11.5cm in C4.

Tube S
Work for 8cm in C3 and 24 cm in C9.

Tube T
Work for 8.5cm in C9 and 23 cm in C3.

Tube U
Work for 9cm in C8.

Tube V
Work for 10.5cm in C10.

Tube W
Work for 13cm in C10.

Tube X
Work for 28.5 (33.5–38.5) cm in C3, noting that when attaching to garment sew extra at end over side seam and on to Left Sleeve.

Tube Y
Work for 13cm in C3.

Tube Z
Work for 8.5cm in C4

Tube AA
Work for 9cm in C10.

Tube BB
Work for 17cm in C4.

Tube CC
Work for 16cm in C10.

Tube DD
Work for 21.5cm in C9.

Tube EE
Work for 7cm in C4.

Tube FF
Work for 14cm in C8.

Tube GG
Work for 8.5cm in C8.

Tube HH
Work for 4.5cm in C9.

Tube II
Work for 8cm in C9.

Tube JJ
Work for 5cm in C11.

Tube KK
Work for 4.5cm in C11.

Tube LL
Work for 5cm in C11.

Tube MM
Work for 7.5cm in C11.

Tube NN
Work for 18cm in C3.

Tube OO
Work for 11 (16–21) cm in C6.

Tube PP
Work for 11cm in C11.

NOTE: *When working from graphs read odd numbered rows (knit rows) from right to left, and even numbered rows (purl rows) from left to right. One square represents one stitch or one bobble.*

NOTE: *Areas on graphs not represented by symbols are labelled, eg MC, C1, C2, etc. Guide lines for sewing on Tubes have circled labels to correspond with instructions at end of pattern, and arrows point to end (cast off edge) of Tubes to indicate which way they should be sewn on. Some Tubes extend from Front and Back across seams to Sleeves and visa versa.*

BIBLIOGRAPHY

Anderson, J. 'The early Work of Sidney Nolan 1939 – 1949', *Meanjin*, Vol 3, 1967

Barber, N. *Conversations with Painters*, Collins, London, 1964

Butel, Elizabeth; *Margaret Preston - The Art of Constant Rearrangement,* Penguin

Chatwin, B. *The Songlines,* pps 50-51, Picador, 1987

Clark, Rowena; Exhibition catalogue for: *The Art of Knitting,* National Gallery of Victoria, 1990

de Teliga, Jane; Exhibition catalogue for: *Art Knits - Contemporary Knitwear by Australian Designers,* Art Gallery of New South Wales, 1988

'Figures in the Landscape', video on Arthur Boyd

Harlow, Eve (editor), *The Art of Knitting,* William Collins, London 1977

Harvey, Michael, *Patons - A Story of Handknitting,* Little Hills Press, St Peters, 1985

Isaacs, J., *Aboriginality - Contemporary Aboriginal Painting and Prints,* University of Queensland Press, Brisbane, 1989

McGrath, Sandra, *The Artist and the River,* Bay Books, Sydney (1982)

McGregor, Sheila, *Traditional Knitting,* Batsford Press, London, 1983

Norbury, James, *Traditional Knitting Patterns from Scandinavia, the British Isles, France, Italy and other European Countries,* Dover Publications, New York, 1973

North, Ian, 'Aboriginal Orientation' from *Creating Australia—Two Hundred Years of Art, 1788-1988,* Produced by the Australian Bicentennial Authority, 1988

North, Ian, *The Art of Margaret Preston,* Art Gallery of South Australia, 1980

Parker, Roszika; *The Subversive Stitch – Embroidery and the Making of the Feminine,* The Women's Press, London, 1984

Preston, M. 'From Eggs to Electrolux', *Art in Australia,* No. 22

Pearson, Michael, *Traditional Knitting – Aran, Fair Isle and Fisher Guernseys,* William Collins, London, 1984

Simpson, C. et al, *A Twentieth Century Colonial 1881-1955,* National Trust of New South Wales, 1980

Thompson, Gladys; *Patterns for Guernseys, Jerseys and Arans - Fishermen's Sweaters from the British Isles,* Dover Publications, New York, 1971

Traditional Knitting with Wool, the Australian Wool Corporation, Melbourne

KNITWEAR DESIGNERS

Kerry Nicholls
PO Box 476
Merimbula
NSW 2548

Libby Jones
Room 4, 1st Floor
Ulster Walk
Edward St
Brisbane
QLD 4000

Ruth Fitzpatrick
'Country Collection'
92 Bradley St
Guyra
NSW 2365

Meredith Russell
515 The Esplanade
Grange
SA 5022

Liz Gemmell
20 Goodsir St
Rozelle, Sydney
NSW 2039

Michael Glover
46 Murchison St
Carlton
VIC 3053

Jenni Dudley
30 Union St
Semaphore
SA 5019

Maria Galinovic
Wilson St
Albury
NSW 2640

Robyn Malcolm
PO Box 442
Fremantle
WA 6160

Robyn McAleer
24 Solomon St
Mosman Park
WA 6012

Moreen Clark
PO Box 78
Mannum
SA 5238

Rosella Paletti
13 Erica St
Heathfield
SA 5153

Amy Hamilton
P O Box 8
Mylore
SA 5153

Ken Killeen
54A Hunter St
Castlemaine
VIC 3450

Meryl Lloyd
9/7 Echuca Rd
Greensborough
VIC 3088

Dariel Brunton
35 Thomas Ave
St Morris
SA 5068

Ros Avent
5 Berkley St
Castlemaine
VIC 3056

Julie Rubenstein
Melbourne
VIC

Libby Peacock
18B Burns St
Fremantle
WA 6160

Accessories used in the photographs were supplied by:

Cheryl Bridgart
PO Box 589
Prospect East
SA 5082

Robyn Russell
P O Box 5
Robe
SA 5276

Lisa Capon
459 Mt Baker Road
Bridgewater
SA 5153

ACKNOWLEDGMENTS

I would like to thank Kim Anderson, the non-fiction publisher at Collins/Angus & Robertson, for the basic concept underlying *The Art of Knitting*, and for her constant encouragement and support throughout the project.

I would also like to thank Sheridan Rogers, Justin Rogers, Skye Rogers, Natali Pride, Linden Pride, Caro Llewellyn, Caroline Caine, Lucy Halliday, Liz Seymour, Michelle Bosworth, John Byrne, Dene Sykes, Adam Hart, Andrew Morrissey, Brent Wong and Ross Emery, who modelled the garments for the photographs: Rae Aonsten, for make-up and hair styling; Rodney Weidland, for photographing the accessories; Denese Coates, for supplying the masks; and Lisa Cummings for supplying earrings. *The Jacaranda Tree* was handknitted by Danielle Cross, with handmade buttons by Beeney Jackson ('Out of the Ordinary'). *Parrot House* was handknitted by Pam Forsythe, with buttons by Beeney Jackson.

My thanks also to Pat and Stephen Blau, Mr and Mrs A.R. Tebble, and Taronga Park Zoo, Sydney, for permission to use their establishments for photographic locations; and to George Lucas, Cleckheaton; and Robert Buckton, BPM Traders, for supplying the yarn used in the garments. A special thanks to Helen Webster and Bojana Kelner from the Australian Wool Corporation for their enthusiastic support and involvement in the project.

TOM ROBERTS 1856–1931
Shearing the Rams, 1890
Oil on canvas (lined onto board)
121.9 × 182.6 cm
Felton Bequest 1932
National Gallery of Victoria

JOHN COBURN
Maquette for tapestry *Summer* 1986
Acrylic and gouache on paper,
48.0 × 72.0 cm
Christensen Fund Collection,
Victoria – copyright reserved

JOHN COBURN
Maquette for tapestry *Spring* 1986
Acrylic and gouache on paper
48.0 × 72.0 cm
Christensen Fund Collection,
Victoria – copyright reserved

JOHN COBURN
Maquette for tapestry *Tree of Life* 1986
Acrylic and gouache on paper
48.0 × 72.0 cm
Christensen Fund Collection,
Victoria – copyright reserved

JOHN COBURN
Maquette for tapestry *Paradise Garden* 1986
Acrylic and gouache on paper
48.0 × 72.0 cm
Christensen Fund Collection,
Victoria – copyright reserved

GRACE COSSINGTON SMITH
Waratahs, c1925
Gouache with pencil and ink
20.5 × 18.5 cm
Signed
Private Collection
Courtesy Bridget McDonnell
Gallery, Victoria

ARTHUR BOYD b. 1920
Shearers Playing for a Bride
Oil on canvas
149.9 × 175.3 cm
Presented by Tristan Buesst 1958
National Gallery of Victoria

WILLIAM HARDY WILSON
Sunlit Hydrangeas
Watercolour on paper 30.2 × 25.7 cm
Purchased 1920
Art Gallery of New South Wales

SIR SIDNEY NOLAN
The Bathers, 1946
Ripolin enamel on canvas
63.5 × 76.2 cm
Heide Park and Art Gallery, Victoria
Photograph: John Brash

DENISE GREEN
City Light, 1989
Oil and wax on canvas
165.5 × 165.5 cm
Roslyn Oxley Gallery,
New South Wales

MARGARET PRESTON
Aboriginal Design with Sturt's Desert Pea,
1943
Masonite cut 30.5 × 38.1 cm
Purchased 1943, Art Gallery of New
South Wales

TREVOR NICKOLLS
Centre Landscape, 1988
Acrylic on canvas 91 × 121.5 cm

SALLY MORGAN
Anxious Angels, February 1989
Acrylic on canvas

SALLY MORGAN
River Picture, October 1989
Acrylic on canvas

MARGARET PRESTON
Australian Gum Blossoms
Oil on canvas 55.5 × 55.5 cm
Purchased 1928
Art Gallery of New South Wales

FRED WILLIAMS
Hardy River, Mount Turner Syncline,
1981
Oil on canvas
122 × 182.5 cm
CRA Ltd, Victoria

BRETT WHITELEY
The Jacaranda Tree (on Sydney Harbour), 1977
Oil on canvas
The Robert Holmes à Court
Collection, Western Australia

HAROLD SEPTIMUS POWER 1878–1951
The Parrot House
Oil on canvas
92.5 × 74.4 cm
Felton Bequest 1928
National Gallery of Victoria

The Cretonne Curtain
Watercolour and gouache over pencil
Gift of Mrs F. Gruen in memory of
her mother Mrs Roy Darvall 1970
Collection: Queensland Art Gallery

JOHN GLOVER
Australia 1767–1849
*A View of the Artist's House and Garden
in Mills Plains, Van Diemen's Land*, 1835
Oil on canvas 76.5 × 114.3 cm
Art Gallery of South Australia, Adelaide
Morgan Thomas Bequest Fund 1951
Art Gallery of South Australia

SALI HERMAN
Parakeets in my Garden, 1967
Oil on canvas, 90 × 70 cm
Private Collection

GRACE COSSINGTON SMITH 1892–1984
The Bridge in Curve, 1926
Tempera on composition board
83.8 × 111.8 cm
Presented by the National Gallery
Society, 1967
National Gallery of Victoria

FRED WILLIAMS
Mount Nameless (Morning), 1981
Oil on canvas
122 × 153 cm CRA Ltd, Victoria

FRED WILLIAMS
Mount Nameless (Afternoon), 1981
Oil on canvas
122 × 153 cm CRA Ltd, Victoria